THE PRIVATE SCHOOLING OF GIRLS
PAST AND PRESENT

THE WOBURN EDUCATION SERIES
General Series Editor: Professor Peter Gordon

Contents

Abbreviations

AHM	Association of Headmistresses
AHMPS	Association of Headmistresses of Preparatory Schools
APS	Assisted Places Scheme
CDT	Craft, Design and Technology
CSE	Certificate of Secondary Education
CTC	City Technology College
DES	Department of Education and Science
ESRC	Economic and Social Research Council
GBA	Governing Bodies Association
GBGSA	Governing Bodies of Girls' Schools Association
GCE	General Certificate of Education
GCSE	General Certificate of Secondary Education
GIST	Girls into Science and Technology
GPDSC	Girls' Public Day Schools Company
GPDST	Girls' Public Day Schools Trust
GSA	Girls' Schools Association
HMC	Headmasters' Conference
IAPS	Incorporated Association of Preparatory Schools
ILEA	Inner London Education Authority
ISAI	Independent Schools Association Incorporated
ISIS	Independent Schools Information Service
ISJC	Independent Schools Joint Council
LEA	Local Education Authority
NCDS	National Child Development Study
SDP	Social Democratic Party
SHMIS	Society of Headmasters of Independent Schools
TVEI	Technical and Vocational Education Initiative

Notes on Contributors

Rosemary Cresser is a researcher at the Social Statistics Research Unit attached to City University. Her past work has mainly been in education and she has carried out research on school differences, teenage smoking behaviour and attitudes, and children's leisure activities. Outside her support work for the Office of Population Censuses and Surveys Longitudinal Study, she devotes a substantial amount of time to her own film distibution business, specializing in Eastern European children's films.

Sara Delamont is Reader in Sociology at the University of Wales College of Cardiff. She was the first woman President of the British Educational Research Association and first woman Dean of the Faculty of Economics and Social Studies at Cardiff. Her books include *The Sociology of Women* (George Allen & Unwin, 1980), *Interaction in the Classroom*, 2nd edn. (Methuen, 1983), *Inside the Secondary Classroom* (with Maurice Galton) (Routledge & Kegan Paul, 1986), *Knowledgeable Women* (Routledge, 1989), *Sex Roles and the School*, 2nd ed. (Routledge, 1990), and *Fieldwork in Educational Settings* (Falmer, 1992).

Elizabeth Frazer is Fellow in Politics at New College, University of Oxford. She has published articles in various academic journals – including *Sociology* and *Culture and Society*.

Brenda Gay was, until recently, head of Lavant House school in Chichester. She is author of *The Church of England and the Independent Schools* (Culham College Institute, 1985). She is an Honorary Research Associate at the Culham College Institute, was part-time co-ordinator of the Oxford Educational Research Group, and also member and secretary of the Bloxham Working Party on Christian education. She has taught in both GPDST and state comprehensive schools.

Kathleen E. McCrone is Professor of History at the University of Windsor, Canada. Her previous books include *Sport and the Physical Emancipation of English Women, 1870–1914* (Routledge, 1988).

Catherine Manthorpe received her doctorate from the University of Leeds in 1985. Her research on girls and science education led to her involvement in the organization of two international GASAT (Girls and Science and Technology) conferences in Oslo and London. Following her doctorate she took up a research fellowship in the School of Education, University of Leeds, working with Professor David Layton and Dr Inge Bates on the definition of school subjects. In 1986 she left Leeds to take up an administrative position at the London School of Economics and Political Science, where she is currently Assistant Registrar for the Graduate School. Her research interests in the sociology and history of women in science are currently 'on hold', pending the introduction of sabbaticals for university administrators!

Jenn Price has worked in the state sector as a science teacher for 20 years, mainly in girls' schools. She currently teaches in Brighton and has responsibility for developing equality of opportunity in a new co-educational school formed from the amalgamation of two single-sex comprehensives. The chapter included here arose from research done while studying for an MA in Women and Education at the University of Sussex.

Debra Roker is Research Associate at the Social and Applied Psychology Unit at the University of Sheffield, currently working with Dr Michael Banks on an ESRC-funded project. This project is comparing the values and experiences of the private- and state-educated samples in the YOUTHSCAN study. Her research interests include identity development in adolescence, youth socialization, young people and politics, and youth policy.

Geoffrey Walford is a senior lecturer in sociology and education policy at Aston Business School, Aston University. His previous books include *Life in Public Schools* (Methuen, 1986), *Privatization and Privilege in Education* (Routledge, 1990) and *City Technology College* (with Henry Miller) (Open University Press, 1991). His most recent edited books are *Private Schools in Ten Countries: Policy and Practice*

(Routledge, 1989), *Doing Educational Research* (Routledge, 1991), and *Private Schools: Tradition, Change and Diversity* (Paul Chapman, 1991).

Introduction

GEOFFREY WALFORD

In Britain, there is surprisingly little research on private education. Furthermore, only a small proportion of the research that exists is concerned with the schooling of girls – the focus of attention has been overwhelmingly on the major boys' boarding schools. This gap in our knowledge of private schooling, and the private schooling of girls in particular, is a serious restriction to informed social and political debate about schooling. For, while private education is currently a very important political issue and the subject of heated controversy, the debate is often conducted more in terms of polemic than rational argument. Many of those on both the political left and the political right seem to believe that the high quality of private schooling is so evident that research is redundant. They differ only in their reactions to this supposed superiority: the left arguing that such elitism in education should eventually be abolished, and the right claiming that parents should be able to buy whatever advantages they wish for their children. Debate proceeds largely in ignorance of the historical development of private schooling, the changing present-day nature of private schooling, and of the wide diversity of provision within the sector.

This collection of research-based chapters cannot hope to fill all the gaps in our knowledge, but it does bring together some important new research that begins a much-needed exploration of some of the major issues. All of the chapters are specially written for this volume and all are previously unpublished. The contributors to the collection take a variety of different theoretical and political perspectives, and do not necessarily agree with one another on the conclusions drawn from research. Such difference of views is an essential part of academic debate, and the book is offered in the hope that it will encourage others to conduct further work in the area.

Within this book, the terms 'private' and 'independent' are used interchangeably to describe the whole range of schools that are not maintained by the state. In Britain, these schools are officially designated as 'independent' schools, which encourages the idea that they are not dependent upon local or central government for financial or other support. In practice, this is not the case, for many of these schools now derive a large proportion of their funding from the state through such means as the Assisted Places Scheme and gain tax exemptions as a result of their charitable status. Private schools are also highly dependent upon the Conservative government's ideological support, which sustains the idea that they are almost automatically superior to maintained schools. In many cases, their degree of independence is less than they might wish their customers to recognize.

In practically every other country, such schools are designated as 'private' schools, a term that in Britain has often carried with it associations of exclusivity and the profit motive, but does not necessarily do so elsewhere. Over the last decade or more, however, the government has shown itself keen to support privatization and various forms of private enterprise over state enterprise, which means that it has now become more acceptable, both within the schools and outside, to use the term 'private' without too great a chance of misunderstanding. Within the discussion of the current situation, the potentially misleading term 'public school' – which historically has been applied to the major schools and, in particular, the boys boarding schools whose headmasters were members of the Headmasters' Conference – is now little used. The various private-school organizations have tried to replace this 'public school' designation with the idea of independence, and the former term is now mainly used only in historical discussions.

Whichever terms are used, one of the most important facts to note is that the distinction between state and private schools is now less clear than it once was. An increased number of private schools now receive substantial funding from the state, and many parents in maintained schools are increasingly expected to contribute to their children's education. The introduction of City Technology Colleges, which are officially classified as independent schools but jointly funded by industry and the state, and grant-maintained schools, which are state-maintained schools outside the Local Education Authority system, adds to the confusion. Such blurring of the boundaries and development of a range of schools can be regarded as an important part of the government's wider privatization strategy for schooling.

The first Chapter of this book acts as an extended introduction to the rest. It presents an account of the development of girls' private education and gathers together data on current educational trends in girls' education. Its purpose is to provide a background within which the other chapters can be contextualized.

The remaining eight chapters in the volume consider various aspects of the private schooling of girls. Chapters 2, 3 and 4 are historical. In Chapter 2, Kathleen McCrone examines the interlinked development of music-teaching and sport and physical education through the second half of the nineteenth century and into the twentieth. While drawing examples from a range of girls' public schools, she concentrates her narrative and discussion on the North London Collegiate School at the time of Miss Buss and the Cheltenham Ladies' College under Miss Beale. She describes the 'double conformity' within which these early reformers were constrained, and argues that the changes in the ways girls' schools viewed and taught exercise and music between 1850 and 1914 were important reflections of the tensions between older and newer concepts of woman, and the degree of continuity and discontinuity between traditional and 'advanced' provisions for educating young ladies. These schools encouraged the development of musical education in part to balance and complement the 'masculine' sides of school life as epitomized in sport and exercise. McCrone argues that while these schools made a major contribution to women's emancipation, they remained essentially faithful to the demands of the traditional female role, and to the idea that they must train girls for suitable matrimony. While they challenged traditional gender relationships by demanding sound education for females, their acceptance of the standards of 'ladylike behaviour' helped to maintain the ideologies, values and attitudes that customarily dominated relations between the sexes.

In Chapter 3, Catherine Manthorpe investigates the somewhat similar dilemmas that faced private girls' schools in including science in the curriculum during the late nineteenth and early twentieth centuries. She also looks in detail at the two leading schools of the time – Cheltenham Ladies' College and the North London Collegiate School – and at the particular views of their headmistresses towards science education. The way in which science education was shaped in these schools is analysed through a discussion of the writings and influence of Sophie Bryant, who was teacher of mathematics, then headmistress of the North London Collegiate School (1875–1918), and of Sara Burstall, headmistress of the Manchester High School for Girls from 1898.

It is shown that by the end of the nineteenth century two models of science education for girls had developed: the academic and the practical. Underpinning both was the idea that science was an intellectual discipline and a means of cultivating the faculties but, while the academic model allowed suitable girls to prepare for university entry, the practical model was more concerned with instilling the skills and knowledge that girls were perceived to require to carry out their domestic duties efficiently. It is argued that, because the girls' schools were newly established, they had a tremendous opportunity to innovate in science education, but that in practice the extent of innovation was severely constrained by the social and political position of women educationists and the social and institutional contexts in which girls' schools developed. The pioneers generally conformed to an existing pattern of education established, or being developed, in the boys' public schools and the universities.

Chapter 4, by Sara Delamont, examines the ways in which girls' private schools have been portrayed to others in the various book-length histories that have been written about them. Through a detailed analysis of 20 such volumes, Delamont shows that most are insider-accounts written by someone who has studied or worked (or both) within the schools described. She examines the internal structure of these books, the nature, number and purpose of illustrations, and the issues that the books cover or omit. Delamont shows that the readers of many of these histories could easily fail to appreciate the historic significance of the issues discussed or omitted in these volumes. Few of the texts, for example, explained why particular rules and regulations for girls were enforced, or why the playing of sports was problematic. Additionally, the feminist spirit of those who founded many of these schools, and the links between education for women and suffrage, were usually ignored. However, Delamont argues that, while there are limitations to such volumes, historians can still derive insights from them and thus increase our understanding of girls' education in areas that have been largely neglected.

While mainly historical, Delamont's chapter also deals with some more up-to-date histories of schools and thus serves as a bridge to the remaining chapters in this book which are concerned with present-day girls' private schooling. Chapters 5 and 6 investigate two important aspects of political socialization. In Chapter 5, Debra Roker presents the results of a comparative study that investigated the political attitudes and values of girls, focusing on both the content and process of their political socialization. Initial questionnaires were completed by 72 girls aged 15–18 who were educated in a girls' private school, and 109 girls from a state school which served the same area of a large northern city in England. This was followed by in-depth interviews with the majority of both groups of girls, where a broad range of political, social and economic topics were discussed. This chapter draws mainly on the results of these interviews and shows that there were significant differences between the two groups. The girls at the private school, for example, were shown to have a greater interest in politics, and showed greater trust in politicians than did the girls from the state school. Very large differences were found in voting intentions, with a far higher proportion of the state-school-educated girls being undecided or unwilling to vote. Not only does Roker establish that in many areas there are differences between the two groups in terms of political content, she also shows that there are considerable differences in their mode of past and current exploration of political issues. The theoretical and practical/policy implications of these differences in the processes of developing political orientations are also discussed.

In Chapter 6, Elizabeth Frazer examines a particular aspect of political socialization in detail. She is concerned with the different ways in which girls from a single-sex private school and a single-sex comprehensive school in the same city talk about social class. Her analysis is based upon several series of group interviews with girls of various ages within these two schools, which were conducted as part of research into teenage girls' experiences of femininity. In analysing the transcripts of these discussions, Frazer distinguishes between 'untheorized discourse' (which corresponds to the girls' practical and articulate social competence – the ability to recognize appropriate and inappropriate behaviour and to spell out rules and procedures for appropriate behaviour) and 'theorized discourse' (which corresponds to theoretical social competence – the ability to subject the existence, validity and specification of a rule or behaviour to enquiry). The chapter focuses on points where theorized discourse is produced, and compares different kinds of 'theory' produced by the various groups. It is shown that girls from both schools shared a basically feminist way of talking about their gender experience, but that the private-school girls had a more conservative understanding of gender relations which was in tension with their feminism. The privately educated girls were highly conscious of their upper-class identity, and they invariably associated issues of gender inequality with class inequality. There were important differences between the two groups of girls in the way they discussed class. For comprehensive-school girls, the subject brought inarticulateness and embarrassment, while it brought clashes between members of the groups in the private school. Frazer argues that, within the private school, the motif of class permeates the school's culture and that there are feelings of guilt at class inequalities which are mixed with contempt and fear of the 'lower classes'. In contrast, class seems to be a taboo subject for the comprehensive-school girls, who seemingly inhabit a classless society.

Issues of class and gender are further discussed in Chapter 7, by Jenn Price, who reports on an investigation of the experiences of girls in the sixth forms of predominantly boys' Headmasters' Conference (HMC) schools. Price's chapter draws upon interviews with a small sample of women who had attended the sixth forms of HMC schools between 1970 and 1986, and upon observation and interviews in three major schools. She discusses what these girls perceive to be the advantages and disadvantages of their decision. The main part of the chapter describes and analyses numerous incidents that were observed while in the schools, and the results of informal interviews with girls about their experiences. It is shown that sexism is alive and well within these schools – in teaching, the curriculum, the school culture, and in the behaviour of both male teachers and boys. The inequalities in provision for sport and differences in the attitude of most boys and staff towards girls' sport and boys' sport are discussed in detail. Price argues that the supposed advantages to girls of moving to a sixth form in a HMC school do not outweigh the considerable problems that they face in such male-dominated schools. She concludes that these predominantly boys' HMC schools do not provide a suitable learning environment for girls.

Chapter 8, by Rosemary Cresser, concentrates on girls' academic achievements. She provides a detailed analysis of the examination performance of girls within the sixth forms of three types of private school: girls only, co-educational, and boys' schools with sixth-form girls. The research draws upon a national sample of 2,385 girls from 78 schools, and considers the extent to which the choice of sixth-form environment influences girls' A-level performance. Taking into account the girls' previous O-level academic achievement levels, the chapter examines overall academic achievement at sixth-form level and the girls' A-level performance in the 'hard' science subjects that girls have traditionally pursued in fewer numbers than boys. The significance of different types of sixth form is considered in relation to the higher A-level grades normally required by the more prestigious universities. The findings suggest that the boys' schools have been successful in attracting the most academically able girls, and in encouraging these girls to take a higher number of A-levels than those who remain at girls' schools. However, against common predictions, the girls who remain in the girls' schools are more likely to be entered for hard science A-levels and subsequently to obtain better results.

In the final chapter, Brenda Gay considers the religious aspect of education within girls' private schools. While the chapter includes some information gathered from informal interviews with heads and pupils of various schools, it draws mainly upon questionnaire responses from 49 heads in the South East region of the Girls' Schools Association. The schools in the survey have a variety of religious denominational affiliations, and the analysis examines differences between schools in terms of these denominational groupings. The study examines, in turn, the various aspects of the religious dimension to these schools. First, it documents the provision for religious worship and the extent to which schools had their own chaplains or had links with the local churches. It is shown that full-time chaplains were rarely found in the schools, but that there were frequent links with parish priests and local congregations. Gay next examines the role that heads saw for school assemblies and for school worship, and it is shown that many heads saw their assemblies as a cohesive force within their schools, and a chance to build a common ethos.

The chapter next documents the position of religious education in the schools and the importance of religious education as an examination subject. It is shown that considerable time was still given to religious education in practically all the schools, with Roman Catholic schools tending to give the most generous time allocations. At examination level, however, religious education was not a popular subject. The chapter also discusses the role that heads see their religious affiliation having on the curriculum, corporate life and ethos of the school. Only a few heads saw their church connection as having any great influence on the curriculum, but many saw it as having clear effects on the corporate life and ethos of their schools. Heads also stated that some prospective parents showed interest in the religious aspects of the school when they visited, and parents often commented on special religious services that were regularly held.

Taken together, these nine chapters present important new research on the history of girls' private schools and on the present-day private schooling of girls. It is our hope that the collection will both enlighten readers and perhaps stimulate some of them to pursue further study of this surprisingly under-researched area.

ACKNOWLEDGEMENTS

I wish to thank the contributors to this volume for their patience and understanding during the long period before publication. Particular thanks are owed to Sara Delamont for her constant enthusiasm and support for this project.

Note: As this book includes chapters representing a variety of academic disciplines, authors have chosen to use a referencing system appropriate to their needs. Thus the two historical chapters (Chapters 2 and 3) use an endnote system of referencing, while the remainder use the Harvard style.

1

Girls' Private Schooling: Past and Present

GEOFFREY WALFORD

This chapter outlines some aspects of the development of private schooling in England and is designed to give a context for the other chapters in this book. It gives particular attention to the changes that occurred in private schooling for boys as well as girls during the Victorian period, because the growth of girls' schools during this time must be seen as part of a complete restructuring of educational provision to accommodate the demands of the late nineteenth century. The chapter also gives a statistical account of contemporary girls' schooling and examines recent trends in recruitment and structure of private-education provision.

EDUCATION FOR THE POOR

The development of private education for girls in England must be understood in its historical, social and political context and, in particular, in relation to the changes in provision for working-class children and for boys of the upper and middle classes. For the last 500 years or more the content and nature of schooling given to children has depended on social class, as well as – and perhaps more than – gender.

In pre-Victorian Britain, the majority of children from what was to become the working class received little or no formal schooling. The education of children was considered to be the private affair of parents and the majority of parents could ill afford to pay school fees or refuse the additional income that a child out at work would bring to the family. If these children received any schooling at all, it was in charity schools supported by the churches or in a variety of dame schools which, in many cases, were little more than a child-minding service to enable women to continue working. A few destitute children and orphans found themselves in charitable hospital schools where they

9

were trained for manual work and service. Nevertheless, as urbanization and industrialization proceeded through the eighteenth century, the sometimes contradictory drives of philanthropy, religious conviction, and the practical need for a better educated and disciplined work-force led to the gradual expansion of a network of schools for the poor.

In the early nineteenth century there were several unsuccessful attempts to establish a national system of schools for working-class children, and to alleviate the grave deficiencies in general provision, accommodation and teaching found by two parliamentary committees. In practice, it was not until 1833 that the government made its first donation to education offered by the two main religious providers of the day. Regular government grants soon followed, and the Newcastle Commission of 1861 found that some 95 per cent of children of the 'poorer classes' attended school, even if only for four to six years. The government made provision for school boards to build and maintain their own schools in 1870, and elementary schooling was eventually made compulsory for all children from 1880.

What is important to note here is that the only schooling available to working-class children before 1870 was private or charitable schooling, and that it was very similar for boys and girls. While there were some differences in the curriculum offered to the two sexes, schooling was available to working-class girls and boys on a more or less equal basis. In the main, this charitable provision was designed to instil a form of religion and morality deemed appropriate for the working class, and to ensure that, as women and men, they took their pre-ordained place in the social hierarchy. For the majority of children, class position rather than gender was the important determinant of life chances and individual opportunity.

VICTORIAN SCHOOLING FOR THE SONS OF THE UPPER CLASS

In contrast to working-class boys and girls who received a fairly similar basic schooling, girls from the upper class and from the expanding middle class of the nineteenth century usually received a very different form of education from their brothers. New schools were established during the reign of Victoria, and a disparate range of existing schools were moulded into a system to educate the upper and middle classes. This restructuring first occurred for boys, but was followed, at a rather leisurely pace, by similar new establishments and restructuring for girls. To appreciate the problems faced during the

Victorian era by those who wished girls to receive an adequate education, it is necessary to understand the deplorable state into which schooling and universities for boys had fallen.

At the centre of discussion of the private schools for upper-class boys is a small group of so-called 'Great Schools', which were investigated by the Clarendon Commission of 1864. By 1820, the seven boarding schools of Eton, Winchester, Westminster, Charterhouse, Harrow, Rugby and Shrewsbury were being linked together as a loose group. These schools were patronized almost exclusively by the aristocracy and landed gentry, and some of those who were rich enough to adopt the gentry's way of life and manners (Bamford, 1967). For the first 50 years of the nineteenth century, each of these seven schools maintained a relatively static social clientele, preferring to risk the uncertainty of lower numbers rather than admit children of lower social rank. They led a precarious existence in which the number of new pupils could fluctuate dramatically from year to year, with wild peaks and troughs, and numbers would often increase markedly on the appointment of a new headmaster. However, even though they could easily have taken children from the new middle class of engineers, scientists and managers and from the upper ranks of the Civil Service, medicine, the Church and the law, they largely chose not to do so, for this would have diluted the aristocratic nature of the schools. It was not until the 1860s and 1870s, after legislative changes following the Clarendon Commission, that curriculum and financial reforms were made and the Great Schools were continuously full (Shrosbree, 1988).

There was considerable variation between the schools, but by the time of the Clarendon Commission all seven schools drew their pupils from all over Britain; however, they still provided a curriculum based only on Latin and the classics. Although there were close links to Oxford and Cambridge Universities, the curriculum offered in these schools was not seen in vocational terms – for the boys who attended these schools were not expected to have to work for their living. The expectation for most of these boys was a life based on their estates, financed from income from property and investments. Some of the younger sons might join the Navy, Army, or the Church, or might train for the Bar, but work in business, medicine or engineering was unthinkable.

In practice, these upper-class schools were 'relieved of the responsibility of providing the basis for a living' (Bamford, 1967: 8), and made little attempt to provide a relevant or up-to-date education. The content of the curriculum had become of no practical importance, and was only maintained through tradition and unchanged statutes. Further, by the early Victorian era, the Wardens and Fellows of Winchester and Eton Colleges, for example, had exploited the endowments for their own use, leaving the boys badly taught, poorly fed and meanly accommodated. The special position of Eton as the training ground for statesmen outweighed these inconveniences, and in 1868 it still had 850 pupils; but the number of boys at Winchester had slumped. Westminster, Charterhouse and Harrow were also doing badly, in contrast to the reinvigorated Rugby and the new Marlborough.

VICTORIAN SCHOOLING FOR BOYS OF THE MIDDLE CLASSES

Throughout the sixteenth and seventeenth centuries, the establishment of a free grammar school for local children was seen as a particularly appropriate way for wealthy merchants or nobility to be remembered, and a large number of endowed grammar schools had been gradually established throughout Britain. The usual pattern was for the foundation to provide a fixed sum for the payment of a schoolmaster from property rents, and for the schoolmaster to be required to provide free teaching in Latin and Greek in return. While this arrangement had originally worked well, gradually the importance of the classics declined, and the growing vocal middle classes of the late eighteenth and nineteenth centuries began to try to divert the endowed schools away from their original purpose. They wanted to exclude the children of the poor and use the endowments to educate their own children and to provide a flow of clerks and office workers for their industries, with the benefit of a wider and more relevant curriculum.

In a few cases, an Act of Parliament was passed to allow particular schools to change their statutes. In 1774, for example, Macclesfield Grammar School was given the right to teach writing, arithmetic, geography, navigation, mathematics, the modern languages, and other branches of literature and education in addition to its main aim of teaching 'grammar and classical learning' (Simon, 1960). Bolton followed this example in 1784, Haydon Bridge in 1785, and Wigan in 1812. In other schools, the statutes were sometimes ignored entirely or evaded by charging extra fees for teaching in subjects other than the classics.

Local dignitaries did not always find change easy, as many of the schoolmasters firmly ensconced in these schools had little desire to change. The statutes often allowed the schoolmaster to take a few pupils from outside the local area and charge them fees, and they had come to rely on the income from these non-foundation pupils. They saw no good reason to change this system. The governing body of Leeds Grammar School, for example, tried for nearly 20 years to get the schoolmaster to broaden the curriculum to include mercantile and commercial subjects. They eventually went to the Court of Chancery with a plan to increase the number of scholars, exclude 'poor' children, and use the endowment to finance the teaching of new subjects. In 1805, in what became a key judgement, Lord Eldon declined the application and allowed only minor changes, which gave incumbent schoolmasters elsewhere greater power to resist change. Unscrupulous schoolmasters in various endowed grammar schools were thus able to continue to exploit their position and live on the income yet do little work, or provide a classical education to the expanding number of fee-paying pupils from outside the town. They thus resisted changes in the curriculum that might have made the schools more attractive to local people. Even after the Grammar School Act of 1840, which legalized the teaching of modern subjects in the endowed school, change could not be made against the wishes of the schoolmaster, and often had to wait until his death.

The result was that those in the middle class who wanted a more up-to-date schooling for their sons patronized various private schools rather than the grammar schools. Such schools had been plentiful since the sixteenth century, and had expanded after the Test Act of 1665 which excluded dissenters from endowed schools. A further boost to their numbers occurred after 1779 when Protestant Noncon-formists gained the right to teach and to own schools. By the early nineteenth century, many such schools had been established in the larger towns to provide a practical education for the sons of the affluent middle-class merchants and manufacturers. A range of schools developed serving distinct social and religious groups.

One popular solution open to those in the major towns was to form a joint-stock company and start a new proprietary day school. The Liverpool Institute was one of the first of these in 1825, and it was rapidly followed by many more in London and the provinces. This included Bristol, Hull, Leicester, Wakefield and Rochester. Brian Simon (1960: 117) argues that the fact that most of these proprietary schools lasted for only 10 or 20 years does not distract from their educational significance. Between 1830 and 1840, these day pro-

13

prietary schools met the needs of the middle class. It was only with the coming of the railways and the social changes of the mid-nineteenth century that boarding-schools were seen as an appropriate way of educating these children.

As the middle class expanded, there grew a demand for boarding-school education; this could not be met through existing provision and thus led to the foundation of new schools. Broadly, these new schools provided the same curriculum as was in the Great Schools, which led to university entry, with the addition of more modern subjects. Many looked to the success that had followed the reforms of Rugby by Thomas Arnold between 1828 and 1842 (Ogilvie, 1957; Honey, 1977) and wished to establish schools run on the same lines. The way was thus paved for a line of new schools, many of which have become major schools. Cheltenham was founded in 1841, to be followed by such schools as Marlborough (1843), Rossall (1844), Radley (1847), Lancing (1848), Bradfield (1850), Wellington (1853), Haileybury (1862), Clifton (1862) and St Edward's, Oxford (1863).

Although these schools are now seen as part of a homogeneous group, they were founded to solve a range of different problems. At Cheltenham, the old grammar school was a typical example of an endowed school that had fallen into disrepute by the first half of the nineteenth century. There were few boys on the foundation, and the growing middle class of the thriving spa town of Cheltenham recognized that, if they wanted a school for their sons, they would have to build one themselves. Cheltenham College was a 'proprietary grammar school for the sons of gentlemen' (Morgan, 1968), financed through share capital. From the start it had two departments – one to teach mainly Latin, Greek and mathematics to those boys destined for universities, and the other offering a wider curriculum for those who might enter the Army, Indian Civil Service or similar occupations.

In contrast, at Marlborough in the 1840s, the Royal Free Grammar School had not fallen into decay. It still educated many boys and maintained close links with the colleges of Oxford and Cambridge. Marlborough College was originally founded to solve the rather different and specific problem of educating clergymen's sons. The number of clergymen had increased dramatically with the rising population, but the salaries of clergy in the new churches were often too low to pay the fees of a 'Great School'. Marlborough was established to provide a cheap public-school education, and the founders intended that two-thirds of the boys would be sons of clergy on reduced fees (Bradley et al., 1923).

14

While some schools can be seen to have been the product of a group of like-minded people working together, individual vision, verging on fanaticism, was at the root of others. By 1836, the Reverend William Sewell had become White's Professor of Moral Philosophy at Oxford, and a moderate follower of the Oxford Movement. He was an influential national figure, with a passion for the Church which, he believed, could only be strengthened through education. He saw a need for smaller schools with more privacy, more contact between masters and boys, a wider curriculum to include aesthetic subjects, and believed that boys should be taught to become 'Christian gentlemen and Christian scholars'. His overall plan was that reform should start with the schools for the gentry, but that the profits of the schools for the rich should finance the schools for the poor. In 1847, he and a small number of others founded Radley College near Oxford, which was sympathetic to the ideals of the Oxford Movement (Boyd, 1948). Fears of Popery made Radley's rise to prominence slower and more controversial than Cheltenham or Marlborough, and Sewell was never able to develop his plan for a network of schools.

In contrast, Nathaniel Woodard, who was firmly committed to the Oxford Movement, was able to develop a group of schools which survive to this day. In 1848, while a curate in Shoreham, Woodard published a pamphlet called *A Plea to the Middle Classes*, which set out what he saw as the need for schools for the middle classes at a price they could afford. He developed a plan that established three grades of school, with the upper grade helping to finance the lower. He rapidly established several small schools and Hurstpierpoint moved to permanent buildings in 1853, Lancing in 1857, and Ardingly in 1870 (Kirk, 1937). The group eventually grew to 19 schools.

The Oxford Movement also strongly influenced another founder of schools, Thomas Chamberlain, who was the minister of a poor church in Oxford. His passion to extend high Anglicanism led him to establish parish schools for the poor, a religious community for women, and a training college for schoolmistresses. During the 1850s he also opened a school for boys under the guidance of his curate; it went bankrupt in three years (Hill, 1962). A second attempt to start a boys' school was made in 1863 which, with better financial management, quickly grew into St Edward's School.

The expansion of many of the major boarding-schools was linked to the growth of the railways, but for Rossall School at Fleetwood, Lancashire, the railways had a rather strange influence. The school was the brainchild of Mr Vantini, who had managed the Euston Hotel at one end of the new North-Western Railway and the North Euston Hotel at Fleetwood which was then the terminus. His original plan was for a profit-making school for 1,000 pupils run on the principle of life insurance (Webster, 1937). The scheme eventually adopted was more modest, and led to a school for 200 boys which opened in 1844.

THE TAUNTON COMMISSION

Although the building of new schools was of considerable importance, the Victorian restructuring of schools to provide a class-delineated system was essentially brought about as a result of the Taunton Commission. Charged in 1864 with the task of examining the state of education for 'those large classes of English society which are between the humblest and the very highest', the Commission reported on nearly 800 endowed grammar schools, and a large number of various private and proprietary schools. While the new proprietary schools were generally found to be praiseworthy, the endowed schools were roundly condemned. Many were unspeakably bad.

The report and recommendations of the Taunton Commission expressed the desire to secure an efficient educational system for the middle class as a whole; however, the middle class was not seen as homogeneous. Echoing the ideas of Woodard and others, the aim was to use the old endowments to create three types of school for the upper, middle and lower middle classes, each type of school charging set fees and having a strictly enforced school-leaving age to ensure that the school kept to its segment of the middle class and defined purpose. The new proprietary boarding schools, such as Malvern and Clifton, and some of the endowed boarding-schools which were aspiring to become Great Schools, such as Repton and Oundle, were to be First Grade schools. These were to aim at university entry. The curriculum was to be classical, but also to include modern studies. Second Grade schools were to be day schools with a leaving age of 16. They were to be established in most towns and prepare children for such occupations as the Army, medicine, engineering, and business. Their curriculum might include Latin, but not Greek. Mathematics, English literature, political economy and practically orientated science were to be central. Third Grade schools were designed for the children of small tenant farmers, small tradesmen, and superior artisans. These were to conclude education at about the age of 14, and provide a limited curriculum which might include the elements of

Latin, but also offer English, history, elementary mathematics, geography and science. The Commission was clear that what it called 'indiscriminate gratuitous instruction' was a waste of endowments. This meant that the working-class children for whom many of the endowments had been intended were to be removed from their free schools. A limited number of competitive scholarships were to be established instead.

The Endowed Schools Act that followed in 1868 led to the appointment of three Commissioners who were given wide powers to rewrite the statutes of schools to fit them into this pattern. Within four years, 97 schemes had been passed by Parliament, often despite strong local antagonism. On a change of government from Liberal to Tory in 1874, the Commission was disbanded and the powers passed to the Charity Commissioners, who pursued their task with less vigour. However, hundreds of local endowed schools were restructured such that free places designed for the working class were removed and fee-paying was introduced. Many of the present-day major private schools originated as endowed charity schools or even hospital schools for the poor, and were able to reposition themselves in the market as a result of this legislation.

PRE-VICTORIAN SCHOOLING FOR GIRLS

The origins of present-day private schools for girls are as varied as those for boys, even though most were founded more recently. A few date back to charitable foundations of the sixteenth century, but most are creations of the nineteenth and twentieth centuries. Only an outline of the development of girls' private schooling is given here; those who require more detail will find the books by Avery (1991), Borer (1976), Burstyn (1980), Dyhouse (1987), Kamm (1965) and Turner (1974) of further interest.

In the Middle Ages, monasteries and nunneries provided an important form of schooling for both boys and girls. Daughters of the gentry would receive a short training in their own homes in religion, reading and writing from a governess or from their own mother. At about the age of ten, some girls (especially those not expected to marry) would be sent to a nunnery where they might continue with their education, while others would be sent to board with a family of a higher social status than their own until marriage at the age of 14 or 15. For girls from the upper class, the nunnery school provided the only type of organized schooling (Kamm, 1965: 35), but the dissolution of the monasteries in the fifteenth century meant that these nunnery schools were also closed. While upper-class boys still had the chance to attend a grammar school, the dissolution of the monasteries meant that their sisters had practically no chance of any organized schooling.

Some upper-class parents still wished to pass on to others the responsibilities of educating their daughters, such that during the early seventeenth century many boarding schools for girls were opened. In the major towns, such as Manchester, Oxford and Leicester and, in particular, near London in Hackney, Chelsea and Putney, there developed private boarding-schools designed to teach girls the 'accomplishments'. Girls were required to learn what was thought to be necessary for 'ladies of leisure', and the curriculum thus included reading, writing and religion, but also a great deal of needlework, music, dancing, household management and French. Some of these schools were evidently quite large. For example, the school opened by Mrs Perwick in London in 1643 lasted for only 17 years, but taught about 800 girls during that time (Kamm, 1965: 69). Moreover, at one point it had 16 masters employed to teach singing and music.

The restoration of the monarchy meant that upper-class girls had to try to conceal whatever learning they had, for it was thought un-ladylike to display any interest in academic matters. However, boarding-schools that taught the accomplishments thrived, such that by the late seventeenth century they had become numerous and offered an alternative for many girls to either being taught at home or being boarded out with another family.

By the 1800s, there were many small individually owned private boarding-schools for girls, which complemented the similar range of schools for boys. It remained true, however, that the majority of upper- and middle-class girls were taught at home by governesses or visiting teachers.

THE VICTORIAN PRIVATE SCHOOLING FOR GIRLS

By the first half of the nineteenth century, women from the upper and middle classes were expected not to work, and only did so if they were unable or unwilling to marry or became widowed. Although badly paid, teaching was the only respectable occupation open to these women, and many teachers had only taken up the work to survive in a socially acceptable way. Teachers and governesses were often uneducated themselves, and resolved the problem by using rote learning and textbooks composed of questions and answers to be learnt like a catechism. Parents wishing to employ a governess and schools looking for teachers faced the same problem of lack of suitably trained women, which the Victorian reformers gradually tried to deal with.

An important development, which linked the need for better educated teachers and governesses with the gradual change in women's position in society, was the formation of Queen's College in 1848. The College developed from regular lectures given by the Reverend Frederick Maurice (a professor at King's College) and others who, as Christian socialists, saw education as a means of wider social reform (Burstall, 1938). The main aim of the College was to provide a supply of well-educated female teachers and to give them certification to distinguish them from the untrained. The College had a school attached which served as a training ground for the women and to prepare future students. A somewhat similar Nonconformist college, Bedford College for Women (originally called the 'Ladies' College in Bedford Square'), opened in 1849. In both cases, these new colleges were not part of the University of London, but the teenage girls and a few more mature women who attended lectures were often taught by men from King's College and University College. The colleges went some way towards providing higher academic education to women who were excluded from the all-male universities of the time.

One of the problems of looking back at the histories of the schools that still exist is that it gives a biased view of the state of schooling in the past. The very many schools that once thrived, but have since closed, get no mention. The many ideas for schools that did not come to fruition are forgotten. This is particularly important in a consideration of the development of girls' private schooling in the mid-nineteenth century, for many of those who established boys' schools were also concerned and involved with schools for girls.

There are several examples of this within the ranks of the major new schools for boys already discussed. For example, the entrepreneurial hotel manager's original plan for Rossall School was for 500 boys and 500 girls to be educated on either side of the River Wyre. The plans for girls were eventually rejected because his backers felt that a boys-only school was a better financial investment. At Oxford in the 1850s, Chamberlain's desire to spread high Anglicanism led to a school for 'the daughters of gentlemen' who were taught by the sisters from the religious order he founded. While the parallel boys' school quickly closed as a result of bad management, the girls' school flourished for many years, and was only later eclipsed by the expanding St Edward's School. Even Nathaniel Woodard, who expressed some ambivalence about boarding-schools for girls, accepted the gift of a small private school for girls in Hove in 1855. Eventually, and primarily as a result of the action of the Headmaster of Denstone (one of the Woodard schools), Abbots Bromley opened in 1874. Seven more Woodard girls' schools gradually followed. Finally, while William Sewell started Radley in 1847, his sister Elizabeth Sewell was running a small school for girls on the Isle of Wight. Elizabeth played a part in developing women's education, and was also a novelist of some repute. In her educational writings she explained that education was 'in the air', and that it was the 'grand problem – the grand interest of the nineteenth century' (Sewell, quoted in Clarke, 1953: 22).

The 'grand problem' and 'grand interest' of education can be seen clearly at Cheltenham. The college for boys opened in 1841, and a training school for masters and mistresses in 1847. The charity school moved to far larger premises in 1847, and the endowed grammar school was resurrected in 1852. The two gaps in the town's provision – 'the daughters and young children of Noblemen and Gentlemen' – were to be filled by the Cheltenham College for the Education of Young Ladies and Children. Two of the six founders of what quickly became Cheltenham Ladies' College were the principal and vice-principal of Cheltenham College, and the Ladies' College, which opened in 1854, was the first to run on a shareholder system in a similar way to several of the new boys' schools. From the beginning, the College was to teach religious education, grammar, Latin and arithmetic as main subjects, along with callisthenic exercises, drawing, French, geography, history, music and needlework.

Discussion of the Victorian development of private schools for girls is dominated by the names of Miss Buss and Miss Beale. Dorothea Beale was closely connected to Queen's College from 1848 until 1856, joining the staff of the school in 1854 (Steadman, 1931). After a brief time as head of the Clergy Daughters' School in Westmorland, she was invited to become the second head of Cheltenham Ladies' College. Frances Mary Buss also attended evening lectures at Queen's College in 1849; at first six, then four, nights per week. She was one of ten children of a poorly paid artist and, to make ends meet, her mother, Frances Buss, opened a small private school in Kentish Town, London in 1846. Frances Mary took over as first head of the reorganized North London Collegiate School in 1850 after obtaining her diploma from Queen's. The school became so successful that she founded Camden School in 1871.

Queen's College not only trained women to teach, but educated them to expect to change society. The Cheltenham Ladies' College under the guidance of Miss Beale, and the North London Collegiate School under Miss Buss, became in their different ways examples that other schools followed. In essence, Cheltenham became the first of a line of public boarding-schools for girls, while North London Collegiate acted as a pattern for the girls' day schools. What distinguished these two schools from most other contemporary girls' schools for the upper and middle classes was that the curriculum centred on academic interests and had university entry as the goal. Music and the accomplishments were still taught, and the girls' lives were closely regulated, as was thought appropriate for 'young ladies', but they were also expected to work hard at academic subjects.

As women gained entry to university examinations, and the role of women in society gradually changed, the influence of these two schools spread. St Leonards School became the first girls' boarding-school to be run on the house system of the boys' public schools. Its founding headmistress was Miss Louisa Lumsden, who had been one of the first six women to attend Emily Davies's new college at Hitchen, which was to become Girton College, Cambridge (Bennett, 1990). The deputy head, Miss Jane Frances Dove, had attended Queen's College before Girton, and both women had taught at Cheltenham under Miss Beale. Miss Dove followed Miss Lumsden as the second head in 1882, and later founded Wycombe Abbey School in 1896. All of these schools wished to educate women to enter higher education, and modelled themselves on the major boys' public schools.

The North London Collegiate School became a model for the growing number of day schools, including those established through the work of Maria Grey and Emily Shirreff who suggested a 'National Union for improving the education of women of all classes above elementary'. This led to the formation of the Girls' Public Day School Company (later Trust) (GPDST) in 1872, which played a major part in providing schools for girls aiming to go to university. By 1876 schools had been started at Chelsea, Notting Hill, Croydon, Norwich, Clapham, Hackney, Nottingham, Bath and Oxford. Two indications of the changing attitude towards girls are indicated by the fact that all of these schools were formed as a result of local demand, and that

Princess Louise became the Patroness of the Company's schools. All of these schools were modelled on the North London Collegiate School in all matters except religious affiliation, where they were Non-denominational rather than Anglican. They also followed Miss Buss's example in aiming to have a social class range of pupils wider than the girls' boarding schools or the boys' public schools (Kamm, 1971). They were not designed to be socially exclusive. By 1971 there were 23 GPDST schools in existence; a further 15 had closed, merged with other GPDST schools, or transferred to other ownership. Outside the GPDST, day schools for girls that had similar aims were gradually developed from existing girls' private schools by a process of change, and through the foundation of other new schools.

The establishment of the Taunton Commission in 1864 acted as an important spur to girls' education for the middle classes. It had originally been intended that the Commission would only examine the private and endowed grammar schools for boys, but, as the girls' schools were not explicitly excluded, pressure from such activists as Frances Buss and Emily Davies led the commissioners to include them. Emily Davies conducted her own survey of schools (Bennett, 1990) so that, when she became the first woman to give evidence at a Royal Commission, she was well armed with information. The final report officially recognized the general deficiency in girls' education and pointed to the problems of lack and misuse of school endowments.

The Taunton Commission found that in 1868 there were 820 endowed schools for boys, but only about 20 comparable schools for girls (Avery, 1991). In some cases, the original benefactions had been given specifically for the education of boys, but in many others the sex of the children who were to benefit was left unstated in the original will or statutes, and it was the governors of the schools who had interpreted the donors' intentions as being for boys only. The commissioners made it clear that this was an inappropriate interpretation, but most of the schools showed little haste in complying with the new policy.

One exception was the very rich Harpur Trust in Bedford, which already funded Bedford School and Bedford Modern School for boys of various social classes. In 1873 it appointed five women as governors and started planning two corresponding schools for girls. These were opened in 1882. In contrast, the new Manchester High School for Girls had to fight to obtain a share of the William Hulme charitable bequest. The charity commissioners eventually conceded in 1884, and the school obtained a regular income and a substantial lump sum (Avery, 1991).

Even where the original endowment specified that only boys were to benefit from a school, the Taunton Commission often decided that it should be extended to support girls as well. Merchant Taylors' School, Crosby, for example, was founded in the early seventeenth century for 'male children only', but in 1874 it decided that it would spend two-fifths of the income on girls. Not until 1888 was a girls' school actually opened (in the renovated old buildings of the boys' school), but it was still a significant step forward.

Where the foundations were supporting both boys' and girls' schooling before the Taunton Commission, the usual pattern was that boys received a far greater share than girls of the foundation income. Christ's Hospital, for example, which was established by charter of King Edward VI as a school for destitute children in London, first opened in 1552. Both girls and boys were accepted, but for 250 years the girls were only taught reading of the Bible and needlework, while the boys had a wider curriculum. Girls had a shorter time at the school, had poorer facilities, and were also always in the minority. In the decade or more before 1870, the number of girls had been kept to just 18 (Avery, 1991). The Taunton Report suggested drastic restructuring, but the governors fought against the proposals and finally made changes as late as 1891.

RECENT HISTORY OF PRIVATE SCHOOLING

In January 1989, there were 2,270 registered independent or private schools in England, representing just over eight per cent of the total number of schools. They educated some 532,500 pupils, or 7.3 per cent of the total school population (DES, 1990). This is a considerable rise from 5.8 per cent in 1979. However, the majority of the percentage increase in the private sector is attributable to the decline in the absolute number of pupils in the maintained sector, as a result of a change in the birth rate rather than increases in the private sector.

These overall figures conceal large differences in the proportion of children in private schools according to geographical region, age and gender. For example, over half of the pupils in private schools are to be found in London or the South East region. Seventeen per cent of private schools are in Greater London, and 34 per cent in the rest of the South East. Table 1.1 gives the overall figures for full-time primary- and secondary-school pupils in England from 1970 to 1989. It excludes children in special schools.

TABLE 1.1
FULL-TIME PRIMARY AND SECONDARY SCHOOL
POPULATION, ENGLAND, 1970–89 (THOUSANDS)

Year	Total (all ages)	Private	% private
1970	7,998	521	6.5
1971	8,188	515	6.3
1972	8,378	516	6.2
1973	8,521	521	6.1
1974	8,864	528	6.0
1975	8,915	530	5.9
1976	8,960	523	5.8
1977	8,955	519	5.8
1978	8,861	510	5.8
1979	8,755	512	5.8
1980	8,593	517	6.0
1981	8,377	516	6.2
1982	8,147	510	6.3
1983	7,905	503	6.4
1984	7,717	501	6.5
1985	7,569	501	6.6
1986	7,441	504	6.8
1987	7,332	515	7.0
1988	7,211	523	7.3
1989	7,144	532	7.4

Source: DES (1990)

The overall number of pupils in private schools can be seen to have fluctuated a little over the years, with a dip in the early years of the 1980s and a rapid increase in the last three or four years of the decade. The percentage of children in private schools fell to a low of 5.8 per cent in 1977 and has since gradually risen to 7.4 per cent in 1989.

Further details are given in Table 1.2 for the years from 1982. In terms of age range, it is immediately evident that secondary private schooling is far more popular than primary private schooling. In 1989, the size of an average primary year group (aged five to ten) was only 60 per cent that of an average secondary year group (11–15). This may show a greater level of parent satisfaction with maintained primary schools, but it could also be the result of the absence of private primary schools near enough for parents to use for these younger children. It is worth noting, however, that the percentage of pupils in private primary schools has risen considerably during the last decade, and the primary level is the major growth area for the private-school sector as a whole.

24

At the secondary level, if the old direct-grant schools are counted within the private sector, Halsey, Heath and Ridge (1984) have shown that the absolute number of pupils remained relatively steady over a 30-year period from 1951. There were declines in the proportion of privately educated secondary children caused by the two 'baby booms' of 1946 and 1961, but the private sector did not markedly increase the number of places to take account of this larger potential market. Over the last decade there has been a small increase in pupil numbers, even though there has been a large decline in the overall secondary-school population. Nationally, the number of 13-year-olds reached a peak in 1978 and declined by over 30 per cent from that year until 1990. That the secondary schools have been able to maintain their pupil numbers and actually increase their market share has been widely argued to indicate a major growth in popularity of private schooling. In practice, however, the decline in the school-age population has been predominantly to parents of social classes III to V (Registrar General's Classification), while the number of children of social classes I and II has remained far more constant (Smithers and Robinson, 1989). Since children from these two social classes dominate the private sector, these schools have not experienced the same decline in potential customers as have state-maintained schools. In fact, the proportion of the population in social classes I and II has risen over the years as a result of changes in the class structure, so an increase in the number of parents wishing to use the private sector might be expected, rather than a decrease.

A rather different pattern is seen at the post-16 age level. The size of the average year group in private schools after age 16 has been

TABLE 1.2
FULL-TIME PUPILS IN INDEPENDENT SCHOOLS IN ENGLAND

	1982	1983	1984	1985	1986	1987	1988	1989
Boys:								
5–10	90,801	88,619	87,318	87,295	87,773	91,010	93,802	96,487
11–15	132,787	132,207	131,982	132,264	131,385	132,793	129,958	128,386
16–19	39,508	39,136	38,998	38,323	38,299	38,715	40,403	42,270
Girls:								
5–10	82,286	79,435	77,997	77,821	78,595	82,241	85,638	89,262
11–15	111,181	111,827	111,256	111,417	111,334	113,165	112,022	110,865
16–19	27,722	27,458	27,740	27,761	28,335	29,563	31,605	33,178
Boarders:								
Boys	80,542	–	–	–	74,863	73,458	71,382	70,552
Girls	42,529	–	–	–	41,721	42,034	42,199	41,371

Source: DES (1990). Figures for boarders 1983–85 not available.

consistently smaller than in the rest of secondary education, but the difference was far less than in the maintained sector, where only about one-third of 16-year-olds stay at school. At post-16 level, about 20 per cent of school pupils were in private schools.

Table 1.2 also shows the continuing differences between the numbers of boys and girls in private schools. Over all, in 1989, 46.6 per cent of pupils were girls, and this proportion had only slightly increased from the 45.7 per cent in 1982. In each of the age ranges, there were more boys than girls in private schools, but with a greater proportion in primary and a lower proportion in post-16. In 1989, beyond the age of 16, only 44 per cent of private-school pupils were girls, but this was up from 41.2 per cent in 1982.

There are many possible reasons for this imbalance. The most obvious is simply that parents might still perceive education as being more important for boys than girls, and thus be more willing to pay for private education for their sons. This explanation appears so obvious that it is tempting to look no further, but the reason may not be this simple. That parents may favour boys is only one of a number of possible factors, and may not even be the main one.

Only scant information is available on why parents are prepared to pay for private schooling (see, for example, Fox, 1984, 1985; Johnson, 1987), but, from the little we know about choice of school, some alternative explanations can be proposed. For example, it would appear that it is not uncommon for parents to consider private schooling only if the child is having problems with maintained-sector schooling (Johnson, 1987). If boys are perceived to have more problems with schooling than girls (which we know is true generally), this would lead to a greater number of boys in private schools than girls. Alternatively, it could also be that parents see boys as problems more than they do girls, and simply want to get rid of them to boarding school. Table 1.2 shows that there were far fewer girl boarders than boy boarders. In 1989, some 37 per cent of boarders were girls. For the number of girl boarders to match that of boys, a further 29,181 girls would be needed, which (if they were new to the system) would bring the total percentage of girls up to 49.6 per cent.

A further possibility takes into account the views of the child in choice of school (Walford, 1991a). It may be that boys are more willing to go to private schools than girls, both as boarders and day pupils. As many pupils join the private system at 11, it may be that the pulls of friendship between girls are stronger than those between boys, so that girls persuade their parents that they wish to go on with most of their friends to the local maintained school, while boys are more prepared to take their chance in a more distant private school with few of their friends making the same transition. In particular, the attractions of good sports facilities may be more likely to persuade boys than girls to leave the safety of what and whom they know.

CONTEMPORARY GIRLS' PRIVATE SCHOOLING

One of the characteristics of the private sector of education is its diversity (Walford, 1991b). Not only are there boarding schools and day schools, Anglican and Catholic schools, large and small schools, but there is great variation in the level of fees that parents pay. Although there is no direct relationship between level of fee and quality of education received, those at the lower end of the spectrum sometimes offer little more than snob appeal, and have poor facilities and teaching.

The majority of the major schools have grouped themselves together into seven organizations that represent their interests. These societies and associations are linked together through the Independent Schools Joint Council and the Independent Schools Information Service, which provides detailed annual census data on the schools (further details are in Walford, 1990). At the beginning of the 1970s, these associations were firmly divided by gender. For secondary boys, the major schools had headmasters who were members of the Headmasters' Conference (HMC). Less prestigious schools for boys had membership of the Society of Headmasters of Independent Schools (SHMIS) or the Governing Bodies Association (GBA). For secondary girls, the main schools were in membership of the Girls' Schools Association (GSA) and the Governing Bodies of Girls' Schools Association (GBGSA), while the Independent Schools Association Incorporated (ISAI) included heads of both boys' and girls' schools. The heads of the major preparatory schools were members of the Incorporated Association of Preparatory Schools (IAPS). The schools in these associations currently educate some 80 per cent of the children in private schools.

In the 1980s and 1990s, the gender segregation within the associations has become less rigid, and there have been important changes in the composition of HMC schools and IAPS schools in particular. Until the 1960s, all HMC schools were for boys only. Schools that were recognized as having a similar standing, but that were co-educational, were excluded. Girls were first introduced into the senior

27

part of a formerly boys-only HMC school in 1969, when John Dancy admitted girls into the sixth form of Marlborough College. After a slow start, many other schools followed, and some existing co-educational schools were invited into membership. By 1990, about 75 of the 231 HMC schools were fully co-educational and a further 85 admitted some girls at sixth-form level. Eight HMC schools had more girls than boys. Unlike some of the HMC schools that followed Marlborough's example, Dancy's motives were not economic, but part of a genuine desire to open the Major Schools to a wider clientele (Rae, 1981: 132). Other schools were less altruistic, and it is clear that many schools saw the introduction of girls as a way of civilizing the boys, boosting the academic standing of the school, and keeping their schools full without reducing academic entry standards. Girls have

TABLE 1.3
PERCENTAGE OF GIRLS IN HMC SCHOOLS

	% girls	% of boarders who are girls
1975	4.82	2.92
1976	5.88	3.81
1977	6.37	4.16
1978	6.82	4.69
1979	8.17	5.78
1980	9.15	6.53
1981	9.98	7.31
1982	10.67	8.04
1983	11.23	8.80
1984	12.24	9.57
1985	13.04	10.84
1986	14.19	12.50
1987	14.54	13.43
1988	15.39	15.13
1989	16.00	15.74
1990	16.67	16.90

Source: Successive ISIS Surveys.

often been particularly welcome in isolated rural boarding schools that have had to face a decline in popularity of boarding. For some schools, girls were a more agreeable and less problematic way of maintaining numbers than expanding into the foreign-pupil market (Walford, 1983). In other schools, the moves to co-education came from the teachers at the schools. Teachers often obtained very greatly reduced fees for their sons at their own schools, but were unable to afford to send their daughters to similar schools elsewhere. By persuading their school to become co-educational, they received this advantage for all their children.

Table 1.3 shows that the total proportion of girls in HMC schools has gradually risen from about five per cent in 1975 to 16.7 per cent in 1990. This is a result of more schools gradually allowing girls into the sixth forms, or throughout the school, in previously boys-only schools, and of the inclusion within the HMC of co-educational schools that were formerly excluded precisely because they were co-educational. Not all of these girls are in the secondary parts of the schools, however, for some HMC schools have their own preparatory schools which are run as part of the secondary school. In 1975, some ten per cent of pupils were aged below 11, with about 11 per cent being girls. In 1990, this had fallen to eight per cent, but with 24 per cent being girls. Very few of these girls aged under 11 were boarders.

Table 1.3 also shows the proportion of boarders who were girls. It shows that initially there were proportionally fewer girls who boarded than girls in the schools – girls were disproportionately day-girls. But, as the numbers of girls has increased, girls are now just slightly more likely to board than are boys. This is in part related to the proportionately greater number of girls in the sixth forms of these schools. In 1990, there were 9,267 girls in HMC schools aged 16 and over, out of a total of 46,806 sixth-form pupils (19.80 per cent). About half of these sixth-form girls entered the schools at the age of 16. While 39.40 per cent of the sixth-form boys boarded, 44.96 per cent of the girls did so. At age 13 there were only 13.53 per cent girls (12 per cent of whom boarded).

Not surprisingly, many heads of girls' schools have viewed with dismay what they regard as the poaching of their girls by HMC schools. The decision to transfer is often couched in terms of higher quality of teaching and facilities in the HMC schools, but the heads of girls' schools argue that they are equally well able to provide an academic education for those entering higher education. They see the HMC schools as being highly selective (especially at 16) and merely getting the academic honours that should have gone to their schools. In practice, the motives for attending such a school are complex. One contributing factor is that girls' schools usually start at 11 rather than the 13 of many boys' predominantly boarding schools, which means that girls have already been at the same schools for five years by the time they start A-levels. The wider pressures within society towards co-education have also meant that some single-sex schools have found themselves fighting a hard battle to survive, with some of them being forced to close.

A few of the GSA/GBGSA schools have tried to attract boys and become co-educational but, in 1990, only 24 out of 220 GSA schools had more than five per cent boys, and practically all of these were at primary level. Those schools in membership of GBGSA had managed a little better, with nine of the 21 schools having more than 5 per cent boys. The schools have been more successful in attracting girls from overseas. In 1990, 6.2 per cent of the girls in these schools were foreign nationals, and a further 1.2 per cent were children of ex-patriates. The corresponding figures for HMC schools were 4.8 per cent and 2.2 per cent.

The figures in Table 1.4 cannot be compared directly with each other year by year as the number of schools in membership of GSA/GBGSA and giving census data has gradually risen. However, the average size of school in membership has remained at about 440 to 450 pupils throughout, while the percentage boarding has fallen from 22.8 per cent in 1982 to 19.1 per cent in 1990. The schools appear to have maintained numbers over the years, but the proportion of girls boarding has decreased. This does not mean that these girls' schools have been without problems, for what the table does not show is that there has been a gradual increase in weekly boarding at the expense of full boarding (14 per cent in 1990), and that the schools are taking a higher proportion of younger pupils. In 1982, 19 per cent of pupils were aged under 11, but, by 1990, this percentage had increased to 25 per cent. Clearly, in order to make up for numbers of girls leaving at or after the age of 16, the schools were taking in younger girls and boys instead. Where there were 11,544 girls aged 17 or over in 235 GSA/GBGSA schools in 1982, there were only 9,712 in 263 schools in 1990. During a period when an increasing number of pupils were

TABLE 1.4

NUMBER OF GIRLS IN GSA/GBGSA SCHOOLS

Number	of schools	Number of pupils	Number of boarders
1981	232	104,848	–
1982	235	104,797	23,912
1983	243	105,354	24,103
1984	247	108,252	24,492
1985	245	108,364	24,526
1986	248	109,253	23,936
1987	250	112,176	24,155
1988	259	116,418	23,981
1989	258	116,352	23,587
1990	267	120,878	23,140

Source: Annual ISIS Census

staying on at school to take A-levels, some GSA/GBGSA schools experienced severe losses at this level.

At the primary level, co-education has been always more common than at secondary. There are only slightly more boys than girls in private primary schools (48.1 per cent in 1990, aged five to ten), yet figures for the main preparatory schools association, the Incorporated Association of Preparatory Schools (IAPS), appear to indicate otherwise. Although the IAPS includes co-educational schools and single-sex schools for boys and girls, the total proportion of girls in these schools was only 29 per cent in 1990. Part of the reason is simply that the major boys' schools have traditionally taken boys at 13 rather than 11, while the number of girls' schools delaying entry until this age has been much smaller. The preparatory schools for boys thus take seven to 13-year-olds, while the preparatory schools for girls more usually end at the age of ten. The IAPS was originally founded for headmasters of preparatory schools and, in 1932, women who were heads of preparatory schools were forced to form their own Association of Headmistresses of Preparatory Schools. The number of girls' preparatory schools was smaller than that for boys, because many of the secondary girls' schools had preparatory departments that were not run as separate schools. In 1971, the growing number of co-educational schools in IAPS led to headmistresses being allowed to join, and in 1981 the AHMPS and IAPS merged to form a new association. The retention of the male association's title is an indication of the gender imbalance that now exists in the organization.

REFERENCES

Avery, G. (1991) *The Best Type of Girl. A History of Girls' Independent Schools*. London: André Deutsch.
Banford, T.W. (1967) *The Rise of the Public School*. London: Nelson.
Bennett, D. (1990) *Emily Davies and the Liberation of Women*. London: André Deutsch.
Borer, M. C. (1976) *Willingly to School. A History of Women's Education*. London: Lutterworth Press.
Boyd, A.K. (1948) *Radley College 1847–1947*. Oxford: Basil Blackwell.
Bradley, A.G., Champneys, A.C., and Baines, J.W. (1923) *A History of Marlborough College*. London: John Murray.
Burstall, S. A. (1938) *Frances Mary Buss. An Educational Pioneer*. London: SPCK.
Burstyn, J.N. (1980) *Victorian Education and the Idea of Womanhood*. Beckenham: Croom Helm.
Clarke, A.K. (1953) *A History of Cheltenham Ladies' College 1853–1953*. London: Faber & Faber.
Delamont, S., and Duffin, L. (eds.) (1978) *The Nineteenth Century Woman. Her Cultural and Physical World*. Beckenham: Croom Helm.

DES (Department of Education and Science) (1990) *Statistics of Schools in England –
January 1989*, Statistics Bulletin 6/90. London: DES.

Dyhouse, C. (1987) *Girls Growing up in Late Victorian and Edwardian Society*. London:
Routledge & Kegan Paul.

Fox, I. (1984) 'The Demand for a Public School Education: A Crisis of Confidence in
Comprehensive Schooling?', in G. Walford (ed.), *British Public Schools: Policy and
Practice*. Lewes: Falmer.

Fox, I. (1985) *Private Schools and Public Issues*. London: Macmillan.

Halsey, A.H., Heath, A.F., and Ridge, J.M. (1984) 'The Political Arithmetic of Public
Schools', in G. Walford (ed.), *British Public Schools: Policy and Practice*. Lewes:
Falmer.

Hill, R.D. (1962) *A History of St Edward's School 1863–1963*. Oxford: St Edward's School
Society.

Honey, J.R. de S. (1977) *Tom Brown's Universe. The Development of the Public School in
the Nineteenth Century*. London: Millington.

Johnson, D. (1987) *Private Schools and State Schools. Two Systems or One?* Milton Keynes:
Open University Press.

Kamm, J. (1958) *How Different From Us: A Biography of Miss Buss and Miss Beale*.
London: Bodley Head.

Kamm, J. (1965) *Hope Deferred. Girls' Education in English History*. London: Methuen.

Kamm, J. (1971) *Indicative Past. A Hundred Years of the Girls' Public Day School Trust*.
London: George Allen & Unwin.

Kirk, K.E. (1937) *The Story of the Woodard Schools*. Abingdon: Abbey Press.

Leinster-Mackay, D. (1987) *The Educational World of Edward Thring*. Lewes: Falmer.

Morgan, M.C. (1968) *Cheltenham College. The First Hundred Years*. Chalfont St Giles:
Richard Sadler.

Ogilvie, V. (1957) *The English Public School*. London: Batsford.

Ollerenshaw, K. (1967) *The Girls' Schools*. London: Faber & Faber.

Rae, J. (1981) *The Public School Revolution*. London: Faber & Faber.

Shrosbree, C. (1988) *Public Schools and Private Education. The Clarendon Commission.
1861–64, and the Public Schools Act*. Manchester: Manchester University Press.

Simon, B. (1960) *The Two Nations and the Educational Structure 1780–1870*. London:
Lawrence & Wishart.

Smithers, A., and Robinson, P. (1989) *Increasing Participation in Higher Education*.
London: BP Education Service.

Steadman, F. C. (1931) *In the Days of Miss Beale*. London: E. J. Burrow.

Turner, B. (1974) *Equality for Some. The Story of Girls' Education*. London: Ward Lock.

Walford, G. (1983) 'Girls in Boys' Public Schools: A Prelude to Further Research', *British
Journal of Sociology of Education*, 4, 1: 39–54.

Walford, G. (1990) *Privatization and Privilege in Education*. London: Routledge.

Walford, G. (1991a) 'Choice of School at the First City Technology College', *Educational
Studies*, 17, 1: 65–75.

Walford, G. (1991b) (ed.) *Private Schooling: Tradition. Change and Diversity*. London:
Paul Chapman.

Webster, F.A.M. (1937) *Our Great Public Schools. Their Traditions, Customs and Games*.
London: Ward Lock.

2

'Playing the Game' and 'Playing the Piano':
Physical Culture and Culture at Girls' Public Schools c. 1850–1914

KATHLEEN E. McCRONE

The link between 'playing the game' and 'playing the piano' may at first glance appear tenuous. However, in fact, the two types of 'playing' were important aspects of girls' public-school education during the second half of the nineteenth century. On the one hand, they represented very different and contradictory educational trends and goals. On the other, they shared unexpected similarities regarding some of the ways they were approached, the ends towards which they were directed, and the ways the limitations upon them perpetuated perceptions of women's 'inferiority'.

The expansion of the educational opportunities available to middle-class women and girls was one of the major feminist achievements of the nineteenth century, for it released the stifled intellects of a large and important segment of the community and was crucial to the whole question of women's advancement. The first condition of emancipation being that women themselves should be able to demand it, they had to develop self-and gender-awareness through education. So long as many remained ignorant, they could neither notice nor challenge their inferior status in sufficient numbers to transform the complaints of individuals into an effective movement. Furthermore, as long as women were under-educated, critics of their liberation could claim with some justification that they were ill-equipped for broadened vocational, legal and political horizons.

According to Frances Power Cobbe, the prominent mid-nineteenth-century upholder of women's rights, in the early-Victorian period, 'The education of women was probably at its lowest ebb. It was ... more pretentious than it had ever been before ... and it was likewise

33

more shallow and senseless ...[1] Based on ornamental accomplishments, it eschewed anything resembling genuine mental and physical training. Many people of both sexes honestly believed that God and nature had created women different from, and inferior to, men, and had given them separate spheres. This view was reinforced by female education and by the rising middle classes' new ideal of femininity, to which passivity, delicacy, gentility and obedience were intrinsic. Since society considered marriage the only legitimate vocation for respectable ladies, things perceived as militating against it – such as too much education – were considered undesirable. Traditionalists thus argued for many years that if girls received intellectual training, they would probably become coarse, unpleasant creatures, unattractive to men, and inclined to forsake matrimony and maternity for a love of quadratic equations.

Changes in education in general, and female education in particular, came with timid slowness. Through a combination of lethargy, jealousy and desperate determination, outworn aims and methods endured until mid-century, when the new forces produced by the Industrial Revolution finally began to alter the outlook of increasingly large numbers. During the 1850s, the need to abolish the barriers that hindered people of both sexes and various classes from attaining genuine education finally began to emerge from the Victorian era's general impulse towards emancipation and reform. Indeed, even conservatives came to realize that all children had to be prepared by various types of training for different kinds of lives, and that the ignorance of substantial segments of the population could be dangerous.

On no other aspect of female life was there eventually as much agreement as on the almost universal weakness of female middle-class education. Critics had been relatively easy to find since the late eighteenth century, but only from the mid-Victorian period did they become numerous and determined enough to accomplish anything significant. While they could never agree completely on the reasons reforms should be made and what the reforms and their results should be, much more important was the fact that reformers' criticisms and proposals coalesced for the first time into an effective movement that produced major public and private initiatives for change.

Although affecting only a minority of females, the new girls' public day and boarding schools, which were founded during the second half of the nineteenth century – particularly from the 1870s onwards – proved to be especially powerful agents in the educational revolution.

Differing markedly from the private ladies' academies of the past in size, financing, goals, organization, curricula and methods, virtually all with pretensions to excellence sought to prepare girls from business and professional families for more active and useful roles in the public and private spheres by giving them a sound and broadly based liberal education.

Educational pioneers generally agreed that females were intellectually and physically deficient not because they lacked ability, but because they had been denied opportunities to develop and apply their talents. Girls as well as boys, they argued, had a right to, and a need for, solid academic and physical training, in order to prepare them to be better wives and mothers and to support themselves should – as demographic realities guaranteed for many – they not marry. If women were to cease being considered inferior, reformers held, and if they were to have productive and fulfilling lives, they required opportunities for intellectual and personal development similar to those of males. While adaptation rather than slavish imitation was their watch-word, and they endeavoured to avoid some of the errors of the male experience, they usually perceived masculine subjects and activities as desirable norms and traditionally feminine ones as less so. With certain notable exceptions, their highest priority thus became the provision of sound intellectual and physical education through the introduction of curricula, examinations, activities and rewards similar to those in boys' schools.

At the same time, however, many reforming headmistresses were progressive conservatives who eschewed social radicalism and whose strategies manifested striking contradictions and ambivalences. As several scholars have convincingly demonstrated, the fulfilment of their goals necessitated accommodation of the demands of femininity and social class, along with a revision of the feminine ideal to include the possibility of intellectual and physical development and careers other than marriage. To put it another way, the reformers embraced a 'double conformity' or 'divided aim' involving the simultaneous acceptance of things apparently mutually exclusive: 'male' academic and atheletic programmes and the constraints of womanliness. Most were highly respectable ladies who remained committed to traditional values and to a sexual division of labour. They therefore aimed to redefine rather than reject the meaning of womanliness and woman's mission. Most also appreciated that the invigorating educational diet they proposed would arouse acute criticism and parental fears, because it appeared to violate many 'sacred' tenets about the training and socialization of female adolescents. To succeed in the long run, they realized they would have to proceed cautiously. Hence, even the most advanced girls' schools continued to insist on impeccably feminine behaviour, and to include certain reassuringly ladylike accomplishments in their curricula.[2]

During the past two decades, historians of women's education have carefully scrutinized the new girls' public schools and the reform movement to which they were integral. But aspects of the schools' 'divided aims' warrant further examination, for they manifest particularly effectively the tensions and cross-purposes that have plagued female education until recently. An analysis of girls' schools' treatment of sport (traditionally a male preserve) and of music (traditionally a female one) is especially revealing.

In the educational old regime, sport and physical education played a minor part, and music a major part. Early-Victorian girls were constantly reminded of their sex's purpose and nature. They were taught that facial colour and muscular strength were unrefined, and that physical effort could damage their reproductive organs as well as their attractiveness to men. Not surprisingly, most girls' schools deliberately avoided genuine physical training, and condoned only demure walking, gentle callisthenics and decorous dancing, which supposedly contributed to the becoming postures and social skills required of a polished lady.

This situation was widely condemned, but not until publication of the harsh criticisms of the famous Schools' Inquiry (Taunton) Commission in 1868, was national attention drawn to the problem. After describing 'the important subject of bodily exercise' as 'imperfectly attended to', and the 'want of systematic and well-directed physical education' as a major impediment to good health and academic success, the Commissioners noted the absence of competition in girls' leisure pursuits, a tendency to consider vigorous exercise undignified, and a general lack of playgrounds and provision for outdoor exercise and games.[3]

At the time the Commission reported, a revolution in sport was underway in English society. An influential aspect of this was the development – at the public schools where bourgeois boys were turned into gentlemen – of a unique cult of athleticism centred on organized team games and the idea that they produced manly men with sterling characters. Manliness and the strength and assertiveness it implied, of course, were considered the complete opposites of femininity. Yet the significance of games-playing at boys' schools for

36

the education of girls was considerable, since it was the boys' scholastic and athletic programmes that many reformers of female education sought to emulate; and it was at similar institutions for girls that organized female sports made some of their earliest appearances.

Most reformers of female education believed that intellectual and physical health were intimately connected; and in time they voiced the distinctly unconventional view that competitive sports and sound physical training should be integral to the education of girls. Games-playing in particular, they argued, would improve health and reproductive potential and counteract mental overstrain. Above all, it would impart valuable moral qualities, such as loyalty, discipline, determination and resourcefulness, that had previously been identified exclusively with males.

Because of the necessity to accommodate reforms to prevailing rules of propriety, the transition from gentle callisthenics to real physical education and competitive games was gradual and did not occur to any extent before the 1880s. From the first, however, many of the best of the new girls' schools, both day and boarding, deliberately tried to educate female bodies as well as minds by providing more opportunities for exercise than had been customary, with the result that they eventually became centres of athletic as well as academic pioneering. A balanced and integrated programme of physical education evolved, which included attention to the physical development and therapeutic needs of individuals, scientifically designed systems of exercise supervised by professionally trained mistresses, regular inspection by qualified medical practitioners, and an elaborate system of organized and competitive games. This comprehensive programme put girls' schools well ahead of their male counterparts, where a simplistic cult of athleticism continued to dominate.

Aesthetic subjects such as music, which had been part of the traditional system of ladylike accomplishments and which had no models in male education, continued to be taught at these pioneering schools. The difference was that the new schools no longer considered accomplishments of prime importance and usually attempted to teach them systematically, to make them optional, and to relegate them to free afternoon hours – thus making sure they did not impinge on the more demanding academic objectives. All the same, few schools dreamed of completely omitting 'aesthetics' because of their feminine imputations and parents' insistence that they be taught.[4]

The cornerstone of popular musical life was the home, for music was considered an effective means of assuring that the ideal home was a kind of Ruskinian 'sacred temple'. Central to domestic music were women, for they were the main performers; and, as was so often the case, they were expected to subordinate their personal inclinations to the pleasure of others, particularly their menfolk.[5] While not new to the period, the musical evening became extremely fashionable among middle-class Victorians, where the onus for entertaining family members and guests by singing and playing the piano fell primarily on ladies whose delicacy of touch and expression was considered more important than the quality of their execution and musicianship.

The piano, a major status symbol in the Victorian home, was the instrument on which domestic music particularly centred, and it took on definite gender connotations. While a not-quite-manly hobby for gentlemen, piano-playing for ladies became identified as an essential accomplishment – a sign of undoubted gentility and an indispensable aid to romance. Thus, throughout the nineteenth century, girls from respectable families were taught to play the piano, regardless of their abilities or inclinations, much as they were taught embroidery or French.[6]

Some women whose musical efforts were purely domestic undoubtedly became outstanding musicians. But it was generally taken for granted that, apart from singing, females were incapable of substantial musical attainment, and that if music were pursued too seriously it had dangerous potential. 'Young ladies singing or playing were expected to charm but in no way to disturb or challenge their listeners.'[7] For years they were warned against approaching the study of music professionally, on the ground that musical ability was to be used as a means of pleasure at home and never of public display. After all, argued Matilda Pullan, what young lady with any sense would put a love of serious music before her desire for a good marriage? 'Who would wish a wife or daughter ... to have attained such excellence in music as involves a life's devotion to it?'[8]

For the production of drawing-room songbirds and pianists, tuition, of course, was necessary. This was most commonly offered by professional musicians of both sexes to supplement their incomes, by genteel ladies of modest talent and limited training who were forced by circumstances to support themselves, and by governesses whose taste and skill were similarly limited. In addition, at all but the cheapest of the unreformed girls' schools, class singing was compulsory and piano and solo singing lessons were provided for an extra fee by teachers of varying qualifications.

The Schools' Inquiry Commission reported that, unlike boys'

schools where 'music is so little learnt as hardly to call for separate remark',[9] 'the great and obvious feature of all Girls' Schools, except those of the humblest type, is the enormous preponderance given to accomplishments over solid acquirements',[10] to satisfy parents' demands. The state of musical instruction was identified as particularly deplorable. Of all the accomplishments, the Commissioners said, playing the piano encroached most on intellectual improvement, in many schools occupying as much as one-quarter to one-third of the working time at a girl's disposal. Furthermore, the common way of teaching was 'a nauseous process' – 'without intelligence', unscientific, irrational and wasteful. Too much emphasis was placed on the acquisition of mechanical accuracy for purposes of display, and too little on training the mind and playing with taste and feeling. As a result, between the ages of eight and 18, girls with little talent and less inclination were likely to spend over 5,000 hours practising the piano, and their time was wasted, the Commissioners concluded, since competence, commitment and genuine musicianship rarely resulted.[11]

As has been noted, while the new girls' public schools deliberately introduced an academic and athletic regime based on male models and put intellectual education first, they did not ignore 'refinements'. The old tradition of private teaching of the piano and of private and class tuition in singing was largely preserved in the form of compulsory class singing and optional individual vocal and instrumental instruction. At a few schools such instruction continued to stress display.[12] At most establishments, however, a deliberate effort was made to teach both the theory and practice of music more scientifically, in accordance with their general aim to treat all aspects of education seriously. The reasons schools continued to teach music at all, though, remained closely connected to their 'double conformity' to male standards in intellectual training and female cultural and behavioural norms. The majority of schools did not consider the prime importance of their improved musical instruction to be preparation for higher musical studies and professional careers, but rather the production of an appreciation of the fine arts and of a tone of refinement among the gifted and ungifted alike, and the counter-action of 'what is low and base and [the cultivation of] all that is true, pure and lovely'.[13]

The new schools' pattern of 'double conformity' and 'divided aims' is revealed with particular clarity by an examination of the place that games (representing the advanced 'masculine' orientation) and music (representing the traditional 'feminine' one) occupied at the two earliest and most famous establishments, the North London Collegiate School for Ladies and the Cheltenham Ladies' College. The former was a day school founded in 1850 by Frances Mary Buss (1827–94) for the daughters of professional men, clerks and respectable tradesmen. The latter, primarily a boarding school and more exclusive, was founded in 1853 for the daughters of noblemen and gentlemen, and from 1858 to 1906 its principal was Dorothea Beale (1831–1906). Both headmistresses became legends in their own lifetimes.

THE NORTH LONDON COLLEGIATE SCHOOL

Frances Mary Buss was brought up and educated by unusually enlightened parents. At an early age she became aware of the educational needs of both single, middle-class women who were forced to live with friends or relatives or take up uncongenial occupations because they had not been trained to earn an independent living, and of married women who as mothers were responsible for diffusing 'amongst their children the truths and duties of religion, and ... a portion of that mass of information placed by modern education within the reach of all'.[14]

At the North London Collegiate School, Miss Buss set out to provide girls with an education that would develop their morals, character and intellect to the fullest, and thus prepare them for any position in life. From the first she introduced a 'dangerously advanced' academic programme; and because she considered health a primary concern, she required students to take physical exercise. She did not, however, completely reject ladylike accomplishments. Class singing was made a compulsory subject, and private music lessons were provided as 'extras'.

Miss Buss believed schoolgirls needed far more exercise than they normally received in order to improve health and to counteract the potentially ill-effects of strenuous mental work. So from the first, although moving cautiously, she required older students to attend callisthenics classes several times a week and younger ones to play outdoors. In the 1870s, she successfully gained access for students to the St Pancras Baths, London, and engaged a swimming instructor. She also persuaded the school's governors to include a gymnasium (the first in a girls' school) in the new school building that opened in 1879. Then, commending gymnastics for enhancing health and improving educational efficiency while 'admirably ... cultivating ... grace and elegance of movement',[15] she ensured that the whole school in different divisions participated in short daily drills, and that optional gymnastics lessons were offered during the free afternoon hours. An eclectic method with a German bias was used, since it included dancing and was thus, Miss Buss considered, more feminine than the more popular Swedish system.

Because she shared the widely held belief that many girls were physically abnormal, Miss Buss also concluded that the management of exercise should be in the hands of female experts. She thus engaged a trained physical education teacher and a part-time woman doctor, innovative steps that were widely imitated. All gymnastics students were required to undergo inspection by the physician who prescribed remedial exercise under the supervision of the physical training mistress and then recorded the improvements.

Although the development of athletic games and sports was seriously handicapped for years by the lack of adequate grounds, during the 1880s and 1890s a sports programme quietly evolved. Students established a games club to organize badminton, fives and ninepins contests in the gymnasium, then the different created separate games clubs for outdoor play in rounders and fives. A few students began competing for prizes in swimming races, which were the prelude to the introduction of races against other schools – the North London's first outside sports competitions. These heightened interest in swimming to such an extent that a swimming club was formed to arrange lessons, life-saving classes, aquatic sports days and form, school and inter-school contests. In addition, squash rackets, intra- and inter-school tennis matches and annual athletic sports days were introduced. By 1900 there were sports clubs for gymnastics, tennis, rounders and fives, while netball, which was begun in 1899 and was considered by school authorities to be particularly conducive to developing self-control and unselfishness, was becoming competitive at the form and inter-school levels.[16]

The appearance of the great team game of hockey was delayed until after Miss Buss's death because she feared that it would cause overstrain and that only rough girls would participate. However, her successor, Mrs Sophie Bryant, was an ardent sportswoman, and in 1896, shortly after she became principal, hockey was finally introduced by mistresses who had learned to play at Girton College, Cambridge. Soon, teachers and senior students started a club which hired grounds for practices, joined the All England Women's Hockey Association, and arranged various internal and external matches. Finally, in 1909, hockey and other sports received a much-needed boost when the school acquired a 2.5-acre sports ground, the governors having finally recognized the lack of athletic facilities as detrimental to the school's otherwise progressive image.

Although 'playing the game' was never as significant a part of life at the North London Collegiate School as at other notable day schools, such as those of the Girls' Public Day School Company (1872–), for which it was the model, and St. Paul's School for Girls (1904), exercise – and eventually competitive sports – were fundamental to the North London's primary aims – the development of the whole woman and the demonstratation of female abilities by challenging and cultivating both mind and body. The result was the gradual implementation of a comprehensive programme of physical education directed towards the needs of individuals, which included optional games-playing and compulsory, supervised gymnastics. At the same time, the frequency of sports participation was always carefully restricted in order to protect the 'play' and 'fun' elements, and to prevent an excessive interest in games having deleterious effects on health and schoolwork.[17]

The ideal North London Collegiate product was the 'new girl' described by the school magazine in 1900 as rational, strong, loyal and willingly co-operative. She could swim, cycle and play hockey. Indeed, she could do virtually anything a boy could as a result of a 'true instinct of sport'.[18] At the same time, however, she appreciated the importance of retaining her femininity. The enforcement of strict rules of behaviour on and off the playing field and the inclusion in the North London Collegiate curriculum of such a traditionally womanly subject as music were intended as a guarantee.[19]

Frances Mary Buss regarded musical proficiency as excellent mental and moral training and as a desirable accomplishment, even for advanced young ladies. She disapproved of the showy, superficial and time-wasting way the subject was often taught, and the low standards of taste and skill that resulted. From her school's foundation, she determined 'to make music an earnest and educational part of school work',[20] 'to teach music grandly, thoroughly ... to make each girl understand what she plays ...'[21] As a result, music came to play a prominent, though always secondary, role in school life, and its quality gradually improved. The school's music staff – which included men and women – never averaged more than five, some of whom were part-time; but their effectiveness increased over the years as teachers with better qualifications and a more systematic approach were appointed.

Class singing was compulsory from 1850 for the conservative reason that it would enable students to 'contribute not only to congregational singing but to innocent and cheerful amusement at home'.[22] Private, and later class, piano, singing, harmony and composition lessons were 'extras', taken advantage of by approximately one-quarter of the students. In 1875, violin lessons were added because Miss Buss thought it 'a great advantage to have different instruments taught',[23] and because of a growing demand – society having finally recognized that violin-playing was not unfeminine.

From 1877 onwards, visiting inspectors conducted annual examinations in harmony and performance, an arrangement the school's board of governors made official in 1886. From 1889, a number of students sat the examinations of the Associated Board of the Royal Academy/Royal College of Music, despite a lack of encouragement because they were not considered part of the school's overall scheme. After 1903, there was more encouragement for students to take the examinations in music conducted by the University of London as part of a plan for the examination and inspection of school studies. A few ex-pupils of the North London Collegiate School went on to the major colleges of music and became teachers – and even professional performers.

In 1886, a school choir was formed, and from time to time guest lectures were given on musical subjects. For several years during the 1890s there were singing contests between forms for a challenge cup. Annual concerts performed by students before family and friends, designed 'to give a definite point to Musical teaching'[24] and to raise money for good causes such as the repair of the school organ, were major, if at times painfully long, events each autumn. Musical performances were also integral to such special occasions as prize days, where awards in harmony and vocal and instrumental music were distributed along with those for academic and athletic achievements. For a few years, from 1898, these special days were embellished by the performances of a small string orchestra – which, alas, did not survive.

Such musical activities and the time and attention devoted to them were fairly typical of large girls' public day schools, although they were less extensive than at some other institutions. Several of the schools of the Girls' Public Day Schools Company (GPDSC) were considerably more musically orientated;[25] for example, one such was St Paul's, where music featured prominently, because the first high mistress considered it a necessity which studied 'Beauty' and led to 'Truth', and was thus integral to the whole scheme of education.[26]

THE CHELTENHAM LADIES' COLLEGE

Important as exercise and sport became at prominent day schools, their role was never as significant as at the great girls' boarding-schools, which emulated male models particularly closely, and wherein, as a result, the games-playing phenomenon reached its peak. At some such schools as well, the halls were 'alive with the sound of music' for the same reason as at the day schools – conformity with female rather than male norms.

Something of an exception to the game-playing ethos, at least initially, was the Cheltenham Ladies' College, whose aim was to give the girl from an upper- or upper-middle-class family

> an education based upon religious principles which, preserving the modesty and gentleness of the female character, should so far cultivate intellectual powers as to fit her for the discharge of those responsible duties which devolve upon her as a wife, mother, mistress and friend, the natural companion and help-meet for man.[27]

Through adaptation rather than slavish imitation, Dorothea Beale was determined to apply the boys' public-school system to the education of girls, 'so that they may best perform the subordinate part in the world, to which ... they have been called'.[28] Convinced that women with fully developed minds and bodies were healthier and more womanly than those without, she committed herself to offering sound and balanced religious, intellectual and physical training in a way that would magnify femininity and cultivate minds and morals.

Cheltenham's early prospectuses listed callisthenics as part of the regular course because Miss Beale considered them an antidote to excessive brainwork. Before long, she terminated the school day at 1 p.m., partly in order to allow more time for outdoor exercise, and over the years she gradually endorsed an improvement of exercise facilities. By 1890, the full system of Swedish gymnastics was offered in a well-equipped gymnasium under the supervision of a qualified teacher. By 1905, Cheltenham's staff included six trained physical-education mistresses who were responsible for superintending games and teaching gymnastics, fencing, swimming and remedial exercise.

Because Miss Beale considered competition of any sort for girls as productive of too great a desire for success and incompatible with their unique emotional and intellectual needs and family responsibilities, and because she regarded sporting contests as particularly masculinizing, for years she prohibited them – apart from occasional 'quiet' games of rounders, tennis and fives. Not until 1890 did Miss Beale finally rent a playing field, apparently having become convinced that the introduction of games in some form was inevitable. At the same time, however, she ordained that they would develop in harmony with the school's general purposes by insisting that play be in a feminine manner and costume, by prohibiting inter-school matches for fear they would foster the type of emulation and overstrain she tried to avoid in the classroom, and by rejecting the awards for excellence in sport and the elements of compulsion that were becoming common at other boarding schools.[29]

Even Miss Beale could not forestall the march of progress, however. As a result of demand by students and mistresses and pressure resulting from the revolution in women's sport under way in society at large and in girls' schools in particular, she soon found herself permitting competitions within and among Cheltenham's 18 boarding houses in tennis, hockey and cricket. By the turn of the century, there was scarcely a school in England with better or more extensive sports facilities, or one that was more of 'a hotbed of hockey'.[30] Games may have been a less prominent part of the overall Cheltenham scheme than at such notable boarding schools as St. Leonards, Roedean and Wycombe Abbey, but their gradual institution, despite Miss Beale's deeply rooted suspicions and resistance, indicates the inexorable growth of their influence and acceptance, as does the choice, as her successor, of a prominent sportswoman. At the time of Lillian Faithfull's appointment to Cheltenham (1907), she was president of the All England Women's Hockey Association, and, as the school council must have anticipated and desired, under her aegis sport received much greater official encouragement and became competitive externally.

Long before they learned to 'play the game', however, Cheltonians learned to play the piano. Their school's founders disliked the fashionable practice of compelling every young lady to perform on the piano, because the time wasted attaining slight proficiency detracted from mental cultivation. None the less, they conceded to fashion and parental demand so far as to include class piano and singing lessons among the accomplishments that were retained in the regular curriculum. When Dorothea Beale became principal, she de-emphasized accomplishments in favour of more demanding academic subjects. Music, apart from class singing, was made an 'extra'.[31] But some 'extra'! In time, the Ladies' College became famous as a kind of unofficial conservatory for the whole Cheltenham area.[32]

Just as facilities for sport were improved over the years, so also were those for music. The seven small music rooms – little better than cupboards – that were included in the new building that opened in 1873 were replaced in 1882 by a whole fine-arts wing that was enlarged in 1898. In its 30 sound-proof music rooms an unusually large music staff comprised of a 'galaxy of brilliant musicians'[33], three-quarters of whom were female, and who possessed the best English and foreign credentials, gave an amazing number of individual lessons on the piano, and in voice, violin, cello, organ, harp, zither, mandolin, banjo and guitar, and group lessons in harmony, theory, sight reading and singing.[34] Towards the end of the summer term, just before final examinations, every music teacher's pupils gave a succession of concerts before parents and friends, which were considered an important part of the school regime. Further, despite Miss Beale's dislike of competition and rewards, in-house music examinations and prizes were introduced, and, after her death, folk-song contests between houses.[35]

In other corners of their musical world, from the 1890s a number of Cheltenham students sat the examinations of the Associated Board, and a significant minority went on to English and German conservatories. They listened to guest lectures on musical subjects and enjoyed musical 'at homes' and occasional recitals by ex-students and regular ones by members of the music staff, often in aid of charity. They participated in a quartet class, in a choir and later a choral society and in a string orchestra comprised of staff members and past and present students and conducted by a man, which made 'steady progress in its more artistic treatment of high-class music'.[36] Additionally, following the acquisition of a new organ for the Great Hall in celebration of Miss Beale's twenty-fifth anniversary as principal, the music provided daily at school prayers became a feature of school life in which she took particular delight.

Finally, Cheltenham students were encouraged to take advantage of their town's extremely full musical life. The local philharmonic society put on regular concerts, and distinguished soloists – Joachim, Pachmann, Paderewski, Patti, Sarasate, Sibelius, Sir Charles and Lady Hallé, Fanny Davies, John McCormack – appeared regularly, sometimes at the school. By the time she graduated, a Cheltenham girl was likely to have heard many of the greatest musicians of the age.[37]

CONCLUSION

By 1914, there were over 200 girls' public schools catering for different ranks within the middle class. Enrolments varied from about 80 to 650, while opportunities for exercise ranged from dancing only to comprehensive sports and physical training programmes; and for musical training, it varied from a little amateurish instruction in singing and the piano to the extensive, professional regime of Cheltenham. Numerous small private ladies' academies survived, largely unaffected by the movements for educational reform and women's rights, where parental permission was required for anything resembling games-playing, and where girls could be forced to practise their music in tiny box-like rooms in which pianos might be sandwiched between beds and wardrobes. Nevertheless, the change that had occurred in girls' schooling since mid-century was nothing less than a revolution.[38]

Whereas it would have been impossible for a mid-Victorian school to boast that 'outdoor games and physical culture play an important part in school life',[39] by the turn of the century it was generally recognized that girls required regular exercise and that athletic games should form an integral part of students' activities. School prospectuses boasted proudly of playing fields and gymnasia, opportunities for sport and systematic physical education, and trained physical educators on the staff.

The section on 'Games for Girls' in *Girls' School Year Books* reveals just how important sport had become. Calling sport the perfect antidote to academic overwork and the means to produce valuable moral qualities, it identified the numerous sports played, and explained their organization and the roles of mistresses and students. It noted further that the time spent on exercise and sport averaged one to two hours daily, that participation was often compulsory at boarding schools, that the number of inter-school matches was usually limited so as to detract as little as possible from internal play and study, and that competition within schools was particularly encouraged to give students of varying proficiency an opportunity to participate.[40]

The *Year Books* also recognized the importance of school music. Its proper place in the curriculum may still have been a subject of considerable debate among educational authorities, but each edition included a lengthy section on 'The Musical Profession', which gave advice to students on specialization, the chief schools of music in London and the provinces, and the various musical examinations and examining bodies. The professional position in music anticipated for most women with training was usually that of music mistress in a good school. But at least the possibility of performance was considered as well, which attests to the evolution since mid-century of more progressive views on appropriate musical activities for ladies.[41]

The 1909 and 1910 editions published the results of a special enquiry into music in girls' schools. The enquiry concluded that while the time assigned for daily practice varied widely – from 20 minutes to four hours – the average was 30 to 60 minutes. In most schools, it observed, 'the subject of music is given most careful thought ... and. ... the results ... are eminently satisfactory'.[42] Forty-three per cent of the 16,130 students in the 86 schools examined received instrumental instruction, the piano being studied ten times more frequently than all other instruments combined (6,147 piano/731 others), an imbalance described as regrettable. Class singing was always part of the regular course; and pupils were usually systematically taught elementary musical theory, sight reading, playing from memory and accompaniment of voice and violin on the piano. In addition, almost half the schools had string orchestras, and many endeavoured to cultivate in students the ability to enjoy good music, by means of lectures, musical discussions and special concerts and recitals.

The chief problem the enquiry identified was utilizing fully the small place that could be allotted to music in the average school timetable. As things then stood, it appeared quite impossible to give music its due, as a result of the many other subjects that had to be covered and the necessity to assure that general education did not suffer at music's expense. Yet it was essential, the enquiry said, that talented girls who proposed to become professional musicians could specialize at a comparatively early age.[43]

Although the musical and the physical sides of girls' schooling represented very different aims and attitudes and the physical was much the more important, there are striking similarities in the ways they were approached and the ends that they were thought to accomplish. For example, it was usual for a school's tone in music as well as sport and physical education to be set by the headmistress. If she were interested, things tended to flourish; if she were not, the opposite often occurred.[44] Similarly, the trend in both areas during the late-Victorian period was towards upgrading quality and status, considerably improved facilities and equipment (thanks frequently to the largess of alumnae and friends), increasingly professional teaching by trained and certificated instructors and regular inspection, the reports on which were carefully filed for future reference and comparison.

In addition, 'playing the game' and 'playing the piano' were perceived as having valuable benefits applicable to life as a whole. Just as sport and exercise were promoted because of their health-improving qualities, so it was argued that the breathing exercises required of singing students 'were as important to health as to music',[45] and that the playing of musical instruments provided useful exercise for different parts of the body. At the same time, fears were occasionally expressed that, like too much mental and physical exercise, too much musical practice could prejudice health.[46]

Other interesting similarities included the equation of playing on sports teams and in orchestras and singing in choirs with the merging of the individual in a community and thus the production of the admirable selflessness, good fellowship and collective feeling essential to the creation of *esprit de corps* in a school. Participation in sport and music was also thought to quicken mental processes, thereby laying the foundation for abstract thought; to provide pleasurable recreation, and thus a valuable antidote to the strain of book learning; to arouse healthy enthusiasm and rivalry when competitive; and to cultivate habits of accuracy, concentration, patience, initiative, discipline, balance and self-reliance. Furthermore, the conviction prevailed that good art produced good ethics, and thus that involvement in music, just as in sport, had an important moral influence that elevated character.[47]

On the more negative side, the obsession with cups and colours that characterized sport at a number of schools was paralled in the realm of music by the avid pursuit of the certificates that were awarded rather liberally by some musical examiners. There were also similar elements of compulsion. Class singing was a required part of the ordinary curriculum at all girls' public schools – regardless of whether students wanted to, or could, sing – just as gymnastics was usually compulsory at both day and boarding schools, and games as well, at many of the latter, regardless of desire or talent.

The changes in the ways girls' schools viewed and taught exercise and music between 1850 and 1914 were important reflectors of the tensions between older and newer concepts of woman, and the degree of continuity and discontinuity between traditional and 'advanced' provisions for educating young ladies. Throughout the period, although many schools tolerated a certain amount of liberty on the playing field, even the most progressive went to considerable lengths to avoid serious breaches with the contemporary code of feminine conduct and respectability that might have damaged their reputations and so endangered entire programmes. Although games-playing became increasingly widespread and valued for its physiological and social benefits, reforming educators remained uneasy about serious sports competition, particularly in rough and potentially unfeminine games such as hockey and cricket. The gradual acceptance of sport as compatible with femininity thus necessitated protracted negotiations and compromises that reconciled the apparent conflict between 'playing the game' and appropriate female behaviour.

Many reforming headmistresses remained committed to conventional Victorian values, and to the belief that men and women had different missions. They may have encouraged games-playing among girls, but they continued to perceive it as 'boyish'; and, to counter sport's masculine image, they required students to dress and behave in a manner that projected an image of reassuring moderation. They also accepted the notion of limited sport – that is, that certain sports and ways of playing were unacceptable, such as those requiring physical contact, awkward positions and great endurance or strength, and so far as as was possible they eliminated painful and dangerous elements and the aggressive use of hands and feet. If these conditions hindered the development of skilful play and perpetuated the view that girls' sport was not really serious, the price was considered worth paying to preserve modesty and gain acceptance. Thus, while reforming educators had a major role in making sport a respectable activity for adolescent girls and encouraging them to be physically fit and to develop new character traits, they contributed to the continued identification of vigorous physical activity with masculinity, and so to its use as a powerful mechanism of gender-based social control.[48]

It was to balance and complement the 'masculine' sides of school life that headmistresses encouraged such subjects as music, which were considered aesthetic and therefore feminine, and which were intended to improve the imagination, promote womanly virtues, inspire an appreciation of the fine arts, and improve the tone of refinement even among the untalented.[49] By 1914, the tradition of ornamental accomplishments, which had assured cultural subjects a continuing place in revised curricula in the first place, had abandoned frivolity and become essentially serious and professional, because reformers had deliberately sought to improve their quality and raise their academic status. The result was that some schools (just as in physical education and sport) had built up considerable musical expertise and reputations. Ironically, however, these high reputations tended to reinforce the idea that music was 'feminine' and, because it was particularly important for girls, that it lacked academic integrity.[50]

Although music was often described as 'vigorous' and a 'strong feature' of school life, its variety was generally limited to solo and class singing and studying the piano, violin, and a little theory. Occasionally instruction on the cello, organ, guitar and banjo was offered, but the playing of wind instruments, like the playing of certain sports, was usually not allowed, because the ill-founded views persisted that women lacked the strength to play winds well and the ability to look pretty while doing so. It was not considered 'a pleasing sight to see [brass and woodwind women] struggling with the bassoon or trombone, with starting eyes, swollen lips, and distended cheeks'.[51] In the wider world, what women did in music, as in sport, tended to be considered trivial and unworthy of serious consideration, and only certain activities were accepted as in accordance with socialization for womanliness. It is hardly surprising, therefore, that the limitations imposed by the dictates of femininity on the nature and extent of musical training in schools derogated its status. The upshot was that women were allowed to play music (as to 'play the game') only within limited behavioural boundaries which confirmed the separate spheres of the sexes and the superiority of men.

The ultimate aim of girls' public schools during the second half of the nineteenth century was to develop the character and abilities of students to the fullest in order to turn them into cultivated and useful gentlewomen. Academic, physical and cultural training was thus directed towards this end, and represented a considerable advance over what had gone before. By providing students with unprecedented opportunities for development and independence, the schools made a major contribution to women's emancipation. At the same time, however, they remained essentially faithful to the demands of the traditional female role, and to the idea that they must train girls for suitable matrimony. While the reformed schools broadened views of the female role to include work apart from family service, they continued to identify success with marriage and domesticity.[52]

There remained important discontinuities between female education and what was realizable in adulthood. The broad and solid training girls received in public schools may have made their sex's potential better appreciated, but that potential remained incompletely attainable. Public-school products frequently found themselves in an ambiguous position. They had been freed of a number of traditional trammels in their efforts to acquire knowledge, health and careers, but they remained restricted by social conventions relating to their class and gender, and by the striking contradictions that were implicit in reformed ideas about the socialization of women. Public-school girls were encouraged to develop opposite sides of their personalities at the same time. They were allowed to pursue academic study that was serious and goal-directed; they were encouraged to be ambitious and self-disciplined and to aspire to careers before marriage. They were permitted good health and physical stamina, and to bicycle and play any number of athletic games; and they were offered an increasingly professional musical training. Simultaneously, however, they were taught to be subservient and self-sacrificing, to believe that their highest duty was to perform well as wives and mothers and to accept obediently many of the limitations that society continued to impose on their sex.[53]

The result was that while the public schools challenged traditional gender relationships by demanding sound education for females, their acceptance of the standards of ladylike behaviour helped to maintain and perpetuate the ideologies, values and attitudes that customarily dominated social relationships between the sexes. Despite considerable progress, in both sport and music, the forces of femininity, however redefined, remained the greatest influence on students' lives. Neither the sporting nor musical worlds of the girls' public school, represented by 'playing the game' and 'playing the piano', seriously challenged the sexual division of labour in society at large. Public-school girls continued to have to choose between marriage and a career, between femininity and ambition.[54]

ACKNOWLEDGEMENTS

The author gratefully acknowledges the support provided by research grants from the Social Sciences and Humanities Research Council of Canada.

NOTES

1. F. P. Cobbe, *Life of Frances Power Cobbe*, 2 vols (New York: Houghton, Mifflin, 1895), Vol. 1, p. 50.
2. S. Delamont, 'The Contradictions in Ladies' Education', in S. Delamont and L. Duffin (eds), *The Nineteenth Century Woman: Her Cultural and Physical World* (London: Croom Helm, 1978), pp. 134–63; C. Dyhouse, *Girls Growing Up in Late Victorian and Edwardian England* (London: Routledge & Kegan Paul, 1981), pp. 40–78; F. Hunt, 'Divided Aims: The Educational Implications of Opposing Ideologies in Girls'

Secondary Schooling, 1850–1940', in F. Hunt (ed.), *Lessons for Life: The Schooling of Girls and Women, 1850–1950* (Oxford: Basil Blackwell, 1987), pp. 3–21; K. E. McCrone, *Sport and the Physical Emancipation of English Women, 1870–1914* (London: Routledge, 1988), pp. 61, 88–9.

3. Great Britain, Royal Commission on School Education, *Report* (1868), Vol. 1, p. 522 and Vol. 7, pp. 556–7. See also Vol. 6, pp. 389, 588, and Vol. 9, p. 299.

4. Dyhouse, *Girls Growing Up*, p. 6. The teaching day at most schools ended at about 1 p.m.

5. M. Farningham, *Girlhood* (London: James Clarke, 1869), p. 15, quoted in D. Gorham, *The Victorian Girl and the Feminine Ideal* (Bloomington: Indiana University Press, 1982), p. 38.

6. R. Pearsall, *Victorian Popular Music* (Newton Abbot: David & Charles, 1973), pp. 74–5, 79; W. Weber, *Music and the Middle Class* (London: Croom Helm, 1975), p. 309.

7. N. Temperley, 'Ballroom and Drawing-room Music', in N. Temperley (ed.), *The Romantic Age, 1800–1914*, Vol. 5, *The Athlone History of Music in Britain* (London: Athlone, 1981), p. 120. See also N. Temperley, 'The Lost Chord', *Victorian Studies*, 30, 1 (Autumn 1986): 18.

8. M. Pullan, *Maternal Counsels to a Daughter* (London: Darton, 1855), p. 81, quoted in Gorham, *Victorian Girl*, p. 104.

9. Royal Commission on School Education, *Report of the Schools Inquiry Commission* (1868), Vol. 7, p. 25.

10. Schools Inquiry Commission, *Reports Issued on the Education of Girls*, pref. Dorothea Beale (London: David Nutt, 1869), p. 123.

11. Royal Commission on School Education, *Report of the Schools Inquiry Commission* (1868), Vol. 1, pp. 551–2; Vol. 7, pp. 72–3, 208–9; Vol. 8, pp. 51–2, 240, 476–7, 509; Vol. 9, pp. 298, 814–16; Schools Inquiry Commission, *Reports Issued*, pp. 5, 40–41, 54, 62–3, 114–16.

12. National Association for the Promotion of Social Science, *Transactions* (1878), pp. 675–6.

13. D. Beale, L.H.M. Soulsby and J.F. Dove, *Work and Play in Girls' Schools* (London: Longmans, Green, 1898), p. 320. See also M. Grey and E. Shirreff, *Thoughts on Self-Culture*, 2 vols (London: Edward Moxon, 1850), Vol. 2, pp. 202, 228.

14. R.M. Scrimgeour (ed.), *The North London Collegiate School 1850–1950* (London: Oxford University Press, 1950), p. 30.

15. North London Collegiate School, Prize Day Reports (1885), pp. 90–92.

16. McCrone, *Sport*, pp. 63–6.

17. Ibid., pp. 66–8.

18. North London Collegiate School, *Jubilee Magazine* (April 1900): 40.

19. Information on music at the North London Collegiate School was derived primarily from school concert programmes (1879–1914); Governors' Meeting Minutes (1871–1914); Head Mistresses' Reports to Governors (1871–1914); Prize Day and Prize List Reports (1850–98); Prospectuses (1850–1914); Staff Meeting Minutes (1885–1914); Staff Register (1893–1927); and the school magazine, *Our Magazine* (1875–1920).

20. Letter by John Farmer, the school music examiner, quoted in A.E. Ridley, *Frances Mary Buss and Her Work for Education*, 2nd edn (London: Longmans, Green, 1896), pp. 225–6.

21. Letter by Frances Mary Buss, 1872, quoted in Ridley, *Frances Mary Buss*, p. 205.

22. K. Anderson, 'Frances Mary Buss, the Founder as Headmistress, 1850–1896', in Scrimgeour (ed.), *North London Collegiate School*, p. 45.

23. Ibid.

24. North London Collegiate School, Head Mistress's Report to Governors (4 December 1871), Vol. 1, pp. 4–5.

25. The GPDSC Council had been eager to promote the finest possible teaching in music from the first, and as a result music – particularly class singing – was taught seriously in a number of Company schools for many years. The Company's special interest in, and enlightened attitude to, music was manifested by the appointment of an inspector of music in 1878, and in 1902 by the establishment of a Music Advisory Board comprising

three distinguished Doctors of Music to inspect music and class singing in schools more thoroughly and to submit written reports. Many pupils took the certificate examinations of the Associated Board of the Royal Academy/Royal College of Music, and by 1912 there were orchestras in most schools. The Kensington High School became pre-eminent thanks to the efforts of its headmistress (1901–31), Ethel Home, a musician of substantial aptitude and imagination. With considerable determination and energy, Home attempted to place music on the same footing as other subjects. She personally took a large share of the music teaching, organizing it on original lines, and in 1908 she established a special and much-lauded Music Training Department for teachers. See J. Kamm, *Indicative Past: A Hundred Years of the Girls' Public Day School Trust* (London: George Allen & Unwin, 1971), pp. 130–31.

26. *St. Paul's Girls' School Book* (London: St. Paul's Girls' School, 1925), p. 31. Gustav Holst was the director of music at St. Paul's from 1905 to 1934; and in the sound proof room constructed especially for him in the school's remarkably fine music wing (1913), he composed much of his greatest work, 'The Planets', often trying parts out first on his pupils.

27. E. Raikes, *Dorothea Beale of Cheltenham* (London: Constable, 1908), p. 87.

28. L. Blandford, 'The Making of a Lady', in G.M. Fraser (ed.), *The World of the Public School* (London: Weidenfeld & Nicolson, 1977), p. 200.

29. McCrone, *Sport*, pp. 80–85.

30. *Hockey Field* (17 October 1901): 7.

31. Raikes, *Dorothea Beale*, pp. 89, 110–12.

32. Indicative of just how important music was considered at Cheltenham was the unusual fact that the College magazine, which was intended for ex-students, devoted far more space to music than to sport.

33. A.K. Clarke, *A History of the Cheltenham Ladies' College 1852–1953* (London: Faber & Faber, 1954), p. 79. See also D. Beale, *A History of the Cheltenham Ladies' College, 1853–1904* (London: c. 1904), pp. 11–12, 23–4, 26, 37, 45, 85, 87; The Cheltenham Ladies' College, *Ladies' Field Supplement* (4 May 1907): 3.

34. The music staff grew from two in 1858 to 33 in 1898, nine part-time and 24 full-time. They gave 1,950 lessons a week (1,500 on the piano) to 850 pupils, including about five-sixths of the students in the school, and about 250 from the community. All the music lessons for regular College students were arranged without using the afternoons, and without any special periods being set aside, which meant that music classes cut across timetables and students often missed up to 15 minutes at the beginning or end of academic sessions. See *Cheltenham Ladies' College Calendars* (1908–14); *Cheltenham Ladies' College Magazine*, 31 (Spring 1895): 181, 185; 33 (Spring 1896): 137; 35 (Spring 1897): 182–3; 37 (Spring 1898): 189.

35. D. Beale, *On the Organization of Girls' Day Schools* (London: Longmans, Green, 1873), pp. 8, 11; F. Cecily Steadman, *In the Days of Miss Beale: A Study of Her Work and Influence* (London: Edward J. Burrow, 1931), pp. 21–2, 38, 51–2.

36. *Cheltenham Ladies' College Magazine* (Spring 1894): 114. See also Beale, *History of the Cheltenham Ladies College*, p. 101; Steadman, *In the Days*, pp. 52, 150; *Cheltenham Ladies' College Magazine*, 19 (Spring 1889): 123, 133; 21 (Spring 1890): 107–9, 112–13; 23 (Spring 1891): 2–3; 26 (Autumn 1892): 300–1, 306; 28 (Autumn 1893): 275–6; 29 (Spring 1894): 114–15, 165–6.

37. See *Cheltenham Ladies' College Magazine* (1889–1914). Under Lilian Faithfull and Sir Hugh Allen, the organist of New College Oxford and conductor of the Oxford Bach Choir whom she appointed Cheltenham's first music director in 1910, the teaching of music was revitalized and systematized further.

Music also played a prominent part in life at other great boarding schools, such as St Leonards and Roedean, although the musical world of the Cheltenham Ladies' College was much the fullest.

At St. Leonards School, in St. Andrews (1877), music was first taught after regular school hours, but it soon became an integral part of the regular curriculum, with lessons being fitted in as girls were free. The quality of teaching was apparently high, which probably explains the development of students' enthusiasm for the subject to the point that they formed a Literary and Musical Society in the late 1880s to organize regular musical entertainments. In addition to attending recitals by teachers, students had numerous opportunities to hear first-rate music performed by the great artists who appeared in St Andrews and sometimes at the school. See *St Leonards School Gazette* (1888–1909); J.M. Grant, K.H. McCutcheon and E.F. Sanders (eds), *St Leonards School, 1877–1927* (Oxford: Oxford University Press, 1927), pp. 39, 51–2, 106–7, 158.

A lasting musical tradition was also developed at Roedean School (1885), where tuition in class and solo singing and in the piano and violin were listed in the original prospectus. From the first, the standard of music was high, thanks to music masters and mistresses who 'all had in common distinguished musicianship, teaching ability and enthusiasm'. A unique Old Students' Musical Association was formed in 1897. See D. de Zouche, *Roedean School, 1885–1955* (Brighton: Dolphin Press, 1955), pp. 35, 161.

38. McCrone, *Sport*, p. 86; W. Knox Peck, *A Little Learning: or A Victorian Childhood* (London: Faber & Faber, 1952), pp. 62–3.
39. *Girls' School Year Book* (1906), pp. 28–9.
40. Ibid., pp. 389–95.
41. Ibid. (1909), pp. 414–50. See also B. Harris, 'Music', in S. Burstall and M.A. Douglas (eds), *Public Schools for Girls* (London: Longmans, 1911), p. 182.
42. *Girls' School Year Book* (1909), p. 456. See also pp. 456–65; Harris, 'Music', pp. 182–3.
43. *Girls' School Year Book* (1909), pp. 456–9.
44. The number of physical education and music instructors on a school's staff gave a good indication of how important the subjects were considered.
45. Harris, 'Music', p. 186. See also pp. 185–7; Dr H. P. Allen, 'Music in Girls' Education', *Cheltenham Ladies' College Magazine*, 63 (Spring 1911): 92–6.
46. Beale, Soulsby and Dove, *Work and Play*, p. 334; Ridley, *Frances Mary Buss*, p. 226; E. Shirreff, *The Intellectual Life of Women* (London: James Clarke, 1865), p. 173.
47. Harris, 'Music', pp. 185–8; *Our Magazine* (November 1880): 147; Shirreff, *Intellectual Education*, pp. 119–20, 126, 174.
48. McCrone, *Sport*, pp. 90–93.
49. Grey and Shirreff, *Thoughts on Self-Culture*, Vol. 1, pp. 202, 228.
50. Hunt, 'Divided Aims', p. 12.
51. *Incorporated Society of Musicians' Monthly Journal*, 9 (February 1900): 27.
52. Dyhouse, *Girls Growing Up*, p. 55; Hunt (ed.), *Lessons for Life*, p. xxv; McCrone, *Sport*, pp. 89–90.
53. McCrone, *Sport*, p. 90.
54. Dyhouse, *Girls Growing Up*, p. 78; Hunt (ed.), *Lessons for Life*, p. xxv; P. Summerfield, 'Cultural Reproduction in the Education of Girls: A Study of Girls' Secondary Schooling in Two Lancashire Towns, 1900–1950', in Hunt (ed.), *Lessons for Life*, pp. 149–50.

3

Science Education in the Public Schools for Girls in the Late Nineteenth Century

CATHERINE MANTHORPE

During the 1860s a debate emerged about the place of science in education when pressure from the state and from the emerging science lobby was being exerted upon the boys' public schools to include science in their curricula.[1] The state saw it as 'little less than a national misfortune' that science was almost totally omitted from the education of middle and upper class boys.[2] Scientists began to attempt to modify the rigid concept of liberal education by arguing that a full training of the mind was only possible by the inclusion of science. In order to overcome the problem of the utilitarian nature of science which, for the advocates of liberal education, tainted its educational merits, arguments were constructed that stressed the purity, abstractness and independence of science as a body of knowledge and yet that also showed the dependence industry had upon the pursuit of that particular form of knowledge.[3] In another line of attack, the British Association for the Advancement of Science made its own investigations into the state of science education – in which consideration of girls' education was noticeably lacking – publishing influential reports in 1867, 1888, 1889 and 1890. At the same time there was also a growing movement for the secondary and higher education of girls and women who belonged to 'the classes above those attending the Public Elementary Schools . . . because there is abundant evidence to prove that their education is actually worse and far less adequately provided for than that of the lower class'.[4] The girls' public schools were in a unique position to establish science in the curriculum from the start. This chapter attempts to demonstrate the social and institutional factors that shaped science education for girls at this time, and that had important implications for subsequent developments.

56

EARLY PRECEDENTS FOR THE INTRODUCTION OF SCIENCE
EDUCATION INTO THE GIRLS' PUBLIC SCHOOLS

In the 1860s, education for girls other than those of the 'industrial classes' looked little different from that available in the early 1800s. The institutional emphasis was on private provision – private day or boarding schools or the services of a governess in one's own home – and the curriculum emphasis was laid on the 'accomplishments' such as drawing, music and languages. Where it found its place in such an education, science was taught as an accomplishment like any other skill.[5] As late as 1868, Joshua Fitch in his work as a Commissioner for the School's Inquiry (Taunton) Commission saw 'girls learning by heart the terminology of the Linnean system, to whom the very elements of vegetable physiology were unknown'. Similarly, astronomy was taught by 'twisting the globes round and round'.[6] Even later in the century, science education for middle-class girls was being publicly criticized for cultivating only the faculty of observation and partaking 'more of show than reality'.[7] Two important exceptions were evident in the pages of the Taunton Commission's Report – the curricula of the North London Collegiate School for Girls and the Cheltenham Ladies' College, both of which included natural science. Both schools were acknowledged to have served as models for other girls' public and secondary schools which developed later in the century.[8]

The North London Collegiate School for Girls was a private school catering mostly for the daughters of professional men. Most pupils attended on a daily basis. The headmistress, Frances Buss, had founded the school in 1850, the same year in which the North London Collegiate School for Boys was founded.[9] It was later reorganized as a public school in the 1870s. By contrast, Cheltenham Ladies' College, founded in 1853, was a proprietary school for daughters of the upper middle class and very influenced by Cheltenham College, the public school for boys. The headmistress was Dorothea Beale, who had taken over the school and reorganized it in 1858. The school included day pupils and boarders.[10]

In the 1860s, science teaching of a sort was an established part of the main school curriculum in both schools. Miss Buss disclosed in her evidence to the Taunton Commission in 1865 that, 'the course includes the properties of matter, the laws of motion, the mechanical powers, simple chemistry and electricity, with the outlines of geology, botany, natural history and astronomy'.[11] The first prospectus of the

North London Collegiate School showed that science was included as 'the leading facts of Natural Philosophy and other Branches of Science and Art taught by means of familiar lectures'.[12] The science course was conducted as 'catechetical lessons' – interrogative teaching rather than didactic lectures – illustrated by 'experiments and diagrams as far as possible'. At this stage in the history of the North London Collegiate School, the science lessons were made the 'means of imparting interesting knowledge rather than mental training'. The chemistry lessons, for example, were described as 'popular', as opposed to dealing with subjects like 'the doctrines'. Miss Buss acknowledged to the Taunton Commissioners that science could usefully be taught as a mental discipline, although, at that time at the North London Collegiate School, subjects other than science were depended on for this purpose.

At Cheltenham, by 1866, physical geography and different branches of natural science were taught by a Dr Wright, FRSE, FGS, 'well known for his geological publications in the Palaeontological Society'. In 1865, according to Miss Beale's evidence, 'he gave a course of very elementary mechanics and hydrostatics, simple mechanics etc', and it was her belief that 'his class quite understood the structure of the steam engine in its simple form'. Botany was also taught, stressing the physiology, circulation and structure of plants rather than simply dealing with classification. A Mr Webb, FRSA, taught occasional courses on astronomy, optics and electricity. Miss Beale taught Euclid without the help of books, aiming 'to give as little help as possible, but to lead [the girls] on to find out for themselves; under no circumstances to let them learn by heart, and to induce them to do without explanation as far as they can, so as to call out their own powers'. With the exception of Euclid, the natural sciences were taught at Cheltenham not as a form of mental training, but, as at the North London Collegiate School, 'as a means of widening the views and furnishing pursuits full of interest for life'.[13] At both Cheltenham and the North London Collegiate School, lessons in natural science formed one part of a full school course which included English, history, geography, modern and classical languages, arithmetic and mathematics (if the pupils were sufficiently advanced in arithmetic), as well as the more traditional subjects to be found in girls' education – such as music, drawing, art and needlework.

That these two schools[14] were so different from the generally insubstantial character of education for middle-class girls at this time can be explained by the background and philosophy of Frances Buss and Dorothea Beale. Unlike many other headmistresses, school-mistresses or governesses, for whom teaching was often a way out of straitened family circumstances rather than a vocation,[15] both Miss Buss and Miss Beale had themselves received a reasonably thorough education. Both attended Queens College, which had been estab-lished in 1848 in conjunction with the Governesses' Benevolent Institution to provide lectures to women in order to better train them as governesses.[16] Such experience undoubtedly contributed to their view that, rather than leading girls to proficiency in various ac-complishments, girls' education should cultivate the mind and induce in them the desire to study. Not only would this benefit girls them-selves – leading them to a much fuller and interesting life than was generally to be had by middle-class girls at this time – but it would also be beneficial to society.[17] Both women believed that girls were as capable of academic study as were boys, and that their minds were as worth cultivating. However, an important difference between Miss Buss and Miss Beale was the reasons each held for wanting girls to be better educated. Miss Buss established her school 'to prepare pupils for any position in life which they may be called upon to occupy'.[18] Her views on the education of women and girls fell into the 'uncompromis-ing'[19] camp of educational reformers. She believed that girls' educa-tion should be equal to that of boys and should enable them to lead independent lives if they chose, or were compelled, to do so.[20] By contrast, Dorothea Beale belonged to the 'separatist' school of thought: women's brains were not inferior to men's, but because their role in life was different from that of men', so should their education differ. Thus her view that

> the habits of obedience to duty, of self-restraint which the process of acquiring knowledge induces, the humility which a thoughtful and comprehensive study of the great works in literature and science tends to produce, these we would specially cultivate in a woman, that she may wear the true women's ornament of a meek and quiet spirit.[21]

Unlike Miss Buss, who wanted to see the examinations of the Univer-sity of London open to girls on the same lines as boys, regarding them 'as the only thing at all attainable at present', Miss Beale favoured 'a special examination for ladies up to the standard of attainment of the matriculation, but not necessarily comprising the same subjects'.[22]

In spite of this divergence of views, evidence suggests that the actual curricula of the two schools were very similar. The only differences were that mathematics was excluded from the curriculum of the North London Collegiate School in the early days because of the pupils' lack of knowledge of arithmetic, and at Cheltenham Latin was excluded on the grounds that 'Latin, as generally taught, is [not] well calculated to develop the intelligence of girls'.[23] Even though neither Miss Buss nor Miss Beale considered that boys' education of the time provided a very good model on which to base girls' education,[24] in general the curriculum of both schools' was largely influenced by that to be found in the boys public schools. For Frances Buss, to choose anything except the boys' model would have been damaging to the campaign to get equal treatment for girls[25] and, for Dorothea Beale, who used Cheltenham College as her model, what was suitable for the sons of 'gentlemen and noblemen' was also suitable for their daughters.[26]

Both Cheltenham and the North London Collegiate School, having been established in the 1850s, were in a position in the latter years of the nineteenth century to act as models for the many girls' public schools that were established in the 1870s and 1880s. The curricula and organizing principles of the North London Collegiate School, and Cheltenham Ladies College derived in part from the emulation of existing boys' education; in part from traditional views and expectations of girls; in part from the diverging views of the 'separatists' and the 'uncompromising' camps of the movement for the secondary education of girls; and in part from a changing philosophy of education for girls – one that moved away from the 'accomplishments' tradition and stressed their intellectual capability and need for mental cultivation. These influences were important for the shaping of science education for girls, which is analysed in the following section through the work of Sophie Bryant, mistress of mathematics (1875–95) and headmistress (1895–1918) of the North London Collegiate School, and Sara Burstall, headmistress of the Manchester High School for girls from 1898.

TWO MODELS OF SCIENCE EDUCATION FOR GIRLS

From the beginning of the 1870s, new schools for girls of the middle classes opened in fairly rapid succession. Many of these were under the auspices of the Girls' Public Day School Company (GPDSC) (later Trust), which was formed in 1872. Thirty-eight GPDSC schools were founded between 1887 and 1901. The Church School Company, formed in 1883, established 24 schools by 1896. There were also the endowed grammar schools for girls set up after the 1869 Endowed Schools Act, which allowed for part of the funds of educational trusts to be applied to girls' education. By 1882, 90 girls' schools were listed as 'public schools' (schools with trustees of governors as opposed to private-venture schools) and, of these, only eight were established before 1865.[27] As noted above, such schools were modelled to a great extent on the North London Collegiate School, which itself became public in 1871, governed by a chairman and board of governors.

In spite of the relatively rapid growth in number, these schools offered an education only to a minority of girls. Even by the end of the century, a dominant form of education for middle-class girls was still in school devoted to 'accomplishments' rather than to 'cultivating the intelligence'. Their continued existence was the result of 'the widespread indifference of parents to the education of their girls, to the qualifications and training of their mistresses and the efficiency of the schools'.[28] The new girls' high schools represented a 'very real step in advance', but they were 'educating but a fraction of the population'.[29] The consideration of the development of science education in these high schools is important, for they, and the educational philosophies produced from them, shaped a particular tradition of education that lasted well into the twentieth century, both in the state sector – through the influence of the county and municipal secondary schools set up after the 1902 Education Act – and in the private sector.

The aim of these new girls' schools was self-consciously 'to supply for girls the best education possible corresponding to the education given to boys in the great Public Schools'.[30] How the new headmistresses defined their 'Public' schools was, as Pederson has argued, 'not so much a precise institutional category as a complex ideal'.[31] This ideal distinguished the high schools from private-venture schools, not least by the provision of advanced instruction leading to university. Further, the education in them was intended to be 'liberal'; that is, 'to instil in those qualities of mind and character appropriate to a gentleman or lady'.[32] Not a decorative, empty-headed lady of leisure, but a lady who had a function and purpose in life. Indeed, the overall aim was, as Maria Grey argued in 1888:

> not to fit a young lady for drawing room life, but to fit a human being, through the training of her faculties, the storing and enriching of her mind, for real human life. The main object of the teaching is to develop intelligence, to call out and exercise the various faculties and thus to train habits of observation and reflection, of drawing inferences from facts; in other words forming judgements.[33]

The ideology of the girls' schools – at least as propounded by their chief protagonists – was comfortably compatible with the emerging ideology of science as pure, abstract and independent thought. The writing of Burstall and Bryant shows how science was perceived to be compatible with the women educationalists' ideal of liberal education, although, by the end of the century, a diversity of aim was becoming apparent.

(i) Sophie Bryant

In her book *Educational Ends or the Ideal of Personal Development*, Sophie Bryant argued for the place of science in education on the grounds that 'all science is the attempt to realise in thought this ideal of a self developing whole of law'. Science had its place in the development of the individual towards the ideal end of 'right-thinking' and 'true-knowing'. 'The study of science', Bryant argued, 'in general is conducted most naturally and therefore best, by the distinction of three logical stages', the stages of induction, philosophy and deduction. Such a sequence, she argued, followed from the practical aspects of teaching any science other than the mathematical sciences. In these latter, 'their first principles are also their elementary facts', and thus, 'the beginning of mathematics in a child's knowledge is, therefore, its true beginning in logical development'. This, she maintained, was not the case with physics, in which 'the order of development from true hypothesis ... is not the natural order of discovery, though it is the natural order of reflection and the only satisfactory order to the reflective mind'. As learners generally begin such studies in 'not very reflective days', first principles should follow the study of observed facts, after which the whole should be worked out deductively. Similarly for chemistry and botany, for which it is 'inevitable' that the teacher should begin with the facts.[34]

The importance of Bryant's assertions about science and logical development was in her stress on its wholeness, 'its self-development of subject in logical sequence, each truth appearing as a demonstrated conclusion'. A teaching of science which rested on 'dogmatic assertions' arising from unquestioned statements of theory and hypothesis, she argued, 'breaks and defaces' the 'ideal of knowledge', with the consequence that 'the average student of natural science when he later comes to reject the prevailing dogmatism of childhood is apt to content himself without any inquiry into the first principles of his subject'.[35] Thus for Bryant, science education had an important role to play in the development of healthy minds and true individuals.

Science as a method, as a 'form of knowing' rather than as a practical or vocational pursuit, was of uppermost consideration.

In a later paper, 'The Curriculum of a Girls' School',[36] written after more than 20 years' experience of teaching, these views on science were more specifically related to the education of girls. The governing philosophy in the paper was familiar: 'the school ought to offer an education calculated to develop each one in accordance with his proper end as a moral, rational and serviceable being'. The uncompromising position of Frances Buss was echoed in the view that 'the efficient girl is trained on the same broad lines as the efficient boy', while recognizing for both that the ideal curriculum was a flexible one that met the different needs of different pupils and that 'respect should be paid in the girls' school scheme to ultimate efficiency in the housewifely and social art'. Furthermore, Mrs Bryant argued that because 'the chief function of women is the making of the home and the preservation of the social side of society' and thus less diversified than the male's future role, in the girls' school the ideal curriculum could be found 'in its simpler and more universal form'. For Bryant 'knowledge [is] the same to all knowers' and the unity of knowledge 'in so far as knowledge per se is the end' is best for both girls and boys. The question of the diversity of knowledge only arose for Bryant when she considered different occupations, but in her view this was not the dominant criterion for the curriculum.[37]

In the North London Collegiate School, two science courses were developed, one for those girls 'fit to carry through a complete course of study planned to fulfil a well-balanced ideal of knowledge and development', and another for those 'who are only able to fulfil these ideals in part'.[38] For both courses, the underlying philosophy was that science should be taught with the ideal in mind, and not for imparting scientific information. For both groups of girls, the necessary groundwork was the 'ability to observe and compare, to measure and calculate, to infer and demonstrate, to inquire into the causes, to invent means, to choose ends'.[39] The 'limited course' involved the study of botany and natural history regularly, with occasional courses on the 'semi-scientific' subjects of hygiene, domestic economy and physiography. The purpose of these latter subjects was to introduce practical interests by which the 'scientific habit' could be developed 'by the application of accepted scientific truths to common life'.[40] The following perhaps sums up the approach to the course:

Therein lies the training value of hygiene as a study inferred from physiology. The inference is scientific though the premises are dogmatically given. There should be going on at the same time, or in adjacent terms, a course of reasoned botany, and the contrast between the application of science should be noted for the further inculcation of sound ideas on the nature of scientific knowledge. For even very dull learners can be taught to know where and how it is that their information falls short of the ideal of science.[41]

In Sophie Bryant's scheme, scientific method was the primary consideration, even though the way it was taught, for some girls, might be more 'relevant' to their perceived future role.

The rationale behind the 'complete course' echoed very much Bryant's earlier work on the logical sequence of the sciences. Mathematics, physical and natural sciences would be taught. She argued that logically mathematics should be followed by elementary physics, then chemistry and then biology. However, she realized that

it was necessary to take account of psychological, or, ... subjective considerations and to allow that the foundations of biological science, which call more for observation and vivid perception than for calculation, should be – because they can be – laid early.[42]

Thus, for Bryant, science had an important role in girls' education for two reasons. First it was of great value in training the mind and thus aiding the growth of intellectual skill. Second, because of the unity of knowledge that science education could demonstrate, it could contribute to the moral development of the individual. For the less academic pupil, a greater stress was placed on the more practical and applied aspects of science, but the 'ideal of science' was not absent from this 'dogmatic' treatment of the subject. Importantly, Bryant stressed that the only difference there should be between the science curriculum for girls and boys was in 'the application of science to practice', an important consideration, but one she argued had an 'inconsiderable' effect on school studies.[43]

Bryant's paper on the curriculum of girls' schools was written in 1898, and it is interesting to note how her views changed in the following decade when anxieties about the health of the nation called for domestic education for girls.[44] Contributing a chapter on 'Natural Science' to a book on public schools for girls,[45] it is evident that Bryant was true to her logical, idealist approach to science as a unity of knowledge, but that practical interests merited greater consideration. Thus she indicated that one of the chief objectives for the inclusion of science in the curriculum was

> that it shall lend itself with certainty and ease to develop in the immature but plastic mind of average ability this *scientific attitude* of alert, *individual inquiry*

and

> that *the learner shall work at some nature subject in the spirit of original investigation*, and it is a condition on the other hand, no less to be observed, that *she shall not leave school in such total ignorance as to involve a lack of interest in the scheme of nature knowledge as a whole* (Bryant's emphasis).[46]

But she also noted that the unity of knowledge, which was the educational ideal behind the study of science, was

> just now obscured by the urgency of the practical interests which it subserves in apparent conflict with the intellectual demand for systematic development in which it is rooted. Thus the dialectic uppermost for the moment in teachers' minds is between the claims of the practical and logical interests.[47]

In spite of this 'urgency', Bryant proceeded to outline courses of study in which practical outcomes were incidental to the main object of the course, or were contained in syllabuses designed for the non-specialist. Thus, for example, in the course of elementary physics, which followed nature study in the preliminary course, the study of heat and 'the simpler phenomena of pressure especially as acting on liquids and gases' was necessary for 'the interpretation of everyday events' and 'for the appreciation of those effects of pressure which play so large a part in geographical phenomena'. But their *chief* importance, according to Bryant, was that they were necessary 'for the understanding of all further scientific work'.[48] Similarly, in the discussion of the botany course in the senior school which required an understanding of chemical change, a preliminary course of chemistry preceded the botanical course and such a course of chemistry was to be 'studied for its own sake'. Only at the end of the course were the chemical processes essential to botany to be studied specifically.[49]

In this article Bryant repeated her view that the curriculum should not be rigid, but be adapted to the needs of different pupils[50]. As in her 'limited' and 'complete' courses, it is clear that it was for the non-specialist science student that the 'urgent' practical interests had the uppermost consideration. Thus in schools where girls left at 15 or 16, it was possible that their science work could be 'shaped throughout by reference to the problems of cleaning and cooking; and thus the earlier year or years will be contrived as to appeal to domestic interest and to be of domestic use'.[51] In other schools where the leaving age was higher:

> the senior course must be so contrived as to form a complete unity in itself and the main demand is likely to be for a course designed primarily in the interest of theoretic study to which the special study of domestic science may or may not be attached, either in sequence or as an alternative.[52]

Domestic science or chemistry 'in direct connection with practical domestic work' or 'the chemistry of domestic life' was in Bryant's scheme very much an *alternative* course for girls not taking pure chemistry to matriculation standard, or for those leaving at 16.[53] The 'natural practical interests' of girls in home-making were seen as 'a powerful additional stimulus to scientific motive'.[54] For the specialist, however, it seems that no such concession to sex was made. In one school cited by Bryant in her article, about 75 per cent of the upper sixth form continued with the science course, and selected students specialized in the sixth form. In the latter, 'the first year is devoted to chemistry and the second to chemistry, physics and botany at the Cambridge Higher Local standard'.[55]

Bryant's views on science education, in her stress on the unity of knowledge, the growth of intellectual skill, the development of a scientific attitude and an interest in nature 'as an All', represented one conception of science education for girls established in the girls' high schools by the turn of the century. The practical aims of science education were twofold. First, it gave girls who were aiming for university a sound, basic science education that would enable them to pass the necessary examinations and that would serve as a basis for further study. Second, it equipped less motivated or less academically minded girls with a scientific interest and, in the rhetoric of the day, fitted them for their perceived future home-making role. Importantly, for this model of science education, at least at the level of theory,[56] this latter practical concern was subordinate to the expressed educational aims.

(ii) Sara Burstall, LLD

Sara Burstall was headmistress of Manchester High School for Girls between 1898 and 1924. Her views on science education were undoubtedly influenced by her education at the Frances Buss schools between 1871 and 1878, first at the Camden School for Girls (a middle school with a leaving age of 16) and then for three years at the North London Collegiate School. After taking a degree in mathematics at Girton, she returned to the North London Collegiate School as an assistant mistress principally teaching mathematics.[57] Like her 'honoured leader Mrs Bryant', Sara Burstall 'regarded Nature as part of Divine revelation and natural science as an essential part of education'.[58] Her election to the post of headmistress at the Manchester High School was explained in part because 'certain governors had determined that more science should be taught in the School'.[59] By the 1920s, a strong tradition of science had been established under her lead. As she recalled:

> we had ... four specialist teachers on the staff, all first class honours graduates in chemistry, physics, botany and zoology, and many Old Girls were students at universities or science graduates. Our former specialists had become university lecturers or headmistresses. Best of all a very satisfactory volume of work stood to the credit of Old Girls which had been increased in the period since 1924. After the War we had twenty-five Old Girls in the medical course of the University of Manchester.[60]

Like Sophie Bryant, Sara Burstall organized the school into 'A' and 'B' forms with different science curricula in each. Burstall suggested that in the 'A' forms, in the five-year course before specialization took place in the sixth form, nature study, biology and general elementary science should be taught. By contrast, the 'B' form should not take physics, but nature study and domestic science.[61]

Writing at the end of the nineteenth century, a period noted by Bryant for its urgency of practical interests, Burstall's views on science education had a greater practical orientation than Bryant's. She did not doubt the intellectual capacities of girls. Every girl, she believed, 'is a human being with a right to complete development, to share in the spiritual inheritance of the race, to be given the opportunities of making the best of her faculties, or pursuing even advanced studies if she has the ability'.[62]

However, in contrast to the views of Bryant, in which practical and vocational interests were distinctly secondary to the educational aims of science education, these practical interests appeared to be organizing principles for Burstall. She noted that 'there are specialised functions in practical life for which the sexes should be separately prepared in the school ... it is the natural duty of a woman to do housework and she must learn it at school'.[63] For Burstall, science education was an essential part of every girl's education, not only for its value as mental training, 'but as preparation for domestic duties and the care of children'.[64] This had consequences for the science curriculum for girls: 'For the latter duty [the care of children], nature study going on botany and zoology are as important in the woman's characteristic activity as are physics and chemistry for men's industries.'[65] Burstall maintained that, generally, the specific study of chemistry and physics was not necessary for girls as they would never need them. Rather, for all girls with the exception of those who intended to specialize in science, elementary physics should be taught as 'physics of the household'.[66]

Thus, for Burstall, while science education was an important aspect of the girls' school curriculum, its importance lay as much in its role of preparing girls for their perceived domestic futures as in its contribution to intellectual development.

The work of Sophie Bryant and Sara Burstall has been quoted at length to demonstrate that by the end of the nineteenth century two models of science education for girls had developed: the academic and the practical. Underpinning both was a concept of science education for girls as a 'form of knowing', as an intellectual discipline and as a means to cultivate the faculties. The academic model functioned to enable girls with an interest and an ability in science to pursue its study in the upper forms of the girls' schools in preparation for university entrance examinations. The practical model was generally regarded as a model of science education for less motivated or less academically minded girls, furnishing them both with a scientific interest and, particularly in the early years of the twentieth century, with the skills and knowledge they would require to carry out their domestic duties efficiently.

THE EXTENT OF SCIENCE EDUCATION IN THE GIRLS' HIGH SCHOOLS: CONSTRAINTS AND LIMITATIONS

The writing of Bryant and Burstall illustrates that, although often left out of account in conventional histories of science education, women educationists in the nineteenth century both contributed to the contemporary debate about the place of science in education *and* laid emphasis on the importance of science education for girls. The extent of the establishment of science education in the girls' public schools is less easy to quantify. There is limited evidence available on what actually was being taught to girls. What exists suggests that in the latter years of the nineteenth century there was a wide variation in the range of subjects taught as 'science' in the girls' high schools and the amount of time spent on them. Of the 90 public girls' schools listed in *The Educational Year Book for 1882*, 49 taught mathematics; 40, natural science; 22, 'elements of physical science'; 16, 'physical geography'; only seven taught chemistry and two taught physical science. As the sample curricula in the Appendix of the Royal Commission on Secondary Education (1895) showed, among the girls' schools there was considerable variation in the time allotted to science education and the branches of science pursued.[67]

Many social and institutional factors had a strong role to play in this period in determining the shape and extent of science education for girls. One such factor was the need for girls' schools to attract enough pupils in order to ensure adequate funding for the continuation of the school. Thus the headmistresses not only had to take into account the views of their boards of governors on the curriculum, but also, and perhaps more importantly, the views of parents, who could withdraw their daughters instantly if they felt that the education received was not useful. The extent to which science education was regarded as 'useful' must have depended strongly on the commitment to science of the headmistress herself and the way in which she could convince parents and governors of its proper place in an education for girls. Many headmistresses had little or no scientific training and may, as a result, have biased the curriculum towards literary subjects.[68] Another factor was that in some schools science teaching was mistrusted, as Burstall argues, 'perhaps because of the apparent opposition of science and religion characteristic of Victorian thought'.[69] For this reason, some schools may have favoured descriptive botany as a *harmless* science.[70]

For those headmistresses who wished to introduce science into their school or to teach more science, there were at least two major handicaps that had to be overcome. The first was the conflict with their broad ideal of a liberal and balanced education – science had to vie with all the other subjects for its place on the timetable. The battle waged by the Association of Headmistresses with the Board of Education over the number of hours that should be devoted to science after the Education Act of 1902 showed that although the headmistresses were not against science education, they were concerned at what effect an emphasis on science would have on the teaching of other subjects, particularly literature.[71] This was exacerbated by the limited number of school hours. A traditional feature of the high school well into the twentieth century was that lessons were taught only in the morning. Comparison between the school week of girls' and boys' schools at the end of the nineteenth century shows that, on average, the week for a girls' school was about 19 hours, compared with an average of 27.5 hours for boys.[72] This shorter week severely limited the possibilities for education in science for girls.

The second major handicap was the general lack of equipment for science teaching in the girls' schools. Attention was drawn in the *Journal of Education* in 1894

> to the almost universal lack in girls' schools of suitable equipment for the experimental teaching of science owing to which girls are severely handicapped in the competitions for the scholarships tenable at Local University and Other Colleges.[73]

In the same journal, Miss A.J. Cooper, headmistress of Edgbaston High School, made the point that, 'in some few girls' schools fairly adequate provisions had already been made for science teaching, but in the cases of most, the laboratories etc., left much to be desired'.[74] This lack of properly equipped laboratories undoubtedly had repercussions for the science curriculum. Speaking of the usual curriculum for the sixth form, Sophie Bryant noted that chemistry, biology, mechanics and mathematics were studied 'because convenient'. Physics was 'not universally taken by sixth form science students' because of 'the lack of adequate equipment for the experimental treatment of this subject'.[75]

Non-material considerations were also relevant, and may well have contributed to Bryant's 'A' and 'B' curricula in science. Many of the girls attending the girls' public schools up to the end of the nineteenth century and beyond, would have lacked a good primary education and thus a good foundation upon which to build a scientific training.[76]

These institutional and social factors may explain why science was not a popular choice for specialization by girls. In 1878, only 30 of the 500 women candidates for the Cambridge Higher Local Examinations took science subjects. Of those women who went on to university to take science degrees between 1878 and 1911, they only comprised 16 per cent of all London BSc degrees and only 18 per cent of the women who took a Tripos between 1881 and 1916.[77] Moreover, these women were drawn from a very limited number of schools.[78]

While education in science and education for girls were not considered incompatible in the establishment and development of the girls' public schools, considerable social and institutional barriers served to limit the extent of science education and had implications for the actual content of the curriculum.

SCIENCE EDUCATION FOR GIRLS: INNOVATION AND IMITATION

The view of science education as forming a proper part of a balanced, liberal education by some of the leading proponents of secondary and higher education for girls and women was, in many ways, an advance on comparable education for boys as found in the older, established public boys' schools which showed 'a basic reluctance to countenance science teaching'.[79] In these schools for boys and the older grammar schools, the curriculum for centuries had been based on classics and later mathematics. The school in this tradition was a place for the building of character and the 'inculcation of moral behaviour', whereas science was being advocated for its 'intellectual and utilitarian value'.[80] It was precisely these intellectual, and to a lesser extent, utilitarian, values that aided the inclusion of science in the curriculum of the girls' public schools. Science was not considered contrary to the aim of producing cultured beings. As late as 1900, it was being argued that science had properly found its place in the education of girls before that of boys.[81] The girls' schools, not being weighed down by centuries of tradition, had a tremendous opportunity to innovate and to include in their curricula new subjects and subjects whose educational value was being strongly advocated at the time. As Sophie Bryant argued in 1898, 'in no part of the educational field is there more living thought at the present time than in the domain of the secondary schools for girls'.[82] However, although ahead of some boys' schools in the latter years of the nineteenth century, when science 'took off' as a proper subject of study for boys following pressure from the science lobby and the demands of the state for more scientific and technical education in schools, more time was devoted to science education for boys than girls. At the time when science education was being defined, the seeds of the contemporary under-representation of girls in science education were sown. Although the girls' schools had innovatory possibilities, the extent of innovation was severely constrained by the social and political position of women educationists.

It has been argued above that science found its place on the girls' school's curriculum on intellectual and practical grounds. Contrary to many of the arguments being put forward for the scientific education of boys, which stressed its importance as a prerequisite for future professional training, professional or occupational considerations (other than the occupation of housewife) were not part of the rationale for girls' science education. The new girls' schools had the scope to be innovative and experimental in their approach to science education, but they were not. What happened instead was that the syllabuses were either defined in relation to the demands of external examinations, which were themselves defined by the demands of the ascending scientific profession, or, in relation to a narrow conception of a girl's future vocation – the domestic.

To some supporters of the movement for the secondary and higher education of women, it was a matter for regret that the new girls' schools did not make greater use of their opportunity to move away from the outdated curriculum of the boys' schools and experiment with new courses and methods.[83] However, as a strategy at a time when the idea of education for girls of the middle classes was, in some quarters, vehemently opposed, the proponents of education for girls were forced to proceed pragmatically, 'not seeking to raise large questions of principle, but, hoping to solve practical problems, make limited points acceptable to all but the most entrenched and irrational opposition'.[84] As a note in the *Journal of Education* for April 1888 stated, the pioneers of secondary education for women had 'been forced, for the sake of asserting their rights, to don male attire'.[85] Sara Burstall, recalling the early days of women's education, justified the adoption of such a strategy arguing that 'progress would have been impossible without it'.[86]

There were two reasons at least why conformity to a particular curriculum was necessary. First, to develop a new pattern of education, different from the existing education for boys, was regarded as a dangerous move. Emily Davies and her colleagues in their early campaigns in the 1860s knew that if special examinations, or special regulations, existed for girls, girls' education 'would always be assumed to be less strict and less exacting whether it was or not'.[87] The danger, as Burstyn has argued, was that girls and women would be left with 'a separate kind of education which would be considered inferior to men's and women would never be able to prove that it was equal to that of men'.[88] Second, in matters to do with the curriculum, the existence of external examinations, supervised by the universities, exerted considerable influence. Preparation for examinations such as the Junior and Senior Cambridge Locals, College of Preceptor's examinations and the London matriculation examination was an important feature of many of the girls' high schools,[89] not least 'because in the eyes of the world at large and also of many pioneers of women's education, the capacity to pass examinations was the sole criterion of the educability of girls'.[90] Little evidence is available on what subjects girls took in these examinations. Evidence is available, however, to show that science subjects were slow to be taken up by candidates entering external examinations,[91] so it can be supposed that science was not the first choice for examination by many girls until perhaps the last decade of the nineteenth century when more candidates from girls' schools were entered.[92] In spite of the lack of information on this point, it is clear that the existence of examinations had several effects on the girls' school curriculum. They probably helped to ensure that science teaching became more methodical and systematic, but they also determined what was taught.[93] They 'forced a certain kind of uniformity on science teaching, making innovation comparatively difficult'.[94] They also gave power to the universities to influence what was taught in the science curriculum with the result that the science course in the sixth form often served as a pre-university education.

Thus the women pioneers were not greatly innovatory in their schools and generally conformed to an existing pattern of education established, or being developed, in the boys' public schools and the universities. They were constrained either by the socially delicate nature of their campaign or, as has been argued by some historians, by the fact that 'revolutionary change' was not their intention, but rather a desire to raise the status of their schools.[95] In either view, the only alternative to this curriculum that was heavily defined by the needs of a virtually all-male scientific profession was one that did not drastically confront social ideas about women and yet that allowed for the professional opportunities for which women and the women's movement campaigned. The 'B' curriculum, developed by Bryant and Burstall for the less able or less motivated girls, using girls' 'natural' interest in the home, was the basis of a 'domestic science' which was seen by some as a legitimate alternative science education for girls.[96] Women science teachers, who by 1912 were sufficient in number to form their own professional association,[97] although in a strong position to develop science curricula that would appeal to, and meet the needs of, the wide range of girls they taught, were unable to influence significantly the major developments in the science curriculum that took place in the twentieth century.[98]

CONCLUDING POINTS

From the 1870s onwards, a network of girls' high schools was established. The North London Collegiate School for Girls acted as a model for many of these new schools. From the beginning, science education was included in the curriculum of these schools, and most often one or more branches of the physical sciences were taught as well as mathematics.

The attempt in this chapter has been to demonstrate that the institutional context of the girls' schools and the social context in which they developed were strongly influential in shaping science education for girls. Furthermore, in spite of the innovatory potential of the girls' schools, they tended to embrace the type of education, including the science education, that was to be found in, or being developed in, the corresponding boys' schools. The women teachers were caught in a double bind, having either to conform to these standards set in the boys' schools in order to prove girls' ability; or to develop conceptions of science education for girls that were seen to be particularly suited to the predominant notions of girls' needs – needs related to their expected domestic futures.

Thus, by the beginning of the twentieth century, science education for girls of the middle classes in the girls' high schools was taking on two forms. For the academic, able and interested, the possibility existed of pursuing science in highly specialized courses leading to university. For others, alternative courses stressing the scientific aspects of domestic life were developing.

NOTES

1. This chapter is based on Chapter 4 of my doctoral thesis, 'Socio-historical Perspectives on the Scientific Education of Girls in 19th and 20th Century England', University of Leeds, 1985. The thesis explored the development of science education for girls and asked two broad questions: how far there has been a 'process of differentiation' that has either kept girls out of science or offered them a limited conception of science; how far have women and girls been excluded from, and subordinate in, the complex of activities understood as science because of the male-defined concerns and priorities of science reflective of the male domination of the scientific community? I am indebted to Professor David Layton, Emeritus Professor of Science Education, University of Leeds, for his advice and help on the original work for this chapter.
2. A.J. Meadows and W.H. Brock, 'Topics Fit for Gentlemen: The Problem of Science in the Public School Curriculum', in B. Simon and I. Bradley (eds.), *The Victorian Public School – Studies in the Development of an Educational Institution* (Dublin: Gill & Macmillan, 1975), pp. 95–114.
3. See the discussion of 'The Scientific Movement' in R.L. Archer, *Secondary Education*

in the Nineteenth Century (London: Frank Cass, 1966); E. Mendelsohn, 'The Emergence of Science as a Profession in Nineteenth-century Europe', in K. Hill (ed.), *The Management of Scientists* (London: Beacon Press, 1964), pp. 1–45.

4. M. Grey, 'On the Special Requirements for Improving the Education of Girls', quoted in J. Kamm, *Indicative Past – One Hundred Years of the Girls' Public Day School Trust* (London: George Allen & Unwin, 1971), p. 41.

5. See C. Dyhouse, *Girls Growing up in Late Victorian and Edwardian England* (London: Routledge & Kegan Paul, 1981); J.B.S. Pederson, 'The Reform of Women's Secondary and Higher Education in Nineteenth Century England: A Study in Elite Groups', unpublished PhD thesis, University of California, 1974. For more on science education as an 'accomplishment', see E. Davies's evidence to the Schools Inquiry Commission, minutes of evidence, Vol. 5 (London: HMSO, 1868), p. 289.

6. Quoted in Kamm, *Indicative Past*, p. 86.

7. See L.E. Walter, 'The Teaching of Science in Girls' Schools', *British Association for the Advancement of Science Annual Report for 1896*, p. 761; and D. Mackintosh, 'On the Introduction of Science into Higher and Middle Class Schools', *Association for the Advancement of Science Annual Report for 1883*, p. 622.

8. This was stated in the *Report on the Differentiation of the Curriculum for Boys and Girls Respectively in Secondary Education* (Hadow Report) (London: HMSO, 1923), p. 24.

9. See the Schools Inquiry Commission, minutes of evidence, Vol. 5, p. 252.

10. Ibid., pp. 722–3.

11. Schools Inquiry Commission, minutes of evidence, Vol. 5, p. 267.

12. *The North London Collegiate School, 1850–1950* (Oxford: Oxford University Press, 1950), Appendix II.

13. Schools Inquiry Commission, minutes of evidence, Vol. 5, pp. 239, 727 and 733.

14. There may have been other schools for which documentary evidence is now lost. The histories both of Cheltenham and the North London Collegiate School are quite well documented; also, importantly, the headmistresses of both were asked to give evidence to the Taunton Commission, which suggests that they were certainly the leaders in their field, if not the only players.

15. A useful discussion of this is given in M.J. Peterson, 'The Victorian Governess: Status Incongruence in Family and Society', in M. Vicinus (ed.), *Suffer and Be Still: Women in the Victorian Age* (London: Indiana University Press, 1973).

16. Hadow Report, p. 24.

17. For an example of this view, see Frances Buss's evidence to the Schools Inquiry Commission, minutes of evidence, Vol. 5, p. 261.

18. Quoted in J. Kamm, *How Different from Us – A Biography of Miss Buss and Miss Beale* (London: Bodley Head, 1958), p. 42.

19. To a discussion of the division of the movement for the secondary and higher education of women into 'uncompromising' and 'separatist' camps is given in S. Delamont, 'The Domestic Ideology and Women's Education', in S. Delamont and L. Duffin (eds), *The Nineteenth Century Woman – Her Cultural and Physical World* (London: Croom Helm, 1978), pp. 164–87.

20. Frances Buss co-operated with Emily Davies in her campaign to open the Cambridge Local Junior and Senior Examinations to girls, providing 25 candidates for the first examinations for girls in 1863.

21. Quoted in Kamm, *How Different from Us*, p. 66.

22. Schools Inquiry Commission, minutes of evidence, Vol. 5, p. 434.

23. Ibid., pp. 253, 738.

24. For evidence of this, see the statements of Frances Buss and Dorothea Beale to the Schools Inquiry Commission, minutes of evidence, Vol. 5, pp. 254, 734. There was general discussion throughout the 1860s stimulated by the Clarendon and Taunton Commissions as to what constituted a good education for boys.

25. In her evidence to the Schools Inquiry Commission, Emily Davies argued that the campaign to enable girls to sit the Cambridge Locals was not so that they could 'run a race with boys', but that they could prove themselves with 'a fixed standard which has recognized value' (Schools Inquiry Commission, minutes of evidence, Vol. 5, p. 241).

26. Hadow Report, p. 26.
27. *The Educational Year Book for 1882* (London: Cassell, Petter, Galpin & Co., 1882).
28. Rev. J.M. Wilson, 'Address to Bath High School for Girls', *Journal of Education*, Vol. XII (1890): p. 35.
29. Ibid.
30. Hadow Report, p. 32.
31. Pederson, *The Reform of Women's Secondary and Higher Education*, p. 282.
32. Ibid., pp. 281–2.
33. M. Grey, 'Influence of the Higher Education of Women on Character', *Journal of Education*, Vol. X (1888): 337.
34. S. Bryant, *Educational Ends or the Ideal of Personal Development* (London: Longmans, Green, 1887), pp. 232–9.
35. Ibid., p. 240.
36. S. Bryant, 'The Curriculum of a Girls' School', *Special Reports on Educational Subjects*, Vol. 2 (London HMSO, 1898), pp. 99–132.
37. Ibid.
38. Ibid.
39. Ibid.
40. Ibid.
41. Ibid.
42. Ibid.
43. Ibid.
44. A full discussion on the widespread anxieties about the health of the nation and how this affected the curriculum for girls is given in C. Dyhouse, 'Good Wives and Little Mothers – Social Anxieties and the School Girls' Curriculum' *Oxford Review of Education*, Vol. 3, No. 1 (1977): 21–35. A discussion of the effects on the science curriculum for girls is given in C. Manthorpe, 'Science or Domestic Science? The Struggle to Define an Appropriate Science Education for Girls in Early Twentieth Century England', *History of Education*, Vol. 15, No. 3 (1986): 195–213.
45. S. Bryant, 'Natural Science', in S.A Burstall and M.A. Douglas (eds.), *Public Schools for Girls – A Series of Papers on Their History, Aims and Schemes of Study* (London: Longmans, 1911).
46. Ibid.
47. Ibid.
48. Ibid.
49. Ibid.
50. Ibid.
51. Ibid.
52. Ibid.
53. Ibid.
54. Ibid.
55. Ibid.
56. In the history of science education, more detailed work is needed to find out what happened at the classroom level. How far were these theories reflected in practice? Closer inspection of school records, textbooks in actual use, laboratory design and apparatus, school histories, oral testimony, as well as biography and autobiography, could help provide a detailed picture of the reality of the classroom situation.
57. S.A. Burstall, *Retrospect and Prospect – Sixty Years of Women's Education* (London: Longmans, Green, 1933).
58. Ibid.
59. Ibid.
60. Ibid.
61. S.A. Burstall, *English High Schools for Girls – Their Aims, Organisation and Management* (London: Longmans, Green, 1907), pp. 115–16.
62. Ibid.
63. Ibid.
64. Ibid.

65. Ibid.
66. Ibid.
67. The list of schools did not include private establishments in which, as noted earlier, if science was taught at all, it tended to be botany or 'use of the globes'.
68. See 'Report of the committee appointed to consider and report upon the method and substance of science teaching in secondary schools, with particular reference to the essential place of science in general education', British Association for the Advancement of Science, *Annual Report* for 1917. This report notes that out of 200 headmistresses in public secondary schools for girls, 65.5 per cent had literary degrees, 24 per cent had mathematics degrees, and 10.5 per cent had science degrees.
69. Burstall, *Retrospect and Prospect*, p. 144.
70. J.P. Bremner 'Some Aspects of the Teaching of the Biological Sciences in English Schools During the Second Half of the Nineteenth Century', unpublished MA thesis, London, 1955, p. 24.
71. J. Milburn 'The Secondary School Mistress: A Study of Her Professional Views and Their Significance in the Educational Developments of the Period 1895–1914, unpublished PhD thesis, London, 1969.
72. Figures taken from sample timetables in the reports of the Bryce Commission, Vol. IX, pp. 407–23.
73. 'Technical Education', *Journal of Education*, Vol. XVI (1894): 87.
74. '6th Conference of the Teachers Guild, Bath 1894', *Journal of Education*, Vol. XVI (1894): 87.
75. Bryant, 'Natural Science', p. 134.
76. In his evidence to the Bryce Commission, David Forsyth, headmaster of Leeds Higher Grade School, noted that many girls came to his school at 13, 14 and 15 from private schools and 'not having had any thorough training before ... we have very great difficulties with such girls' (Bryce Commission, Vol. III (1895), p. 191).
77. R. McLeod and R. Moseley, 'Fathers and Daughters: Reflections on Women, Science and Victorian Cambridge', *History of Education*, Vol. 8, No. 4 (1979): 321–33.
78. Bryce Commission, Vol. IX (1895) pp. 428–9.
79. A.J. Meadows and W.H. Brock, 'Topics Fit for Gentlemen: The Problem of Science in the Public School Curriculum', in B. Simon and I. Bradley (eds), *The Victorian Public School – Studies in the Development of an Educational Institution* (Dublin: Gill & Macmillan, 1975), p. 110.
80. Ibid., p. 113.
81. In an article written for a series of special reports on educational subjects, Archer Vassell, a leading figure in the Association of Public School Science Masters, argued that 'now that the large number of subjects included under the head of science are more reasonably taught to elder boys and others, there has arisen a fairly widespread feeling amongst both parents and schoolmasters that some elementary information on scientific subjects should be given to boys while still at Prep Schools and that these subjects afford valuable material for educating the minds of such boys. To their credit, be it said, Board Schools and Girls' Schools have for some time realised this fact and in many of them scientific subjects find a place in the curriculum' (*Special Reports on Educational Subjects*, Vol. 6 (1900), p. 257).
82. Bryant, 'The Curriculum of a Girls' School', p. 99.
83. J.Burstyn, *Victorian Education and the Ideal of Womanhood* (London: Croom Helm, 1980), p. 158.
84. Bryant, 'The Curriculum of a Girls' School', p. 82.
85. *Journal of Education*, Vol. X (1888): 176.
86. Burstall, *Retrospect and Prospect*, p. 55.
87. Schools Inquiry Commission, minutes of evidence, Vol. 5, p. 142.
88. Burstyn, *Victorian Education*, p. 152.
89. See *The Education Yearbook for 1882*. The majority of girls' schools listed provided instruction for one or more of these examinations.
90. Hadow Report, p. 27.
91. B.S. Cane, 'Scientific and Technical; Subjects in the Curriculum of English Secondary

Schools at the Turn of the Century', *British Journal of Education Studies*, Vol. 8, (1959): 52–64.

92. Oxford and Cambridge Schools Examination Board, *Summary Report on the Work of the Board During the Thirty Years 1874–1904* (Oxford: Clarendon Press, 1904), p. 20.

93. In her evidence to the Schools Inquiry Commission, for example, Frances Buss explained that, 'Botany has recently received very much more close attention because it is a subject which would tell in the Cambridge examinations', and also that the lessons were made to suit what was 'demanded by the Cambridge examinations for a pass' (Schools Inquiry Commission, minutes of evidence, Vol. 5, p. 266).

94. W.H.Brock, 'School Science Examinations – Sacrifice or Stimulus', in R.MacLeod, *Days of Judgement: Science Examinations and the Organisation of Knowledge in Late Victorian England* (Driffield: Nafferton Books 1982), pp. 169–88.

95. This is discussed in Bryant, 'The Curriculum of Girls' Schools', Pederson, 'The Reform of Women's Secondary and Higher Education in Nineteenth Century England', and Milburn, 'The Secondary School Mistress'.

96. For a full discussion of this, see Manthorpe, 'Science or Domestic Science?'.

97. See D. Layton, *Interpreters of Science: A History of the Association for Science Education* (London: John Murray, 1984), especially Ch. 3.

98. This is dealt with more fully in Ch. 6 of my thesis, 'Science for Girls: The Work of the Association of Women Science Teachers'. See also C. Manthorpe, 'Reflections on the Scientific Education of Girls', *School Science Review* (March 1987).

4

The Beech-covered Hillside:
Self-presentation in the Histories of the Girls' Schools

SARA DELAMONT

Stands there a School in the midst of the Chilterns
Beech-covered hillsides encircle it round
Ivy and creepers entwine the old Abbey
Health and contentment within it are found
Wycombe Abbey School song, 1901,
(Bowerman, 1966)

This chapter analyses how the histories of independent, private, fee-paying schools for girls present the origins, development and social worlds of those institutions. It examines the histories of the schools as texts, which are the vehicle for conveying certain messages about the schools to an audience. The data for the chapter are 20 book-length school histories from the author's collection.[1] The sampling of the texts is discussed in Appendix 1 on pp. 95–7. The title is taken from the 1901 Wycombe Abbey School song (quoted above).

Beech-covered hillsides are a potent image from which to begin a textual analysis of girls' school histories, and the image of Wycombe Abbey, in its rural setting with its healthy, happy inmates, is the epitome of the tone conveyed by the 20 volumes examined here. This chapter deals with their style, their content, and what is omitted from them. The limitations and the possibilities for historical work based on girls' school histories are also explored.

DEFINING THE TOPIC

This chapter is a study of how girls' schools have presented themselves (or been presented) in their official published histories.[2] Its focus is book-length histories of individual schools, all of which are available to the public. Excluded are books about categories of schools, such as Kirk's (1952) study of the Woodard Schools, or O'Leary (1936) on the Society of the Sacred Heart; general works such as Haddon (1977) or Burstall and Douglas (1911) on the schooling of girls; and biographies or autobiographies of pioneering headmistresses such as Kamm (1958) on Miss Buss and Miss Beale, or Clarke's (1973) account of her rise to the headship of the Manchester High School for Girls. Each of these categories of book would be a suitable subject for the type of analysis offered here (see, for example, Dyhouse, 1987), but such examinations are beyond my present scope. It would also be interesting to compare histories of boys' schools with those of girls' schools,

TABLE 4.1
SCHOOL HISTORIES SELECTED

School and place	Date published	Author(s)
Albyn School, Aberdeen	1967	Duthie and Duncan
Bedford High School	1932	Westaway
Bedford High School	1957	Westaway
Bedford High School	1982	Godber and Hutchins
Cardiff High School	1955	Carr
Cardiff High School	1986	Leech
Cheltenham Ladies' College	1904	Beale
Cheltenham Ladies' College	1953	Clarke
Cheltenham Ladies' College	1979	Clarke
Edgehill College, Bideford	1934	Pyke
Edgehill College, Bideford	1957	Pyke
Edgehill College, Bideford	1984	Shaw
Francis Holland School, London	1931	Dunning (Graham Street)
Francis Holland School, London	1939	Bell (Baker Street)
Francis Holland School, London	1978	Hicklin (Baker Street)
Park School, Glasgow	1930	Anon
Park School, Glasgow	1980	Lightwood
Richmond Lodge, Belfast	1968	Robb
Rugby High School	1969	Randall
Shrewsbury High School	1962	Bates and Wells

but that is also beyond the range of the research described here. This chapter scrutinizes books such as the two volumes of history about the City of Cardiff High School for Girls by Carr (1955) and Leech (1986). Carr's *The Spinning Wheel* covers the 1895–1955 period, Leech deals with 1950–70. Both could be bought in local bookshops, but were mostly sold to ex-pupils. The analysis that follows compares and contrasts a selection of such books.

Table 4.1 shows the 20 books analysed selected in the light of the difficulties that exist in defining the population outlined in Appendix

1. The 20 books deal with 11 schools, including the two 'sister' institutions founded by Francis Holland in Baker Street and Graham Street in London. The full bibliographic details of the 20 volumes are provided in the references at the end of the chapter.

These volumes have been chosen to reflect the following criteria: geographic spread (one Welsh, one from Northern Ireland, two Scottish schools); day and boarding; urban, small town, and rural; elite and expensive (Cheltenham) or ordinary (Cardiff and Rugby); denominational (Edgehill founded by Methodists, the two Francis Holland schools by Anglicans) and non-denominational; privately owned, independent, or part of a group of schools such as the GPDST; much written about and famous (Cheltenham and Bedford) and little known (Rugby, Albyn, Richmond Lodge); celebrated repeatedly (Bedford, Cheltenham, Park School) or only once. There are books published in the 1930s, 1950s, and in the 1980s.

There are works about schools that have vanished (Cardiff) and those that remain (Cheltenham). Eleven of the 20 volumes are listed in Barr (1984), the standard bibliography. Those about Albyn School, Cardiff High School after 1955, the 1934 and 1984 books about Edgehill, the Rugby Girls' High School, the 1980 Park School history, the 1979 account of Cheltenham, and, most oddly, the books about the Francis Holland School in Baker Street by Bell (1939) and Hicklin (1978), are not included in Barr. Only seven of the 20 volumes are in Cunningham's (1976) bibliography. The Scottish and Northern Irish books are beyond his scope, but of the English and Welsh texts, seven are listed.

The sample of 20 volumes covers a good range. However, there is no convent or other Roman Catholic School; there is nothing in England north of the Shrewsbury High School, nothing published in the nineteenth century, and no school known more for sport than anything else.

Table 4.2 shows the schools in order of their foundation.

The origins of the 11 schools were as follows: Albyn School for Girls, Aberdeen, grew out of Miss Warrack's establishment for young ladies, begun in 1867. Bedford High School for Girls was founded in 1882. The City of Cardiff High School for Girls was founded in 1895 and vanished into a mixed comprehensive in 1970. Cheltenham Ladies' College was founded as an Anglican day school in 1853, and was taken over by Miss Beale in 1858. Edgehill College was planned in 1882 and opened in 1884. The Francis Holland School in Baker Street opened in 1878, moving to Clarence Gate in 1915. The younger branch, at Graham Street, opened in 1881. The Park School, Glasgow, opened in 1880. Robb (1968) reports that 'the beginnings of Richmond Lodge are lost not in antiquity but in obscurity' (p. 5). It grew out of a mixed private school owned by three sisters, daughters of a linen merchant. The Misses Hardy were certainly established by 1884, but may have opened a school in 1879. In 1903 it was sold to Miss

TABLE 4.2

SCHOOLS IN ORDER OF THEIR FOUNDATION

School	Date of foundation
Cheltenham	1853
Albyn	1867
Francis Holland, Baker Street	1878
Park School	1880
Francis Holland, Graham Street	1881
Bedford	1882
Edgehill	1884
Richmond Lodge	1884
Shrewsbury High	1885
Cardiff	1895
Rugby	1919

Garrett and became a 'Ladies' Preparatory School', the real beginning of an academic secondary school for girls. Rugby High School for Girls had its origins in the Arnold High School founded in 1903, but dates its opening from 1919. Shrewsbury High School opened in 1885. This spread of dates is expected. Few schools for girls existed before 1860, and the 1880s were the 'great decade' for their foundation.

THE ANALYTIC METHODS AND THEMES

As there are now many computer packages for the analysis of text (see Tesch, 1990), it would be possible to set up files on all these books and run various concordance or analytic programs on them. The analysis presented here was done by hand, in the old-fashioned way, with hash marks in coloured inks on squared paper. The following themes, questions and headings were used in the analysis: the authors and the audience; the internal structure of the volumes; the illustrations; the relative amounts of space devoted to different topics (especially their coverage of six historical controversies); the dates of the volumes. Each of these is explained in turn before the analysis is presented.

1. Author(s), audiences and publishers

The producers and intended consumers are one issue to be explored. Note was made of who wrote the individual chapters or sections of the histories, who edited or compiled the whole volume, who published it, and the intended audience if stated. A book written by one scholar, published by a commercial publisher and aimed at the general public, might be very different in style and content from the reminiscences of former pupils compiled by the history teacher and printed privately for the Old Girls' Association.

2. Internal structure

The organization of the books can be studied. Some are thematic (acting, sport, the staff, the Guides), others are chronological – often following the regimes of the various heads (Miss X, 1880–98, Miss Y, 1899–1907). Some books are a mixture of both.

3. Illustrations

If there are illustrations, it is necessary to see whether these are photographs, drawings or maps and plans, who did them, and what they portray. Are there pictures drawn by girls or only by adults? What do the photographs reveal? Did royalty visit? Did the local bishop visit? Are girls shown going to church or playing netball or acting or working? What periods in the life of the school are illustrated?

4. Coverage of key issues

There are six topics that earlier work on the history of women's education has revealed as being problematic for the schools to deal with. A particular focus of this analysis is the ways in which the histories report these topics, which are: dress and deportment; sport; class and religion; relations with males (masters and boys); curriculum; and feminism, especially suffragism. Delamont (1989) includes a discussion of the strategies adopted by girls' schools to protect the reputations of their inmates (both staff and pupils) from public censure over their clothing, behaviour, curriculum, exercise, relationships across religious and class lines, interactions with men, and political campaigns. The 20 volumes have been examined to see how far, if at all, these issues are presented to the reader 20, 50 or even 100 years after the controversy. It is important to see how much space is devoted to different issues, such as sport, the financial arrangements, the governors, the staff, pupils' funny memories and so on, in the light of the controversial status of some matters.

5. Date of publication

Comparisons of books written between the two world wars, those published in the 1950s and 1960s, and those issued since the reawakening of feminism are also illuminating in the light of the coverage of the six key issues. Additionally, where schools' histories were published after one or both of the world wars, their treatment of women's lives in wartime is worthy of attention.

THE AUTHORS, THEIR AUDIENCES, TEXTS AND PUBLISHERS

Table 4.1 includes the names of the authors of the 20 volumes. There are three people who produced more than one book about 'their' school, making 20 separate authors. Two of these are men (Duthie and Pyke), and the remainder are women. Five of the 20 books do not provide any details about their author(s) at all, although it seems likely that they were written or compiled by either former pupils or staff. Five authors explicitly are identified as 'Old Girls'; eight books are by a teacher, and two by the school's bursar (Pyke). Only two of the books are stated to have a co-author who is a professional historian (Albyn School and the 1982 book on Bedford High School). Essentially, these books are produced by an insider: a person who studied or worked (or both) in the school described.

Half of the authors produced a text with a continuous narrative, but half are edited or compiled: consisting of extracts from letters, diaries, memoirs and so on produced by former staff, past pupils or local people. Thus the 1930 volume about the Park School, Glasgow, contains memories from former pupils, identified only by their initials, dealing with issues such as the first time scenery was allowed for a school play: 'It was a proud day when scenery was first introduced. ... What a thrill it was to lie upon the floor and splash in trees on sheets of brown paper out of huge pots of paint' (Anon, 1930:52).

The texts that have one or two named authors, rather than an editor, mix historical narrative with quotations from former staff and pupils. Thus Bates and Wells (1962:62) tell their readers that: 'Miss Birch, the Head of the Junior House from 1920–1928, was much loved and her death after a short illness was a great shock to the school' (p. 64). They also include a former pupil recalling that: We played Netball, Tennis and Hockey. This last was at first considered not *quite* lady-like – I was only allowed to play when I decided to take up P.T.' (p. 46).

The similarities between the authored and the compiled texts are considerable. The question arises: for whom are these books intended? Nine of the 20 texts make no explicit statement about their intended audience, and another (Hicklin, 1978) talks only of 'the reader'. The remainder make it clear that they are designed for 'Old Girls' or people connected with the particular school. Thus Duthie and Duncan (1967:i) say their book is for 'all who have a connection with the school'. Westaway (1957:i) states hers is for 'all the people who have passed through the school who will . . . read the book'. Carr (1955:ii) addresses hers to those who: 'loving the school or friendly towards it will read its story with charity', and Leech (1986) dedicates hers to 'all who made Cardiff High School for Girls a school worth writing about'. Pyke (1934: 7) believes his book will only make sense to those who 'know Edgehill', and Anon (1930:ii) compiled her material for 'the little world of the pupils and friends of the Park School' and 'many' who 'remember their old school'. Robb (1968:3) explicitly writes for 'any Arellian reader', the Old Girls of the Richmond Lodge School being Arellians. Bates and Wells (1962:14) are not very explicit about their readership, but state that: 'the majority of readers of this history will be familiar with the description of Shrewsbury High School as a "Direct Grant" school'.

The implication of these findings – that the books are written by women associated with the schools, reliance is placed on self-reported memories from other such women, and the end-product is designed to be read by similar women – leads on to the question of who publishes the volumes. Only one of the books (Clarke, 1953) was published by a national publishing company: Faber & Faber. Two were produced by the press of the local university (Aberdeen and Glasgow), and one (Carr, 1955) by the local newspaper. All but one of the remainder were printed by local firms; for example, the history of Richmond Lodge School was printed in Belfast.

The scrutiny of the authors, publishers and readership suggests that, with the exception of Clarke's (1953) history of Cheltenham Ladies' College, these texts are entirely parochial. The next analytic theme, the internal structure of the volumes, will develop from this.

There are three main patterns in the structure and content of the 20 volumes. The books are either chronological, thematic or a mixture of the two. The three histories of the two Francis Holland Schools include one of each type. Dunning (1931) is a mixed compilation. There are 25 chapters arranged in chronological order written by staff and pupils, recalling school life, followed by ten thematic chapters focused on games, art and drama, the Guides, and so on. The first 25 chapters have titles such as 'Notes by one of the first thirteen' and 'Memories of a middle-aged old girl', while those in the latter part of the book include 'The school missions association' and 'The Guide Movement at Graham Street'. Bell (1939) follows the chronological model, and has four chapters, each dealing with the reign of a headmistress. Thus Chapter 2 covers 1891 to 1904, the period when Lilla Blanche Strong led the Francis Holland School in Baker Street. She 'came from a military family and discipline was in her bones' (p. 34). The third book on a Francis Holland School, by Hicklin (1978), is entirely thematic. There are 17 chapters, dealing with such topics as 'Music', 'Kind Hearts and Good Works' and 'Crown and Empire' at Baker Street.

Six of the 20 volumes, including the Dunning one, mix thematic and chronological chapters. Six are thematic like the Hicklin, while eight are chronological like Bell. The content and coverage in the 20 volumes is discussed in detail below.

ILLUSTRATIONS

Illustrations are a feature of most girls' school histories. Photographs, maps, sketches and even paintings are reproduced to adorn the volumes. Photographs are the most common type of illustration; all the books have at least one, while Godber and Hutchins (1982) contains 180. Table 4.3 shows the number of photographs, maps and sketches in each of the 20 volumes. Not only do the books vary in the number of illustrations, there are also differences between them in the objects and people actually shown in the pictures. All three books about the two Francis Holland Schools include a picture of Francis Holland himself; all three volumes about Edgehill carry pictures of the school's bursars; while Cheltenham's histories are unusual in having no pictures of sporting activities at all. Table 4.4 shows the relative frequencies of different subjects for illustrations across the 20 volumes.

Table 4.4 shows that the most frequent subjects for illustrations are the exteriors of buildings and the headmistresses of the schools, followed by a variety of sporting teams and activities. Hockey alone provides 21 pictures in these 20 books, while science teaching is only shown eight times. Hockey is the most commonly shown sport, followed by drill and gym (11 pictures). Within the aesthetic area, drama (shown 22 times) is more often shown than art or music.

In general, the more recently published books have more pictures of all types than do the earlier volumes. This is spectacularly so comparing the 1932 and 1982 volumes about Bedford High School, or the 1930 and 1980 texts on Park School. Given the wide range of both

TABLE 4.3

ILLUSTRATIVE MATERIAL IN 20 SCHOOL HISTORIES

School volume	Photographs	sketches	Maps	Total
Albyn 1967	3	4	–	35
Bedford 1932	11	1	–	12
Bedford 1957	12	–	–	12
Bedford 1982	180	14	3	197
Cardiff 1955	14	–	–	14
Cardiff 1986	48	1	–	49
Cheltenham 1904	12	9	–	21
Cheltenham 1953	20	3	2	25
Cheltenham 1979	42	3	2	45
Edgehill 1934	21	–	–	21
Edgehill 1957	19	–	–	19
Edgehill 1984	58	–	–	58
Francis Holland 1931	7	8	1	16
Francis Holland 1939	1	1	–	2
Francis Holland 1978	29	6	–	35
Park 1930	9	–	–	9
Park 1980	32	–	–	32
Richmond Lodge 1968	10	–	–	10
Rugby 1969	13	–	–	13
Shrewsbury 1962	42	–	–	42

TABLE 4.4

FREQUENCY OF SUBJECTS IN ILLUSTRATIONS

Topic	Number of illustrations
Exterior views of school buildings	91
Headmistresses	85
Sporting activities	59
Staff groups	40
Visiting dignitaries and royalty	36
Pupil groups	33
Drama, art and music	31
School governors	26
Girl Guides	26
Staff and pupil groups	24
Interior views of school buildings	18

the total numbers of illustrations and the variety of their content, it is worth comparing older and more recent volumes to see if the topics illustrated have changed. Table 4.5 divides the 20 volumes between those published up to 1960 and those produced after 1961. It shows that while in most categoies there are more illustrations in the post-1961 books, the differential is especially striking when *pupils* are the subject. There are many more illustrations of girls playing sport, acting, and in the Guides, in the post-1961 books. Depictions of governors are the only type of illustration to be commoner in the older texts than the more modern ones. The school histories appear to have included more evidence of pupils' activities in the later era. Certainly the later books show pupils in informal settings, such as sixth-form

TABLE 4.5

CHANGING NATURE OF PICTORIAL REPRESENTATION:
NUMBER OF ILLUSTRATIONS

	Pre-1960 books	*Post-1961 books*
Exteriors of buildings	37	54
Headmistresses	33	52
Sport and gym	5	54
Visiting dignitaries	2	34
Staff groups	6	34
Staff and pupil groups	2	22
Drama art and music	5	26
Pupil groups	8	25
Governors	17	9
Guides	0	26
Interior views	2	16

common rooms, whereas the earlier ones illustrate pupils *only* in formally posed shots – such as the Hockey XI standing for their team photograph.

SPACE, LENGTH AND COVERAGE

The 20 books vary a good deal in length. Godber and Hutchins (1982) has 554 pages, Pyke (1934) only 80. Ten of the books have an index, ten do not. There is also a wide variety in the amount of coverage devoted to different issues in the written text, just as there is in the illustrations. Thus, for example, the two Pyke volumes deal with the place of Edgehill in the Methodist system of education, while Shaw is predominantly based on pupils' views of the school. Before examining the content of all 20, some of the variations in coverage can usefully be mentioned. The Albyn School history is one of the most idiosyncratic, and makes a good starting point.

Duthie and Duncan (1967) opens with an account of Aberdeen in 1867, drawn from local newspapers. They suggest that the city had 50 private schools, among which was Miss Warrack's: the institution that became Albyn School. There is no explanation for the survival of Albyn. The authors highlight the lack of educational and career opportunities for women in nineteenth-century Aberdeen, including the fact that the local university is all-male in 1867. There is a chapter on Miss Warrack's family, followed by memories of former pupils at the school under the different twentieth-century heads. These are childish memories, of snowballing and cod-liver oil, evacuation in the Second World War, and isolation in the typhoid epidemic of 1964. Then the current (1967) head writes bracingly of the educational scene, and there are lists of governors, and distinguished staff and pupils. None of the anxieties of the pre-1914 era are discussed at all: no mention is made of parental anxieties about the curriculum, or whether pupils were from mixed religious or social backgrounds. The space devoted to Miss Warrack's ancestors and descendants (nine pages out of 84) is considerable in a slim volume. Yet, as the analysis that follows will show, an emphasis on a founder's family is a commoner ingredient than a discussion of suffrage or the local university. Carr (1955) is the only volume to deal with suffrage, while the 1930 volume about the Park School is the only one to have a chapter on life in the local university in the pre-1914 period.

We now turn to an analysis of how the nineteenth-century controversies (dress and deportment, sport, class and religion, men, curricula, and feminism) are treated in the 20 volumes. An analysis of how, if at all, the key themes appear in the girls' school histories reveals variations, but over all the picture is of neglect.

Elsewhere (Delamont, 1989) I have discussed the threats surrounding the pioneering girls' schools in the period before the 1914–18 war, and the strategies employed to defend the schools against them. Potential parents were worried that girls would be corrupted, and their reputations sullied by contacts with fellow-pupils of other religious denominations or other social classes; with males of all ages; by being *seen* acting, playing hockey or cricket; by dressing immodestly; coming under the influence of older women who were suffragists or campaigners for anything to do with gender; or by studying 'masculine' subjects. Schools developed a myriad of procedures to demonstrate that their pupils could learn Latin and play lacrosse without endangering their health, reputations or marriage prospects. A century later it is hard to reconstruct either the parental fears, or the rationale and efficacy of the strategies. It is equally difficult for the contemporary reader to imagine generations of girls who were forbidden to talk to their schoolfriends inside the school, or walk home with them except by parental permission, or were forced to act in skirts even when playing male roles, or had to be chaperoned to receive a piano lesson.

The struggle for girls to be allowed to play tennis or netball, to learn Greek and algebra, to wear a gymslip, and to be a Girl Guide seems quaint. So, too, does loyalty and nostalgia for pioneer schools. As Hicklin (1978:9) points out:

> Sentiments uttered at the turn of the century, and even between the wars, on the subject of the Dear Old School and its denizens might come in for mockery today. The notion that any civilized young women could have actually wanted to wear an old school tie or hatband, ... or to have considered turning up at Harrods clutching a signed authorization from the Headmistress and demanding to purchase the old school blazer ... will seem scarcely credible ...

To recapture the controversial nature of schooling for girls, it is necessary to read autobiographies by pioneering teachers and pupils who lived through the early days, such as Sara Burstall (1933), who became headmistress of the Manchester High School for Girls; or study attacks on the girls' schools by critics such as Meyrick Booth (1927, 1932) or Arabella Kenealy (1899, 1920). These two authors were criticizing women's education during the first 30 years of this century. Kenealy, though herself a doctor, believed that: 'The woman of average brain attains the intellectual standards of the man of average brain only at the cost of her health, of her emotions, or of her morale' (1920:55).

The fee-paying girls' schools, with their sport, had changed the course of evolution, and upper-class women were being transformed by lacrosse and hockey into Amazons who 'lapse to the biological grade, not of cultured, but of rough working men' (Kenealy, 1920: 28) and whose physique resembled 'colts' or even 'bullocks' (p. 87). The working-class girls reaching secondary school, where they en-countered algebra and Latin, were equally damaged. These schools had engendered the race of stunted, precocious, bold-eyed, cigarette-smoking, free living working girls who fill our streets; many tricked out like cocottes, eyes roving after men, impudence upon their tongues, their poor brains vitiated by vulgar rag-tunes and cinema-scenes of vice and suggestiveness (Kenealy, 1920: 230).

Kenealy was very worried about the Girl Guide movement because they sponsored girls to parade in the street in a 'hideous' uniform, encouraging 'a love of publicity and of unwholesome excitement!' (p. 231). Worse than Girl Guides were feminists, who were leading the Anglo–Saxon race into 'Prussianism, socialism, Bolshevism and Anarchism' (p. 285).

Meyrick Booth, writing in 1932, saw the pioneering girls' schools as old-fashioned, because Freud had overthrown the theory behind them.[3] Booth saw Miss Buss and Miss Beale as motivated by 'the sterile rational doctrinairism of the J.S. Mill . . . school' (Booth, 1932: 143), guided by the 'unpsychological ideals of pre-war days' (p. 162), which is a 'utilitarian, pseudo-masculine feminism' (p. 164). The girls' schools were misguided, because they exposed the pupils to: 'the examination cramming; the tennis, hockey and other sports; the conversion of an interest in the other sex into *camaraderie;* the cult of hardiness, independence, and self-assertion' (p. 174).

In the writings of Kenealy and Booth, at a period when the academic schooling of girls was already 50 years old, the bravery of the pioneers is starkly apparent. They introduced Greek and lacrosse in the teeth of views such as these, but, because of these views, they had to do so with caution and precautions. A novel about a scandal threatening one of the Woodard Schools is discussed in Appendix 2.

Careful scrutiny of many school histories, in addition to autobiographies and memoirs, and an examination of archives, reveals the plethora of rules and regulations in their original social context. However, the casual reader of one or two histories, or the former pupil of just one school, could either miss these important issues, or fail to see their historical significance because of their cursory treatment in many of the volumes.

The key themes in women's education may appear in the girls' school histories in one of three ways. Such topics as hockey, Latin, and uniform may appear without any discussion at all, as if they had always been entirely acceptable ('Hockey began in 1892'). Alternatively, they may be introduced with a clear indication that they were problematic, but without any explanations of their dubiousness and risk ('Hockey, played in skirts which trailed on the ground, was introduced as an optional game for those whose parents were progressive'). Thirdly, the text may introduce the theme, *and* explain to the reader why the pioneers behaved as they did. The concrete example of sport will illustrate these three approaches.

Randall (1969: 24–5) reports that at the school that turned into Rugby High School; 'Hockey, tennis and cricket were played ... by 1909 sufficient money had been raised to build a pavilion.' There is nothing here to alert the reader to the controversial nature of such games (see Atkinson, 1978 and 1987). The second approach is epitomized by the Bates and Wells (1962: 40) report that Swedish drill began at Shrewsbury in 1898 and a demonstration was given: 'The visitors, *only ladies*, sat chiefly in the Orchestra.' No explanation is provided for the reader in 1962 about the all-female nature of the audience. Later in that chapter is the quote from an former pupil about hockey being 'not *quite* ladylike' (p. 46) and, later, another former pupil recalls how in 1935 the tennis team 'were allowed to play in socks' (p. 47). Again, a reader in the 1960s is not helped to understand why hockey was risky, let alone that tennis had been played in lisle stockings until 1935. The Lightwood (1980, pp. 51–3) book on Park School, Glasgow, takes the third path, explaining how in 1890 hockey was seen as a 'dangerous' game, 'devastating to good looks', and how carefully the costume was designed to ameliorate 'adverse public opinion'. Finally, of course, one of Delamont's themes may not be mentioned at all: Pyke (1934, 1957) does not discuss physical education in any way, and nor does Beale (1904).

Table 4.6 shows the number of school histories that mention or

TABLE 4.6

TREATMENT OF KEY THEMES

Key theme	Not mentioned at all	Facts only	Theme raised, not explained	Theme explained
Games and gym	2	10	4	4
Dress	8	9	2	1
Chaperonage	11	4	2	3
Mixing of classes/ denominations	15	–	1	4
The male curriculum	5	8	3	4
Suffrage	15	2	1	2

discuss the key themes. It is clear from the table that few of the volumes deal with the themes in a way that makes them comprehensible to a modern reader. Thus half the books tell the reader when hockey began, but not why that matters. Eleven fail to discuss the ways in which schools prevented girls meeting males; and 15 have nothing on suffrage, although many pioneering schools were staffed by suffragists (Kean, 1990). Fifteen of the books do not discuss anxieties about the mixing of pupils of different denominations or social classes, even though it was a major issue in the first 50 years of the schools' existences. We know from other sources that Cheltenham accepted only the daughters of gentlemen, and demanded references to prove claims to gentility (Delamont, 1989:96–7), but the three histories of Cheltenham do not mention this. Cheltenham also had territorial rules to keep the pupils away from areas of the town where they might encounter men or boys. In the pre-1914 era, girls were forbidden to go to the polo ground, the racecourse or the Cheltenham boys' school playing fields (see Delamont, 1989:73). These rules are not mentioned in the three histories either. In contrast, Godber and Hutchins (1982) are careful to *explain* the rules on chaperonge (the girls' school had different hours from the boys' so the pupils would not meet in the street) and on keeping the *social* contacts between girls to a minimum.

Similarly, we know that religious mixing was considered so dangerous that the school for army officers' daughters at Bath nearly failed to get established because admitting Catholics was proposed (Delamont, 1989: 99–100), yet the three histories of Edgehill do not mention any discussions of whether non-Methodists were to be admitted. In fact, Anglicans *were* accepted, but the books do not analyse the debates, if any, over religious 'mixing'.

It is noticeable that the three topics that were no longer controversial when the majority of the books were published (after 1930) – chaperonage, mixing of classes and denominations, and suffrage – are the three topics that are not mentioned at all in the majority of the books. Games, the curriculum and dress issues, which were still educationally significant when the books were written, get more lengthy treatment. Even with these three topics, however, very few of the books try to explain to their readers *why* former pupils had to wear hats and gloves in the street, were forbidden cricket, or had to contend with inadequate laboratories. School historians do not want to remind their readers of rules and regulations that had long since ceased to serve any purpose, and that would smack of religious and class intolerance. The problem with many of the histories of the schools is that they do not help their readers to think like their foremothers, and therefore to understand their own inheritance.

CONCLUSIONS

The chapter has examined the structure and content of 20 school histories, estimated to be approximately a 10 per cent sample of those published for the United Kingdom. In general, these are written or compiled for former pupils and staff, rather than general readers, and they concentrate on the growth of the physical amenities and the lives of the headmistress. The feminist spirit of the pioneers who founded and led them, and the links between education for women and suffrage, were usually ignored.

The historian who wishes to learn about the experience of schooling needs to read them with some care, because very important topics may be missing altogether, and other topics are left unexplained. While it is obvious that some will not be mentioned in these books – those pupils who were expelled, or who hated the place and kept no links to it, or who attended for only short periods, and those teachers who stayed only briefly or left under clouds – it is less obvious that whole themes (such as religious mixing) are absent. Even allowing for these limitations, the historian can derive insights from such volumes. There is plenty of scope for further work to be done on them. It would be possible to trace both special friendships and career chains among the staff of the pioneering schools, for example. There has been a tendency for historians of women's education to focus on Miss Buss and Miss Beale and the GPDST schools, neglecting Wales, Scotland and Northern Ireland, and many less distinguished English schools.[4] Once an accurate bibliography of the girls' schools has been established, further work on better representative sets of school histories will be rewarding. There is a need for a history of girls' schooling in Wales, in Scotland, and in Northern Ireland; and a scholarly book on religiously based girls' schooling which compares Catholic, Quaker, Anglican and Non-Conformist institutions systematically.

The main lesson for the person who wishes to use histories of girls' schools for research purposes is that it is necessary to read a substantial number of them – at least 25 – written over the whole century of such schools' existence, in order to get a feeling for what is and what is not discussed. Even then, certain themes may be more easily discovered from autobiographies or contemporary scholarship – such as Booth's attacks – than from the histories of schools. This chapter has shown them to offer intriguing, but partial, accounts of women's history.

APPENDIX 1

Sampling the texts

It is necessary to explain how the selection of the 20 books examined was made from the large, but indeterminate, universe of such books. It is not entirely clear how many histories of particular girls' schools in the United Kingdom have been published to date. Barr (1984) is the most comprehensive list published, but it is by no means complete. Barr compiled her handlist from information supplied by 27 librarians in charge of educational collections in universities. It lists books about 152 different schools in the United Kingdom and Eire, along with sources of information about an equal number of schools that can be extracted from general works on education and biographies. Barr's list is by no means exhaustive, even of books available before 1984, as she admits in her introduction. For example, there is a book on the Croydon Girls' High School (1954) published to celebrate its fiftieth birthday. There is a copy of it in the main university library at Sussex, but it is not held in the education library there, or in the 26 other education libraries that sent data to Barr, so it does not appear on Barr's list. There are 15 other such school histories that I have found in second-hand shops that none of the 27 education libraries owned, and so are not included in Barr either. Peter Cunnigham (1976) of Leeds University has produced an alternative source in his *Local History of Education in England and Wales: A Bibliography*, which contains 188 pages of small-type listings with many school histories among them. There are two problems associated with using it as a source to try and define the total number of histories of girls' schools. It is now rather out of date, especially as many schools celebrated centenaries in the 1980s with new volumes. More seriously, it is not necessarily clear from the name of any particular school whether it is mixed, or for boys only, or for girls only. Getting hold of all the ambigously titled volumes to check their clientele would be a major piece of research. There are 53 book-length histories of schools known to be for girls listed in Cunningham (1976), which are not in Barr (1984). That suggests there are at least 220 published histories of girls' schools, so the 20 analysed here are about 10 per cent of the total.

The complications around sampling some texts for detailed analysis do not end with the open-ended nature of the 'population'. A further difficulty is that some schools have had multiple volumes prepared about them, especially if they are over 100 years old. Bedford High School was celebrated at 50 years (Westaway, 1932), at 75 years (Westaway, 1957) and at 100 years (Godber and Hutchins, 1982), and Westaway (1945) also wrote a book to commemorate the achievements of alumnae in the 1939–45 war. Thus a list of 100 volumes *could* contain multiple books about 30 schools and one book about each of 20 others.

Another problem is that the girls' schools that exist today (which can be traced from the *Local Authorities Year Book* and the *Girls' Public Schools Year Book*) are not a guide to the range of schools that have closed down, become co-educational, or merged with other schools, all of which should be in the sample. If the city of Edinburgh is taken as an example, the last 30 years has brought several changes in the number and status of girls' schools. George Watson's Ladies' College was merged with its 'brother' school to form one mixed institution. Then there was once a real school in Dick Place called St. Trinneans that has a book about it (Lee, 1962), although the school closed in the 1960s. George Watson's Ladies' College and St. Trinneans are not the only girls' schools to have vanished in Edinburgh. Lansdowne House merged with St. George's, leaving separate histories (Hale, 1959; Welsh, 1939), and eventually, one assumes, generating a joint one. The Edinburgh pattern, with schools merging, closing and amalgamating, is typical of many cities. The published histories do not reflect the currently functioning schools in any simple way.

In addition, it is only the larger and/or more famous schools that will generate histories. Very small, very new, or very private schools will not be listed in the published guide books at all, and their histories are most likely to be missed by libraries. There is a need for a regularly updated, complete listing of the histories of girls' schools in order to reduce these complications. In the light of all these difficulties in establishing the total universe of girls' school histories, there is no ideal way to choose a sample for the analysis conducted here. This chapter is based on detailed study of the 20 volumes about the 11 schools listed in Table 4.1. All the books are owned by the author;

they may be said to represent the major dimensions along which girls' schools are distributed.

APPENDIX 2

The importance of respectability as late as the 1930s is best captured from a curiosity – a 'novel' privately printed in 1930, entitled *The Diary of a Public School Girl and Other Documents*. The first, private printing was only 50 copies, but this was followed by a second printing of 450 copies, and later in the year a further 1,000 were published. The book purports to be the diary of a pupil at St. Mona's School for Girls, Sparrington, which is described as being one of the 'Horsham Schools' founded by 'the late Canon Henry Horsham' (p. v). In my copy, a previous owner has written in 'Woodard' over 'Horsham', and 'Queen Ethelburga's School, Harrogate' over 'St. Mona's School, Sparrington'. The book was published in Harrogate, and deals with the damage that could be done to a school if a pupil were involved in a sexual scandal. The publisher states firmly that 'all the names and dates throughout this book are substitutes'. The author of the diary is named – presumably pseudonymously – as Hilary Sherburn of Form Va. The diary covers her life as a boarder at St. Mona's and at home, and, whether fact or fiction (or a mixture), it is an interesting record of everyday school life in the north of England in the 1920s. The central threads of the book, however, are the romance of Hilary and a young man called Rodney (which is very innocent, and brings no disgrace upon the school) and the scandalous conduct of an older girl called Nathalie Goring. In April, on her way home for the holidays, Hilary sees Nathalie 'being kissed by a boy' (p. 34) in a railway carriage. Nathalie claims to be secretly engaged to this male (Eric), and swears Hilary to silence. Subsequently, Hilary discovers that Eric is climbing into the school at night, and in July she comes upon Eric and Nathalie when they are about to elope.

Nathalie says:

'Goodbye. I shan't be coming back to St. Mona's.'
It is awful. I said:
'Can't you wait till we break up?
Think of the disgrace to the school' (p. 58).

The elopement is foiled, and schooldays proceed, with Hilary becoming a house captain. However, at the end of the book, the real reason

97

for Nathalie's scandalous behaviour is explained. Her father tells Rodney the following story:

You have heard of Canon Henry Horsham, who founded St James's School, Litterham, and the organization which gave rise to St. Mona's School? Well, there was once a boy at St. James's, who, on the night of the 5th of November, was confined to bed in the school infirmary ...

Goring claims that Canon Horsham entered his room and committed a nameless crime upon him. So:

Horsham is dead, but his memory is revered and his life's work remains. I have worked much for its destruction.... I sent my own daughter to St. Mona's with the sole object of disgracing it by a scandal which should have rung through England.

Whether the 1,500 purchasers of *The Diary* believed this story is unclear. However, the idea that the elopement of a girl from a boarding school could seriously damage the Woodard Schools in 1930 is obviously meant to explain Nathalie's otherwise incomprehensible behaviour.

Today the innocence of *The Diary* is as far in the past as the Francis Holland Old Girl's blazer described earlier.

NOTES AND ACKNOWLEDGEMENTS

1. The author owns 143 volumes of histories of girls' schools in Great Britain and Eire, plus two Australian ones, one New Zealand study, and two American histories.
2. I am grateful to Mrs Elizabeth Renton for word-processing this chapter more times than I had a right to expect. The students on the MA course on Women and Education at Sussex University discussed this project with some vigour in June 1990, and I am grateful to them for their healthy scepticism.
3. The Freudian challenge to the schools established by pioneering nineteenth-century feminists is discussed in Delamont (1989) and Vicinus (1985).
4. Scotland does have a bibliography (Women in Scotland Bibliography Group, 1988) and the volume edited by Paterson and Fewell (1990), and for Wales there is Evans (1990).

REFERENCES

Anon (1930) *The Park School, Glasgow 1880–1930*. Glasgow and Edinburgh: William Hodge & Co.
Atkinson, P.A. (1978) 'Fitness, Feminism and Schooling', in S. Delamont and L. Duffin (eds.), *The Nineteenth Century Woman*. London: Croom Helm.
Atkinson, P.A. (1987) 'The Feminist Physique: Physical Education and the Medicalization of Women's Education', in J.A.Mangan and R.J. Park (eds.), *From 'Fair Sex' to*

Feminism: *Sport and the Socialization of Women in the Industrial and Post-Industrial Eras*. London: Frank Cass.

Barr, B. (1984) *Histories of Girls' Schools and Related Biographical Material*. Leicester: The School of Education.

Bates, H., and Wells, A.A.M. (1962) *A History of Shrewsbury High School (Girls Public Day School Trust) 1885–1960*. Shrewsbury: Wilding.

Beale, D. (1904) *History of the Cheltenham Ladies' College 1853–1904*. Cheltenham: 'Looker On' Printing Works.

Bell, E.M. (1939) *Francis Holland School*. London: Waterlow & Sons.

Booth, M. (1927) 'The Present-day Education of Girls', *The Nineteenth Century and After*, 102, pp. 259–69.

Booth, M. (1932) *Youth and Sex*. London: Allen & Unwin.

Bowerman, E. (1966) *Stands There a School*. Brighton: Privately printed.

Burnett, J.F. (ed.) (1984) *Girls School Yearbook, 1984*. London: A. & C. Black.

Burstall, S. A., and Douglas, M.A. (1911) *Public Schools for Girls: A Series of Papers on Their History, Aims and Schemes of Study*. Guildford and London: Lutterworth Press.

Burstall, S. (1933) *Retrospect and Prospect*. London: Longman.

Carr, C. (1955) *The Spinning Wheel: City of Cardiff High School for Girls 1895–1955*. Cardiff: Western Mail & Echo.

Clarke, A.K. (1953) *A History of the Cheltenham Ladies' College 1853–1953*. London: Faber & Faber.

Clarke, A. K. (1979) *A History of the Cheltenham Ladies' College 1853–1979*. Great Glenham, Saxmundham: John Catt.

Clarke, M.G. (1973) *A Short Life of Ninety Years*. London: A and M. Huggins.

Croydon, GPDST (1954) *Croydon High School 1874–1954*. Croydon: Privately printed.

Cunningham, P. (1976) *Local History of Education in England and Wales: A Bibliography*. Leeds: Museum of the History of Education, University of Leeds.

Delamont, S. (1989) *Knowledgeable Women: Structuralism and the Reproduction of Elites*. London and New York: Routledge.

Dunning, B. (ed.) (1931) *Graham Street Memories: Francis Holland Church of England School for Girls*. London: Hazell, Watson & Viney.

Duthie, G.I. and Duncan, H.M.E. (1967) *Albyn School Centenary*. Aberdeen: The University Press.

Dyhouse, C. (1987) 'Miss Buss and Miss Beale', in F. Hunt (ed.), *Lessons for Life*. Oxford: Basil Blackwell.

Education Authorities Directory and Annual (1986). Merstham: The School Government Publishing Company.

Evans, W.G. (1990) *Education and Female Emancipation: The Welsh Experience 1847–1914*. Cardiff: University of Wales Press.

Godber, J., and Hutchins, I. (eds) (1982) *A Century of Challenge: Bedford High School 1882–1982*. Bedford: The School.

Haddon, C. (1977) *Great Days and Jolly Days; The Story of Girls' School Songs*. London: Hodder & Stoughton.

Hale, E.M. (1959) *Lansdowne House School, Murryfield, Edinburgh 1879–1950*. Edinburgh: Lansdowne House Old Girls' Guild.

Hicklin, S. (1978) *Polished Corners: Francis Holland School 1878–1978*. Hatfield: Stellar Press.

Kamm, J. (1958) *How Different from Us: A Biography of Miss Buss and Miss Beale*. London: Bodley Head.

Kean, H. (1990) *Deeds not Words*. London: Pluto.

Kenealy, A. (1899) 'Woman as an Athlete', *The Nineteenth Century*, 45, pp. 635–45.

Kenealy, A. (1920) *Feminism and Sex-Extinction*. London: Fisher Unwin.

Kirk, K.E. (1952) *The Story of the Woodard Schools*. Abingdon: Abbey Press.

Lee, C.F. (1962) *The Real St Trinneans, with Tributes to the School by Former Pupils*. Edinburgh: W. Brown.

Leech, B. (1986) *Full Circle*. Risca, Newport, Gwent: Starling Press.

Lightwood, J. (1980) *The Park School 1880–1980*. Glasgow: Robert Mac Lehose.

O'Leary, M. (1936) *Education with a Tradition*. London: The University Press.

Paterson, F.M.S., and Fewell, J. (eds.) (1990) *Girls in Their Prime*. Edinburgh: Scottish Academic Press.

Pyke, R. (1934) *Edgehill College 1884–1934*. London: Epworth Press.

Pyke, R. (1957) *Edgehill College 1884–1957: A Triumph of Faith*. London: Epworth Press.

Randall, G.F. (1969) *Rugby High School Golden Jubilee (1919–1969)*. Rugby: George Over.

Robb, N.A. (1968) *A History of Richmond Lodge School*. Belfast: The School.

Shaw, A.M. (1984) *When You Were There: 1884–1984: Edgehill College*. South Molton, Devon: G.P. Printers.

Sherburn, H. (1930) *The Diary of a Public School Girl and Other Documents*. Harrogate: Waldo Sabine.

Tesch, R. (1990) *Qualitative Research: Analysis Types and Software Tools*. London: Falmer.

Vicinus, M. (1985) *Independent Women*. London: Virago.

Welsh, W.B. (1939) *After the Dawn: A Record of the Pioneer Work in Edinburgh for the Higher Education of Women*. Edinburgh and London: Oliver & Boyd.

Westaway, K.M. (1932) *A History of Bedford High School*. Bedford: Hockliffe.

Westaway, K.M. (1945) *Old Girls in New Times: The Story of Some of the Work Done by the Old Girls of Bedford High School During Nearly Six Years of War 1939–1945*. Bedford: Hockliffe.

Westaway, K.M. (ed.) (1957) *Seventy-five Years: The Story of Bedford High School 1882–1957*. Bedford: Diemer & Reynolds.

Women in Scotland Bibliography Group (1988) *Women in Scotland*. Edinburgh: The Open University in Scotland.

5

Private Education and Political Socialization

DEBRA ROKER

My parents have always been Labour Party people, and I suppose I always thought I would be too. But since getting the scholarship here [the private school], it's all changed. People here believe different things and have very strong views. I'd say I definitely support the Conservatives now, and I really do believe their policies are best for the country, which is odd really because I don't come from that sort of background. I think that's one of the things that the private schools do to people like me. You come to believe that the only sensible party is the Conservative (16-year-old; private school).

This chapter describes research undertaken between 1987 and 1989 in the north of England, aimed at exploring the political attitudes and values of girls educated in private schools, focusing on both the content and process of their political socialization. The framework of the study was social–psychological, aiming to integrate the investigation of structural factors (such as education system and social class) with psychological factors (including the development of political identity) in exploring the political socialization of those in private schools.

A brief history of research on the political socialization of youth is included, to demonstrate how the privately educated have generally been excluded from this area of research. It is shown how previous work undertaken on the privately educated has revealed that their political development is distinctive from those educated in the state sector. The nature of the private-school environment is described as a particularly isolated arena for the development of political orientations, and factors relating to both the school and the home environment are identified as contributing to the political socialization of girls in private schools.

POLITICAL SOCIALIZATION RESEARCH

The 1980s witnessed a rise in work investigating young people and their political attitudes. Much of the research in Britain found these attitudes to be characterized by political distrust, disinterest and alienation (e.g. Cochrane and Billig, 1983; Mardle and Taylor, 1987). However, the basis of such conclusions was studies of similar groups of young people: often male and working class, politically extreme or very alienated. Also, most of this work had a *content* bias, focusing on outcomes in the form of attitudes and opinions. Few researchers have addressed the issue of the *process* of political socialization, investigating how young people deal with and explore political issues.

Researchers exploring the political socialization of youth have largely neglected several important groups. The academically able, for example, have only rarely been the focus. Significantly, the political socialization of young people educated in private schools has been neglected by researchers. In turn, the narrow focus of much private-sector research is typified by its restriction to boys only, leading Fox (1989) to claim that there are 'virtually no details about girls in the private sector' (p. 334). Much work has also focused only on the experiences of the privately educated in the 'top' public schools (Walford, 1986); less is known about the privately educated in not so well-known private schools.

Researchers in the field of private-sector research have focused largely on easily defined and observed aspects of private education. For example, research has explored the motivation of parents of the privately educated (Bridgeman and Fox, 1978; Fox, 1985), the occupational and career outcomes of a private education (Eglin, 1984; Halsey, Heath and Ridge, 1984), and the wide-ranging arguments for and against the existence of the private sector (Griggs, 1985; Cibulka and Boyd, 1989). In comparison, the impact of a private education on the attitudinal and value development of young people has been only briefly explored, a deficiency that this chapter goes some way towards correcting.

In investigating the development of attitudes and values in young people, the research is exploring one aspect of youth socialization, a concept utilized within both sociology and psychology. Socialization is seen as being characterized by certain key features. First, it is a process of adaptation to new roles and experiences in adolescence, comprising the development of attitudes, values and goals. Second, it is part of the overall process of child and adolescent development.

Third, it comprises different component parts: for example, socialization to work, to politics, and to gender, although there is considerable overlap between these areas. Fourth, there are different 'agents' of socialization, these influences including the family, the school, the peer group and the media. Finally, socialization is both an *outcome* (comprising the development of specific attitudes, values and goals), and a *process* (involving particular modes of exploring alternatives and establishing commitments).

Early work on political socialization was conducted mainly by political scientists interested in explaining 'systems persistence': that is, how different political systems persist over time (e.g. Easton, 1965; Greenstein and Polsby, 1975). These studies explored the origins of individual political outlooks, and how such aspects as attitudes to authority and to political leaders emerged: these findings were then related to the characteristics of individual political systems (see Merelman, 1986, for a full discussion). More recent work has moved away from this global perspective, with researchers aiming to explore how different social, economic and educational groups develop their ideas about social and political reality. Much of this work, however, has focused on only one or two political phenomena, such as level of political knowledge (Furnham and Gunter, 1987) or explanations for unemployment (Lowe, Krahn and Tanner, 1988).

A broad definition of 'politics' was adopted in this study, with political behaviour viewed as the development of rules and norms governing human relationships. Thus the study included the investigation of overtly 'political' areas explored in most political socialization research: voting behaviour and attitudes to political parties; interest in politics, use of political media, and level of discussion of politics; trust in politicians and engagement in political activity. The remit of 'political' adopted also led to the investigation of broader issues: attitudes to the overall political system; perceptions of the rule of law and civil disobedience; notions of class; attitudes to taxation, trade unions, (in)equality, and the redistribution of wealth.

The broad remit of the political arena adopted led to the incorporation of economic and social concepts in the study. As such, the author agrees with the view of Furnham (1987) that, ... 'economic and political beliefs are inextricably intertwined ... a study of the structure and determinants of the one, will inevitably involve the other' (Furnham, 1987: 370). Socio-economic socialization includes such things as personal career planning, attitudes to work, work commitment and training, issues of job entitlement and perceptions of the local and national labour market. It also includes views as to the causes of unemployment, success, wealth, and poverty, and view of overall socio-economic organization. Thus the study of such things as preferences for government expenditure and views of the causes of unemployment are economic concepts that are inseparable from the study of politics.

It was proposed earlier that a key characteristic of youth socialization is the role of the socializing 'agents'. The concept of socializing agents suggests that different individuals, groups or factors are involved in youth socialization, each influencing to a different extent and in different ways. In the area of political socialization, various agents have been identified as influencing the political development of young people, including the family, the school, social and peer groups, and the mass media. Much of the research undertaken to date has identified the family (including socio-economic background) as being the major influence on youth political socialization. For example, early work by Hyman (1959) demonstrated the link between the political values of parents and those of their children, while later work identified the ways in which parents influence the political socialization of their children (Dawson, Prewitt and Dawson, 1977). These influences included the degree of parental interest in politics, and their articulation of political views.

However, despite some research that has highlighted its importance, the role of the school and educational experience in the political socialization process has been largely neglected by researchers, and by social psychologists in particular. Thus, although some researchers in the past have suggested different school structures have little or no influence on political socialization (e.g. Hyman, 1959; McQuail, O'Sullivan and Quine, 1968), other research has identified the school experience as a major socializing influence. For example, Dawson et al. (1977) claim that schools can influence political development both in formal ways (such as via the curriculum and teacher style) and also in non-formal ways (via the social composition of the school and school ethos). Similarly, work has suggested that school experience determines the 'magnitude and valence' of early political learning (Palonsky, 1987). A longitudinal study by Himmelweit and Swift (1969), on the relative influence of the home and the school on the development of goals and values, revealed evidence pointing to the 'dominant influence of the school' (p. 157).

This study therefore aimed to explore the effect of educational structure, in both private and state schools, on the development of political values. An analysis of some of the literature to date indicates that differences do exist between these two groups, although the studies were often limited in scope to one or two areas of attitudes and values, rather than to a broad range. Nevertheless, a clear picture does emerge. For example, researchers in Australia demonstrated that young people in private and state schools had very different beliefs about employment and unemployment (Feather, 1983). Work on private- and state-school boys in Britain found that the two groups had quite different views about poverty and its causes; the private-school group were more likely to blame the poor for their situation, with the state-school group naming the government and societal factors (Furnham, 1982).

Differences between private- and state-educated young people have been demonstrated in other areas of political and socio-economic orientations. For example, Hewstone, Jaspars and Lalljee (1982) found that private- and state-educated boys gave different explanations for success and failure at exams: whereas the private-school sample were most likely to talk about ability and effort, the state-educated sample mainly focused on luck. Similarly, researchers have identified the different perceptions of class of girls from private and state schools (Frazer, 1988), and also different perceptions of social inequality between the two groups (Emler and Dickinson, 1985). The latter study found that private-school pupils perceived incomes generally as higher, and were more likely to view inequalities in income as justified.

SOURCES OF EMPIRICAL DATA

In the present study, two groups of girls were sampled, one from a private school and one from a state school. Both schools were in the same area of a large northern city. The state school was large, with an active sixth form and a good academic reputation. The private school, which took pupils from age four to 18, also had a good academic reputation and participated in the Assisted Places Scheme. Pupils, who were all aged 15–18, each initially completed a questionnaire (adapted from a larger, national study of young people; see Bynner, 1987, for details). The final sample size was 72 girls at the private school and 109 at the state school, making a total sample of 181.

The majority of the sample were also individually interviewed to gain in-depth insight into their political values. In order to control for the possible effects of social class and family background, only those at each school with at least one parent in a professional or managerial occupation were selected for interview. The research rationale was therefore to sample two groups of girls matched for socio-economic background, but who had experienced different types of education. Thus interviews were conducted with 67 girls at the private school and 60 at the state school, most interviews lasting one to two hours and conducted in the pupils' homes. The majority of empirical data presented in this chapter are drawn from the interviews, which investigated the broad range of political, social and economic areas described earlier.

Thus a broad range of topics were covered, but the results presented here will focus mainly on the political attitudes and values of the girls in the private school; comparisons with the state-school group will be made where appropriate. Two aspects of the results will be presented. First, some selected findings on the *content* of political socialization will be presented. This information, which is mainly descriptive, includes the following: interest in politics; voting intent and perceptions of the main political parties; view of the government and its policies; view of democracy, politicians, and the workings of the political system; political activity and view of violent overthrow. Most of this information was gained from the individual interviews, with responses content analysed or coded according to category responses.

Second, the results of a more unusual form of analysis will be presented, exploring the *process* of forming a political identity. This method of analysis emerged from a psychological theory of development in adolescence, and investigates whether private- and state-school pupils differ in the way they approach the exploration of political issues, and also in how they make commitments to particular political ideologies. This approach is proposed as a particularly valuable one in the study of political socialization and the privately educated.

THE CONTENT OF POLITICAL VALUES

This section details the content of the political values and attitudes of the private- and state-educated girls interviewed. Recent evidence (e.g. Mardle and Taylor, 1987) has suggested low levels of interest in politics among most groups of young people. However, the private-school girls in the study did not demonstrate this, and many expressed a considerable degree of interest in current political activity and issues. Table 5.1 details the numbers in each category of interest ('very', 'quite', 'not very', or 'not at all'), and also the percentages per school.

This same table shows that over half of the state-school group were 'not very' or 'not at all' interested in politics, whereas the majority of pupils at the private school were 'very' or 'quite' interested in politics. This higher level of interest in politics by those at the private school was reflected in the level of political discussion they reported with parents/family and also with friends. The private-school girls reported higher levels of discussion of politics, with 64 of the 67 interviewed saying they discussed politics with their family once or twice a week or more; only 37 of the 60 at the state school reported this, the remainder

TABLE 5.1

LEVEL OF INTEREST IN POLITICS AMONG
PRIVATE-SCHOOL AND STATE-SCHOOL PUPILS

	Private school (n=67)		State school (n=60)	
Very interested	8 }	73%	8 }	43%
Quite interested	41 }		18 }	
Not very interested	17 }	27%	22 }	57%
Not at all interested	1 }		12 }	
	(= 100%)		(= 100%)	

saying they discussed politics 'hardly ever' or 'never' with their family. Similar results were found for level of political discussion reported with friends.

The private-school pupils also showed a greater degree of trust in politicians and the political system. The questionnaire used in the study included a three-item scale which measured the degree of positive/negative feelings towards politics and the political system (see Banks and Ullah, 1987).

The three items were:

1. Politicians are mainly in politics for their own benefit and not for the benefit of the community.
2. It does not really make much difference which political party is in power.
3. None of the political parties would do anything to benefit me.

A statistical test showed that the state-school girls had much lower scores on this scale, indicating a greater degree of agreement with the items than the private-school sample.

The in-depth interviews with each girl explored attitudes to politics and the political system still further. The state-school girls' more negative views about politicians and the political process were reflected in the following two comments, typical of many:

Umm ... well, I just don't think politicians can really do anything ... and most of them wouldn't do anything that wasn't good for them anyway. Politicians are all the same really (16-year-old; state school).

They're all hopeless really, aren't they? I don't think governments and politics can ever actually change things or improve things (18-year-old; state school).

However, although the private-school girls generally had more positive attitudes towards politics and the workings of the political system, there were clearly different views among this group about the ultimate purpose of politics. The key difference lay in the degree to which politics was seen as a means of change in society, or as a controlling force that promoted political stability and individual freedoms. Both views were frequently expressed, and comments from two private-school girls reflect this distinction:

I think politics is really important. People work together and through debate and argument settle on policies that are best for society. I mean, if you look at the changes between the 1950s and today ... there's the health service and help for the unemployed. I think it's only through politicians working for what they believe that's made all these changes possible (17-year-old; private school).

Well, you see, I think governments should not try and alter everything and impose lots of laws. Politics should aim to give people freedom to live their lives.

[D.R.: In what ways?]

Well ... the political system should just monitor and organize things. For example, by protecting people through the law and by running local government. Outside that, people must be free to do what they want ... make money, set up companies, travel, things like that .... That's why I agree with Mrs T. (17-year-old; private school).

Linked to differences between the private- and state-school girls on perceptions of politics, were differences in voting intent. Table 5.2 details the responses in the sample when asked who they would vote for 'if there was an election'.

Several aspects of Table 5.2 are important. Over all, the private-school girls were overwhelmingly supporters of the Conservative Party, while at the state school there was little support for the Conservatives. However, it is interesting that this low level of support for the Conservatives at the state school was not reflected in high levels of support for any of the other major parties; rather, the majority of the state-school girls (41 of the 60) were either undecided about how they would vote, or would not vote at all. This lack of political commitment in the state-school girls was of note in other areas explored in the study, and will be returned to later in the chapter.

Subsequent questioning showed that two subjects at each of the schools would vote tactically if there was an election, in order to prevent a particular party or person from being elected in their area. Thus the two tactical voters at the private school said they were actually Conservative supporters, and the two tactical voters at the state school were Liberal/SDP supporters. Thus the level of Conservative support among the private-school girls was actually higher than it appears from Table 5.2 (i.e. 52 of the 67 pupils). Further questioning on length of time the girls had supported their chosen party was revealing, with a much longer length of support for preferred parties among the private-school group. Forty-two of the 67 at the private school had supported their chosen party for two years or more; only 12 girls at the state school had supported a party for this length of time. This suggests a much earlier development of political commitments among the private-school girls.

TABLE 5.2

VOTING INTENT AMONG PRIVATE- AND STATE-SCHOOL PUPILS

	Private school (n = 67)	State school (n = 60)
Conservative	50	4
Labour	4	9
Liberal/SDP	5	4
Green	1	2
Would not vote	1	17
Don't know/uncertain	6	24

The majority of the private-school girls were very supportive of the present Conservative government, as was evidenced by the high numbers who said they would vote Conservative in a general election. Many commented on their support not only for specific policies, but on their general belief in a right-wing political and economic ideology. The following comments are representative of many of the comments made by the private-school girls:

> Well, I support the Conservatives because of their view about people and how we should live. Like ... everyone has an opportunity to do well and make something of themselves. You can work your way through education, set up your own business, whatever you want. You're free to live your life as you want (17-year-old; private school).

> Oh, well, I support the Tories because I believe in capitalism and the free market. I believe people should be responsible for their own lives and ... well ultimately do things for themselves. Like Mrs T., I believe in individuals and families (18-year-old; private school).

There was evidence of widespread support at the private school for both the economic and the social policies of the Conservative government. At the private school, 51 of the 67 girls said they 'strongly supported' the government's economic policies, or that they 'supported most aspects'; this compared with only seven of the 60 girls at the state school in these two categories. Similar results were demonstrated for opinions about the government's social policies.

Perceptions of the different policies of the main political parties reflected the different concerns of the private- and state-school girls. Subjects in the interviews were asked what the Labour and the Liberal/SDP Alliance would do if they were in power. Although just under a quarter of the girls at both schools thought these two parties would do 'everything different' if in power, the remainder of pupils at each school had very different thoughts. At the private school, 45 of the girls commented that the Labour Party would close private schools if in power, and many of them added that this effectively prevented them from ever considering giving support to the Labour Party. The state-school girls were more likely to say that the Labour Party and the Alliance would spend more in the public sector if in power, and also that they would get rid of nuclear weapons. Many of the girls, however, commented that they found it difficult to imagine anything other than a Conservative government, as they were too young to have had any experience of any other party in government.

It was suggested earlier that the private- and state-school girls had different views about the nature of politics and the working of the political system. This was further reflected in the girls' anticipated involvement in protest activity, as well as their views about the possibility of violent change ever happening in Britain. Subjects were asked whether or not they would undertake four different political actions if the government passed a law that they thought was 'really wrong'. The four types of political acts, and the number at each school saying they would 'definitely', 'possibly' or 'not' do them, are given in Table 5.3.

TABLE 5.3
POLITICAL ACTIVITY CONSIDERED

		Private school (n = 67)	State school (n = 60)
1.	Write a letter to an MP		
	Definitely	36	22
	Possibly	31	32
	No		3
	Don't know		3
2.	Sign a petition		
	Definitely	34	20
	Possibly	32	32
	No	1	4
	Don't know		4
3.	Take part in a demonstration		
	Definitely	24	14
	Possibly	37	34
	No	6	7
	Don't know		5
4.	Break the law		
	Definitely	1	1
	Possibly	6	36
	No	55	12
	Don't know	5	11

The results of Table 5.3 suggest that most pupils at both schools would be prepared to take part in some sort of peaceful protest, including writing a letter to an MP, signing a petition, or taking part in a demonstration. However, the private-school girls were more likely to reject political action that broke the law. The following comment from one of these girls reflected the thinking of many at the school:

You see, I believe people should act if they think the govern-

111

ment does something wrong ... it's important people are active to get things changed. That's why I said I'd sign a petition or go to a demonstration.... . But no, not break the law, ever. If everyone did that when they disagreed with something, the whole system would break down wouldn't it? (16-year-old; private school.)

The rejection of protest action that broke the law by the majority of the private-school girls was clear, as was their belief that a violent overthrow of the government would never happen in this country. Those saying that this would definitely not happen accounted for 59 of the private-school sample, but only nine of the state-school group; the latter group generally felt that the political situation was not sufficiently stable to say this would never happen. Further, the two groups reacted differently when asked how they would feel if a violent overthrow did happen. The majority of the private-school group (56 of the 67) said they would be 'very against it'; however, the most common response at the state school (38 of the 60) was that they would 'support it in certain circumstances'. The view of most of the private-school girls in the sanctity of the democratic process was reflected in the following exchange:

... it just wouldn't be right ...

[D.R.: Why?]

Well, because we elect the government and whatever they do we have to put up with it. That's democracy ... and the British people would never have any sort of coup or overthrow anyway. But if there was one, I think it would be dreadful (17-year-old; private school).

The results presented above suggest that private- and state-educated girls reveal differences in the content of their political attitudes and values. It is worth noting at this point that these differences cannot be explained in terms of the different socio-economic backgrounds of the two groups, as the results presented are only for those girls at both schools with parents in professional and managerial backgrounds. Further, *both* schools were in an economically advantaged area of the city and known for their high academic standards.

Having established differences in political *content*, however, it was important to then explore whether girls educated in the private sector have different *processes* of developing political orientations.

THE PROCESS OF POLITICAL SOCIALIZATION

During the individual interviews, the author noticed differences between the two groups that were not being picked up using the traditional content approach – that is, concentrating on political *attitudes*. The private-school girls appeared to have not only different political beliefs and values, but seemed to have developed politically in quite different ways to the state-school girls. In order to explore this further, theoretical and analytical frameworks were utilized from the psychological literature on identity development. Primarily informed by the psycho-social development theory of Erikson (1965; 1968), the identity literature explores development across the life-span, with negative and positive psychological outcomes possible at each of eight 'critical periods', of which adolescence is one.

Erikson (and later theorists such as Marcia, 1966; 1980) identified development in adolescence in terms of periods of exploration of alternatives and commitment to particular goals and values. Adolescence was seen as characterized by spirals of exploration and commitment in four main areas or domains: occupation, politics, religion, and gender roles. Erikson viewed the development of a political ideology in particular as a key achievement of the adolescent period. (A further discussion of these concepts and a review of the relevant literature is given in Waterman, 1985, and Kroger, 1989.)

Researchers using an identify focus therefore concentrate not on overt identity 'elements' – for example, individual political attitudes or vocational goals – but on processes of change and development in the four domains. Thus the focus is on which young people have (or have not) explored in an area, and whether (or not) they have achieved a secure identity in the area. This is the central tenet of the process approach, in comparison to the content one detailed earlier. Over all, adolescence is viewed as the development of more mature modes of functioning, seen as the move through exploration towards commitments.

Researchers in the field have identified four possible categories that can be applied to each of the four domains (in this case, politics), and it is this classification that was used in the current study. Two of the categories apply to those with clear political commitments (categories 1 and 4 below), and two apply to those without a political commitment (categories 2 and 3). The categories are distinguished by the way subjects have reached their current status. The four categories (based on Marcia, 1966) are as follows:

113

1. *Identity achievement*: Individuals in this stage have seriously explored options and alternatives and have come to a decision to which they are fully committed.
2. *Identity diffusion*: Individuals in this stage have no commitments, and show no evidence of trying to form any; they may or may not have experienced a period of crisis in the past.
3. *Moratorium*: Individuals in this stage are in 'crisis', exploring among alternatives in an attempt to form commitments.
4. *Foreclosure*: Individuals in this stage have firm commitments, but have *not* experienced a period of crisis; generally, their commitments are taken from their parents.

In the current study, the notion of exploration and commitment, and the four categories above, were utilized to investigate the process of political socialization. To achieve this, key sections from all 127 interviews were transcribed, the sections relating to interest in politics, voting behaviour and reasoning, past support for political parties, and attitudes to the current government and its policies. The author then undertook two analyses for each pupil:

Task 1 Deciding whether or not the subject showed evidence of having, or not having, a political identity. This was defined as evidence of clear, firm and integrated commitments to a particular ideology.

Task 2 Deciding which of the four identity categories (above) the subject was in; that is, how the subject had arrived at their current stage of development.

This method was clearly open to subjective bias, and consequently two other coders repeated the procedure, independently undertaking Tasks 1 and 2 from anonymous scripts. Agreement between all three coders was achieved for 94 per cent of cases for Task 1, and for 90 per cent of cases for Task 2. Remaining cases were allocated on the basis of two out of three rater agreement; there were no cases for which all three coders disagreed. These figures for inter-rater reliability compare very well with other equivalent research (e.g. Kroger, 1986), where such high levels of inter-rater agreement are usually limited to only two raters.

Table 5.4 gives the results for Task 1, which explored whether or not the girls had achieved a political identity. (Numbers and percentages per school are given for each category.) The results of Table 5.4 demonstrate that the majority of the private-school girls (60 of the

67 interviewed) had achieved a political identity. In other words, they showed evidence of having clear, firm and integrated commitments to a particular ideology. Less than a third of the state-educated girls demonstrated such an ideology.

When the results for Task 2 (i.e. the identity categories) are added to these Task 1 results, further differences between the private- and

TABLE 5.4

POLITICAL IDENTITY COMMITMENT IN PRIVATE-SCHOOL
AND STATE-SCHOOL PUPILS

	Private school (n = 67)	State school (n = 60)
Political identity commitment	60 (89.6%)	18 (30.0%)
No identity commitment	7 (10.4%) =100%	42 (70.0%) =100%

state-school girls become evident. Table 5.5 demonstrates that the process of political identity exploration and the making of commitments are different for the two groups of girls. As was shown in Task 1, only a few of the private-school girls were in the moratorium or diffusion statuses – that is, without a political commitment. Of the remainder (i.e. those with a political commitment), the private-school group were equally divided between the achievement status (those with commitments after exploration) and the foreclosure status (those with commitments, but with no evidence of exploration).

The state-school girls, however, revealed a quite different process

TABLE 5.5

POLITICAL IDENTITY CATEGORY IN PRIVATE-SCHOOL
AND STATE-SCHOOL PUPILS

	Private school (n=67)	State school (n=60)
Identity achievement	30 (44.8%)	16 (26.7%)
Identity diffusion	2 (3.0%)	28 (46.7%)
Moratorium	5 (7.5%)	14 (23.3%)
Foreclosure	30 (44.8%)	2 (3.3%)

115

of political identity formation. Of the 18 girls who did reveal an identity commitment, the majority were in the achievement status; only two girls were in the foreclosure status, a much smaller number than at the private schol. Further, of those who had not achieved a political identity commitment (42 of the 60), only one-third of these (14 girls) were currently exploring among alternatives (i.e. in the moratorium status); two-thirds of those without a commitment (28 girls) were in the diffusion status. These girls (nearly half of the state-school sample) had no political identity and showed no evidence of trying to form one.

These results suggest that the private- and state-school girls in the study may have developed politically in quiet different ways. Over all, the majority of the state-school girls had not developed a political identity, and many were also not interested in doing so. At the private school, the majority of girls did have a political identity; however, of these, 30 of the girls had a political commitment without experiencing a period of exploration; that is, they were in the foreclosure status. This is a particularly interesting finding. The literature suggests that those in the foreclosure status are functioning at a less mature level, as their political commitments have generally been taken without question from their parents or significant others. More mature modes of functioning are the achievement and moratorium categories, where individuals have thought issues through for themselves and settled on commitments, or are currently questioning early commitments. The finding of differences in the process of political development between those at private and state schools have not been previously described in the identity literature.

COLLECTIVE REPRESENTATIONS?

Differences in the content of political values in the two groups were extensive. The content of political orientations of the majority of the private-school girls can be summarized as follows: high levels of interest in politics and engagement in political discussion; trust in politicians and the workings of the democratic system; support for the Conservative Party and its policies; support for political activity, but only forms that are within the law; a belief that violent overthrow is very unlikely, and that they would be against if it it did happen.

The privately educated group were distinctive in all areas of political and socio-economic development (see Roker, 1991, for details). The sample demonstrated agreement with policies associated with a right-wing political and economic philosophy, supporting an extensive programme of privatization and viewing trades unions as having too much power. There was support for strict social-security regulation and the encouragement of an obligation, rather than an entitlement, culture among the poor and unemployed. Capitalism as an economic system was viewed positively, socialism negatively; inequality was seen as natural and inevitable under the free-market form of social organization.

Over all, the private-school girls revealed a philosophy of individualism and freedom from state control: their views on most current and topical issues reflected this. These beliefs and values were also revealed in the socio-economic orientations of the group (see Roker, 1989, 1990, 1991, for more details). The majority of the girls at the private school showed very similar political values and beliefs. This was not the case for the state-school girls, who revealed very varied and disparate political orientations. The small number of girls at the private school whose views were markedly at odds with those of the majority merit further attention.

Essentially, the majority of girls at the private school showed evidence of a collective representation of political reality. One theoretical approach viewed as a possible explanation for this is social representations theory, a social-psychological theory proposed by Moscovici (1984). The theory has been used by psychologists to explore how members of different social groups create and represent knowledge about social reality, and social representations have been increasingly used in the 1980s to help explain a range of social and behavioural phenomena. For example, Emler and Dickinson (1985) utilized social representations theory to explain their finding that middle-and working-class children offered quite different explanations of economic inequalities.

Although usually applied to explain the different values and behaviour of social-class groups, it is possible that young people educated in different types of educational establishment will form different representations of political and socio-economic reality. The social isolation of many private schools may mean that those attending the schools will be characterized by a group-based and group-reinforced framework that guides the development of thoughts, behaviours and aspirations. (For other work exploring the notion of social representations and educational groups, see Hewstone et al., 1982; Feather, 1983; Emler et al., 1987). The possible effects of the social isolation of private education on political development is returned to later in the chapter, when further explanations for the differences between the two groups are proposed.

COLLECTIVE REPRESENTATIONS: ISOLATING THE SCHOOL EFFECT

In proposing that private- and state-educated young girls reveal different content and processes of political socialization, the question of separating the specific effect of the school from the home and family is clearly important. Some investigation was therefore made of the political values and voting intent of the parents of the sample in the interviews. A small number of open-ended interviews were also held with parents of pupils at the private school, and these confirmed a high degree of accuracy in pupils reporting of parents' political values.

At both schools, parents revealed a wide variety of political views and commitments. Just over half of the private-school parents were found to support the Conservatives, with another third supporting the Liberal/SDP Alliance. The remainder were either Labour supporters, did not vote, or the pupils were unable to say. At the state school there was support for all three major parties, with a third of parents who either would not vote or did not express any opinions. The higher number of Conservative-supporting parents of private-school pupils may, therefore, be claimed as explaining the high levels of support for the Conservatives and their policies at the private school. However, the effect of the private school on the political values of the 21 girls on the Assisted Places Scheme suggests that the impact of private education may be particularly potent. The APS pays all or part of fees for pupils according to parental income. These girls (just less than a third of the private sample) showed quite different political values to

TABLE 5.6
VOTING INTENT OF ASSISTED PLACE SCHEME (APS)
PUPILS AND THEIR PARENTS

	Conservative	Labour	Lib./SDP	Would not vote	Don't know
Mother	2	4	10	3	2
Father	2	4	11	1	3
APS pupils (n = 21)	18	2	1		

their parents. Table 5.6 details the voting intent of the parents of those on the APS, and also their own voting plans.

It is evident from Table 5.6 that the parents of APS pupils supported mainly the Liberal/SDP Alliance, with only a minority planning to vote Conservative. (Note also that none of these were reported as being tactical votes.) However, of the pupils on the APS, the overwhelming majority said they would vote Conservative. Further investigation of the political values of these pupils found that not only would they vote Conservative, but that they shared the right-wing political views detailed earlier. The finding that pupils on the APS revealed the dominant political ideology of the school, generally quite different to their home background, is important. It suggests that in certain circumstances the school experience may override the influence of the home, and become the primary socializing experience.

In investigating the mechanisms by which the school may override the influence of the home, the theoretical model of Himmelweit and Swift (1969) is particularly useful, as it aimed to explore how different school structures affect the development of values and goals. Their longitudinal study revealed that the type of school a young person attended (in this case grammar and secondary schools) predicted later occupational status and value orientation more accurately than family background and social class, or intelligence. They proposed that schools are different types of 'systems', systems that (using certain criteria) can be described as 'strong' or 'weak'. A strong school system (in their study, the grammar school) is able to override the values and orientations children bring to school, and promote acceptance of the school's values. Thus background factors are important where school structure is weak, and less so where school structure is strong.

Himmelweit and Swift proposed a range of characteristics that distinguish between a strong and a weak school system. The school's influence can therefore be determined on the basis of the following factors:

1. The extent to which the school's values are consistent and coherent.
2. The extent to which the school's values and ideology conflict with, or are reinforced by, other people that the pupil is exposed to.
3. The kind of rewards the school can offer the pupil in return for acceptance of its values.
4. The kind of sanctions the school can use for non-acceptance of its objectives.
5. The kind of status the child has within the school.

In applying these criteria to private schools, the first three factors (i.e.

value consistency, reinforcement and rewards) can be seen as particularly important. Private schools often have clear goals and values, made explicit to staff, pupils and the parents who choose to pay specifically for their child to experience these values; consequently, there is also often a considerable degree of support from the home for these agreed goals, and thus a reinforcement of them.

Himmelweit and Swift identified two main aspects in their study that characterized the grammar school as a strong school system. First, the strong school system selects its pupils, whereas a weak school system accepts pupils not selected by others. Second, the strong system has explicit goals that are designed specifically to shape its pupils' futures in key ways. Clearly, both these aspects apply to the private school in the current study. Thus according to Himmelweit and Swift's model, the private school may be a 'strong' school system, confirming and reinforcing the values and orientations of those who arrive at the school already 'appropriately' socialized, and overriding the early socialization experiences of those with vague and uncommitted views, or with values contrary to those of the school.

Thus Himmelweit and Swift's model may help explain the differences found in the current study in the content of political socialization between those girls educated in private and state schools. The private school – a strong school system – promotes and perpetuates a right-wing political philosophy, associated with academic excellence and personal success. It is able in many cases to override other influences, demonstrated by the values of those pupils on the APS. The model may also help to explain the differences in the process of political socialization found. The majority of the private-school girls were found to have achieved a political identity, though for many this was achieved not after a period of exploration, but by adopting the values of a significant other. Usually the significant other is said to be the parent(s), but it is possible that it could also be the school's dominant ideology. Perhaps the notion of the strong school system can be applied not only to the content of political goals and values, but also to how issues are explored and whether commitments are achieved.

EXPLAINING THE DIFFERENCES: THE PRIVATE SCHOOL AS A PARTICULAR TYPE OF SYSTEM

Four main characteristics, primarily relating to the nature of private education, are considered central to explaining the differences found in the current study. Essentially, the characteristics are mechanisms by which the private school may affect the content and processes of political development:

1. The *limited social backgrounds* and experiences of most young people in private schools may help explain the results. Few of the privately educated girls had any immediate experiences of such things as unemployment, poverty, or less-able young people; this was reflected, for example, in inaccurate estimates of the income of the unemployed or those on the YTS. Most of the girls had parents in professional occupations, and some admitted they found it difficult to comment on certain things (such as the experiences of the unemployed) because of their limited experience. The social and political isolation of many private schools may well perpetuate a collective and narrow representation of socio-economic and political reality.

The pupils' friendship groups reflected this social isolation. Questioned in the interview about how they spent their time out of school, the majority of the girls socialized with other pupils from the same school. Further, the small numbers of girls at the school who did not reveal the dominant political ideology were often found to associate outside of school hours with a quite different circle of friends. In two cases, these friends were from campaigning groups (one environmental, one a political party), and for three others these were religious groups. All five girls located the origin of their political beliefs in these reference groups.

2. Associated with social background is the *ideological similarity* of pupils at the private school, which may help explain the results found in the current study. The private-school girls revealed a singular political orientation shared by the majority of its pupils (a shared social representation). In this environment there is little incentive for pupils to re-evaluate their views, and few opportunities to experience either criticism or competing viewpoints. Thus pupils arriving at the school with right-wing political ideologies have them confirmed, and those uncommitted find only one 'choice' of political orientation available at the school. The ideological similarity of pupils at the private school may explain the difference found between the two groups in terms of identity commitment and identity status (described earlier). The existence of higher numbers of girls at the private school with a political-identity commitment can be interpreted in terms of the lack of political 'options' presented. (See also characteristic 4 below.) At the state school, the girls experienced a much wider range of socio-

economic and political values, and consequently a wider range of political orientations were evident.

3. The *academic emphasis* of the private school may also be an important factor in explaining the results. The clear and stated aims of the private school were to achieve excellent academic results, obtain university places for its pupils, and subsequently secure entry to the professions. Pupils are encouraged to have very high academic aims, and there is an efficient and well-organized careers system to promote this. This has two implications for the development of political values. First, there may be an element of anticipatory socialization in relation to expected career path and political standpoint. Pupils planning professional and managerial careers may begin to adopt the political orientations they associate with these careers; this process was very clearly articulated by one girl:

> ... well, it's difficult. I'm not really totally happy with the Conservatives. I disagree with nuclear weapons ... and I do think they could do more for the less well off. But I want to join the police more than anything else, and it's just logical that you support the Conservatives if you're in the police. So yes, I'd say I do support the Conservatives, mainly because I know I will in a couple of years' time (17-year-old; private school).

The second implication for political development of the academic emphasis of the school lies in identity theory. Theorists in this area have identified a pattern in adolescence, where young people explore mainly in just one of the identity domains (such as occupation or politics), and then move on to another area. The academic emphasis of the private school meant that over 90 per cent of the girls had achieved an *occupational* identity; as a result, the girls were free to move on to explore in another area, such as politics. The numbers of privately educated girls who had achieved a political identity at the time of the research indicates this might in fact be happening.

4. Finally, the *organizational culture and educational ethos* of the private school may explain the differences found. The school's stated aim was to encourage the early development of clear personal and vocational goals, and in particular the ability to coherently express a viewpoint; this latter aspect was regarded as a skill important for both academic work, success at interviews, and in future careers. Thus the organizational 'culture' of the school was what the careers teacher described as a focus on individuals and their abilities. In particular,

the small number of pupils in each class (often only four or five pupils) allows a focus on individual articulation of views and opinions. This may explain the clear and integrated political identities of the private-school girls, and also the early development of these identities.

CONCLUSIONS

This chapter has gone some way to answering the question posed at the beginning: What is the influence of private education on the political socialization of young people? The study reported here demonstrated that there were clear differences in the content of political attitudes and values between the two groups, with a right-wing ideology shared by the majority at the private school. The state school, conversely, showed a wide range of political ideologies, and a majority of girls with no political commitment. These aspects were further reflected in differences in the process of political development, with the two groups varying both in terms of whether they had a political commitment, and also in their mode of past and current exploration of political issues. Thus both the content and process of political socialization was found to be different for private-and state-school girls, with the suggestion made that the private school is a 'strong' school system and a major influence on development.

This finding clearly has implications at both a theoretical and a practical/policy level, and these will be briefly outlined. First, the findings have implications at a theoretical and methodological level relating to research into private schooling and political development. The results confirm the need to adopt a broad definition of politics in exploring political development, rather than taking one or two aspects of political phenomena (such as attitudes to trade unions). As a result, the process approach revealed differences in the way in which private-school girls explore political issues, as well as finding differences in a wide range of political attitudes and values.

Further, the findings of the study demonstrate the need to explore the effects of different educational experiences on political development. Much previous political socialization research offered general rules about the effects of education on attitudinal and value development; these rules were then applied to all types of educational experience. The findings suggest that different educational structures may in fact be more or less important in influencing political development. The experience of private education in particular has been shown to be a powerful socializing agent. Two important concepts explaining this are the development and perpetuation of political knowledge (conceptualized in terms of social representations), and the notion of the strong/weak school system. Further research exploring educational influence using these two theoretical frameworks would be useful.

The practical and policy implications of the study are considerable, and centre on the role of private schools in Britain. Very little research has been conducted on the attitudinal and behavioural outcomes of private schooling; rather, work has focused on generalized outcomes such as educational attainment or employment status. The current research therefore suggests that the experience of private education is, in fact, a major socializing influence on attitudes and values.

The desirability of this situation is a question for educational policy-makers as well as for society as a whole. Private schools have long been associated with both a right-wing political ideology and support for the Conservative Party. However, although rarely articulated, this ideology was mainly associated with large public schools or the later political commitments of adulthood. The current findings demonstrate that private schools may actually inculcate a right-wing ideology – for many, very early on in life. For the politics of the APS, this is particularly important: taking more able pupils out of state schools and offering them a 'wider range of educational experience' (DES, 1985) may actually be applicable in academic terms but not in the political arena. Private schooling may actually restrict the social contact of young people and the political options presented to them. Attending a private school on the APS may lead to large groups of young people supporting the Conservative Party who, if they had remained in state schools, may not have done so. Whether or not this was the intention of Conservative policy-makers when they introduced the APS is a point for debate.

In drawing conclusions from the results of the current study, it is important to stress that political orientations are not static, and considerable change is possible over time. New experiences (such as in higher education and in the work-place) may lead the sample to re-evaluate and alter the political stance reported here. In response to this, a two-year follow-up study of the private-school group is currently under way, aiming to assess the degree of change in political views; two years on, the girls are currently aged 17–18 and 19–20, and many have now left the school. Past work, however (see, for example, Dawson et al., 1977), suggests that while changes in specific political attitudes may occur in adulthood, it is during childhood and adolescence that broad, general, and enduring orientations towards politics and political issues are developed. Early indications from the follow-up study suggest that this proposal may be confirmed with the private-school girls.

The political socialization of girls in private schools has only been briefly explored by researchers to date. Yet this information is important, as many of the girls will end up in professional careers and positions of power in the legal, business and policy-making fields. Knowledge about how these girls think about political issues is therefore vital, and researchers need to address these questions further. This chapter has indicated the areas this new research may want to address.

ACKNOWLEDGEMENTS

The research reported in this chapter was supported by a doctoral studentship from the Medical Research Council. The author gratefully acknowledges the comments of Dr Michael Banks on an early draft of this chapter.

REFERENCES

Banks, M., and Ullah, P. (1987) 'Political Attitudes and Voting Among Unemployed and Employed Youth', *Journal of Adolescence*, 10: 201–16.

Bridgeman, T., and Fox, I. (1978) 'Why People Choose Private Schools', *New Society*, 29 June: 702–5.

Bynner, J. (1987) 'Coping with Transition: ESRC's 16–19 Initiative', *Youth and Policy*, 22: 25–8.

Cibulka, J.G., and Boyd, W.L. (eds.) (1989) *Private Schools and Public Policy: An International Persective*. Lewes: Falmer.

Cochrane, R., and Billig, M. (1983) 'Youth and Politics', *Youth and Policy*, 2(1): 31–4.

Dawson, R.E., Prewitt, K., and Dawson, K.S. (1977) *Political Socialization*. Toronto: Little, Brown & Co.

DES (Department of Education and Science) (1985) *Assisted Places at Independent Schools: A Brief Guide for Parents*. London: DES.

Easton, D. (1965) *A Framework for Political Analysis*. New Jersey: Prentice-Hall.

Eglin, G. (1984) 'Public Schools and the Choice at 18+', in G.Walford (ed.), *British Public Schools: Policy and Practice*. London: Falmer.

Emler, N., and Dickinson, J. (1985) 'Children's Representations of Economic Inequalities: The Effects of Social Class', *British Journal of Developmental Psychology*, 3: 191–8.

Emler, N., Ohana, J., and Moscovici, S. (1987) 'Children's Beliefs about Institutional Roles: A Cross-national Study of Representations of the Teacher's Role', *British Journal of Educational Psychology*, 57: 26–37.

Erikson, E.H. (1965) *Childhood and Society*. New York: Norton.

Erikson, E.H. (1968) *Identity: Youth and Crisis*. London: Faber & Faber.

Feather, N.T. (1983) 'Causal Attributions and Beliefs about Work and Unemployment among Adolescents in State and Independent Secondary Schools', *Australian Journal of Psychology*, 35: 211–32.

Fox, I. (1985) *Public Schools and Private Issues*. London: Macmillan.

Fox, I. (1989) 'Elitism and British Public Schools', in J.G. Cibulka and W.L.Boyd (eds), *Private Schools and Public Policy: An International Perspective*. Lewes: Falmer.

Frazer, E. (1988) 'Teenage Girls Talking about Class', *Sociology*, 22, (3): 343–58.

Furnham, A. (1982) 'The Perception of Poverty among Adolescents', *Journal of Adolescence*, 5: 135–47.

Furnham, A. (1987) 'The Determinants and Structure of Adolescents' Beliefs about the Economy', *Journal of Adolescence*, 10: 353–71.

Furnham, A., and Gunter, B. (1987) 'Young People's Political Knowledge', *Educational Studies*, 13, (1): 91–104.

Greenstein, F.I., and Polsby, N.W. (eds) (1975) *Handbook of Political Science (Vol.2): Micropolitical Theory*. Reading, MA: Addison–Wesley.

Griggs, C. (1985) *Private Education in Britain*. Lewes: Falmer.

Halsey, A.H., Health, A.F., and Ridge, J.M. (1984) 'The Political Arithmetic of Public Schools', in G. Walford (ed.), *British Public Schools: Policy and Practice*. London: Falmer.

Hewstone, M., Jaspars, J., and Lalljee, M. (1982) 'Social Representations, Social Attribution and Social Identity: The Intergroup Images of "Public" and "Comprehensive" Schoolboys', *European Journal of Social Psychology*, 12: 241–69.

Himmelweit, H., and Swift, B. (1969) 'A Model for the Understanding of the School as a Socializing Agent', in P.Mussen, J.Langar and M.Covington, *Trends and Issues in Development Psychology*. New York: Holt, Rinehart & Winston.

Hyman, H. (1959) *Political Socialization*. Glencoe, IL: Free Press.

Kroger, J. (1986) 'The Relative Importance of Identity Status Interview Components: Replication and Extension', *Journal of Adolescence*, 9: 337–54.

Kroger, J. (1989) *Identity in Adolescence: The Balance Between Self and Other*. London: Routledge.

Lowe, G.S., Krahn, H., and Tanner, J. (1988) 'Young People's Explanations of Unemployment', *Youth and Policy*, 19, 3: 227–49.

Marcia, J. (1966) 'Development and Validation of Ego Identity Status', *Journal of Personality and Social Psychology*, 3: 551–8.

Marcia, J. (1980) 'Identity in Adolescence', in J. Adelson (ed.), *Handbook of Adolescent Psychology*. New York: Wiley.

Mardle, G., and Taylor, M. (1987) 'Political Knowledge and Political Ignorance: A Re-examination', *Political Quarterly*, 58: 208–16.

McQuail, D., O'Sullivan, L., and Quine, W.G. (1968) 'Elite Education and Political Values', *Political Studies*, Vol.XVI: 257–66.

Merelman, R. (1986) 'Revitalizing Political Socialization', in M.G. Hermann (ed.), *Political Psychology*. London: Jossey–Bass.

Moscovici, S. (1984) 'The Phenomenon of Social Representations', in R.M. Farr and S. Moscovici (eds), *Social Representations*. Cambridge: Cambridge University Press.

Palonsky, S.B. (1987) 'Political Socialization in Elementary Schools', *The Elementary School Journal*, 87, 5: 493–505.

Roker, D. (1989) 'The Socialisation of Elites: Economics Values in the Privately Educated', paper presented at the 4th West European Congress on the Psychology of Work and Organisation, 10–12 April, Cambridge, UK.

Roker, D. (1990) 'The Economic Socialisation of British Youth: The Impact of Different School Types', paper presented at the 22nd International Congress of Applied Psychology, 22–27 July, Kyoto, Japan.

Roker, D. (1991) 'The Political Socialization of Youth: A Comparison of Private and State Educated Girls', unpublished PhD thesis, University of Sheffield.

Walford, G. (1986) *Life in Public Schools*. London: Methuen.

Waterman, A. (ed.) (1985) *Identity in Adolescence: Processes and Contents*. London: Jossey–Bass.

6

Talk about Class in a Girls' Public School

ELIZABETH FRAZER

E.F.:	Has this got something to do with class?
Kate:	Oh, of *course*.
Amy:	*Everything's* got something to do with class.

The above fragment of discussion and the one that follows are between a group of girls from an Oxfordshire single-sex public school and myself. They are lower-sixth-formers, 16 years old. Their parents' occupations are: a retired military officer; a landowner/farmer; two farmers; two company managing directors. They all describe their mothers as 'housewives', except one who is a 'part-time secretary and company director'. They for the most part live in country houses. They are all white.

Extract 1

E.F.:	What about in school? ( )¹ Can you work out, can you imagine the possibility of someone coming to the school who really didn't fit in, was disapproved of—
Amy:	All they'd have to do is put on a pair of white socks in this school.
Arabella:	Or have a name – Sharon.
Kate:	Or have lovely hair, you know [*draws picture in air with her hand*].
E.F.:	Why, what's Sharon, a working-class name?
Arabella:	Oh, it's just that some people —
Kate:	It's a name that a lot of people look down on.
Sara:	Yes, but I don't agree with that, I think that it's just

127

	people's individual opinions here. I think half this form wouldn't take a second's notice, it's just the half with all their stupid prejudices that —
Amy:	And what if she was black?
Kate:	It's more than half who take notice ( ) No, I don't think that would make any difference.
Amy:	Not if she talked with an upper-class accent.
Annabel:	Yes, but what about all those Chinese girls, they had one in the year before last, they had one in the year before that, did they fit in? Did they fit in? Really fit in?
Amy:	No way near it.

[PSB, 5 4][2]

The discussion from which the extracts come was one of a series, in turn part of a wider project with teenage girls, studying their experience of femininity. Among the participants were groups from an Oxfordshire single-sex comprehensive school: their parents included a butcher; secretaries; nurses; a midwife; police officers; and builders. In what follows I shall use extracts from their discussions for comparison.

In the session from which Extract 1 is taken, I had begun by posing a question designed to elicit the girls' normative notions and standards of femininity: How ought you to behave at parties? (Here I was following the method of Marsh, Rosser and Harré, 1978.) Several rules and norms were identified in the discussion: you shouldn't be 'loud-mouthed' or boisterous, you shouldn't flirt (well, at least, not 'obviously'), you shouldn't 'try too hard to impress'. The discussion proceeded at two levels. In Extract 1, we can clearly identify 'the norms': working-class and/or black (indeed any 'non-European') girls would not easily fit into this school; that is very clear. But girls also argue about *whose* rules these are, and who judges what counts as an infraction – who says Sharon is a name to look down on? What counts as a correct upper-class accent? The *status* of 'the norms', and how and by whom they are and should be enforced, is a matter for dispute.

I am drawing a threefold distinction here. As competent participants in any form of social life, people must be able to orientate to the appropriate 'rules and procedures'. ('Orientation', of course, can encompass conforming, criticizing, flouting, breaking, ignoring and so on.) *Practical social competence* involves the ability to recognize appropriate and inappropriate, or breaching, behaviour, in others and in oneself. *Articulated social competence* involves the ability to spell out the rules and procedures – to say in what respects a breach is a breach. The rules and procedures of forms of social life, like parties, are difficult or impossible to specify exactly, but, having recognized the 'over-flirtatious girl', competent actors can supply a locution for the rule she is breaching – for example, 'girls should behave decorously'. But this is distinct from *theoretical social competence*, which is marked by subjecting the existence, validity and specification of a rule or state of affairs itself to enquiry. In analysis of the transcripts it is possible to distinguish between the *theorized discourse* that corresponds to theoretical social competence, and the *untheorized discourse* that corresponds to the girls' practical and articulated competence. The following analysis focuses on the various points at which they produce theorized as opposed to untheorized discourse; and also compares the *kinds* of 'theory' produced by the respective groups.

The main subject of the research, and therefore for the groups, was 'femininity'. It is striking that putting questions about *gender* to the public-school girls elicited the major part of their contribution discussion about *class* and *race*, as in Extract 1. Class is marked by clothes, hairstyles and accent – although, as we shall see later, there is much more than this at stake. Racial difference precludes shared class identity and position for these girls; their identity is racially exclusive. In thinking and talking about femininity, that is, they think and talk about class and race; concomitantly, their experience of and talk about class and race is inextricably bound up with a particular model of femininity. For the public-school girls, but not for the comprehensive girls, *everything*, as Kate and Amy tell me, has something to do with class.

II

FEMININITY AND FEMINISM

Extract 2

Suzanne: They expect you to be, in the end they expect you to be dependent on a man, or be in a relationship where the man is dominant.

Heather:　And men hate it when they're not.
Linnie:　I know.

[CS6, 2 6 – 17 years, comprehensive]

Extract 3

Annabel:　Why is it that nobody takes it seriously if a boy goes
　　　　　　to bed with a girl and yet —
Sara:　　　Yes, the double standard.
Annabel:　I mean really I mean —
Sara:　　　Boys lose their virginity as young as they can, you
　　　　　　know, 'hey I'm cool', but a girl's a slut.

[PSB, 3 7–16 years, public school]

Extract 4

Gill:　　Yeah, but you get treated nicely as well, because if
　　　　　they think you're weaker than them they think —
Sian:　　Yeah, but who ( ) do you *want* to be?
Jane:　　No, I don't wanna be.
Sian:　　I don't wanna be treated any way just 'cos I'm a
　　　　　girl.
Jane:　　I'm as equal as any boy in my year.
Donna:　Yeah, that's right.

[CST, 2 4–14 years, comprehensive]

All the groups, when invited to discuss what they like and dislike about being girls, produce feminist discourse – that is, they focus on the sexual double standard and the injustice of differential treatment of boys and girls. Boys' and men's own treatment of girls and women in interpersonal contexts – calling them slags (Extract 3), hating it if they're not dominant in a relationship (Extract 2) – are discussed; and so are what we might call the ideological context for these actions: a world in which the identical action performed by a girl and by a boy can have a completely different meaning and value (Extract 3), and in which women face oppressive normative expectations (Extract 2). The routine enacting of male dominance, and the role of meanings of masculinity and femininity in perpetuating gender inequality, the social phenomena identified and discussed by the girls here, are central to feminist analysis and theorizing.

However, the following two extracts show that the public-school girls' and the comprehensive-school girls' relationship to feminism is markedly different. The girls talking in Extracts 5 and 6 are from the upper-sixth form in the respective schools – 17 years old and about to take A-levels.

Extract 5

E.F.:	How do you feel about being feminine, or rather, being girls, not the same thing as femininity —
Suzanne:	Oh, I hate the image that girls are labelled with, that they're expected to fit to, I hate that.
Heather:	I hate the way girls are exploited in the papers and all this, you know, when you think of a prostitute you think of a girl ...
Suzanne:	Yeah, and I hate the fact that we don't have as much freedom as we should have, and the fact that you can't walk down the street after dark without some creep jumping on you.
Sarah:	And if you do walk down the street after dark, and you get —
Heather:	And why did you do it?
Sarah:	You're asking for it.
Linda:	Yeah, that's weird.
Sarah:	Or you get the point of view of the hard business-woman, real bitch kind of thing.
Suzanne:	There's nothing in between.
Linda:	You can't be both, can you?
Sarah:	You can't be caring and be a tough nut.
Linnie:	And the way women are supposed to run the home and look after the children
Sarah:	You've either got to be submissive to the husband, or a hard woman, but I think you —
Linnie:	But I think if you choose a career over marriage I think you've got to be tough, though.
Linda:	Mm, you do.
Heather:	That's the thing, see, if you choose a career you have to be tough, if men choose a career they just sail on.
Linda:	Yeah, they can be married.

131

Heather: If a woman chooses a career then she either chooses a career not a family, or she's got to be really tough to make it last.

Sarah: As well as that, if you're a woman you've got to be twice as good 'cos, do you know what I mean, you get the impression that employers aren't willing to take you, or 'what if you leave in five years' time?' you know, 'if you get pregnant', so you've got to make it doubly sure and say, 'well, I'm not —'

Linda: You've got to force yourself.

Suzanne: Twice as well as men have.

Sarah: As well as that, you're twice as wary.

Linnie: Twice the risk, they still think you're a risk.

Suzanne: There's a lot of sexual discrimination in jobs.

[CS6, 2 2–17 years comprehensive]

Extract 6

Caroline: It is true that for a boy to lose his virginity is encouraged and is good, whereas for a girl it's bad.

Fiona: A girl would be called a slut if she behaved in the way boys are encouraged to behave, it really isn't fair.

Clare: Careful, though, this is getting a bit feminist.

Fiona: Well, yes, it is, but —

Jemima: What worries me is that we're encouraged to get married and not have careers and stay at home and look after the children and everything and then what happens when you are divorced? Men can always find a younger woman to look after them and the woman is just left there.

Cressida: But we're talking as though marriage and divorce always go together, that marriage always ends in divorce.

Jemima: But how many is it? One marriage in three?

Candida: In here [*i.e. among the parents of girls in this school* – *E.F.*] it's two out of eight.

Jemima: It's a lot.

E.F.:   And the new Matrimonial Bill means there's a once and for all settlement at the time of divorce and the woman gets nothing after that except support for the children while they're minors.

Jemima: And what do the feminists think about that?

E.F.: Well, it's one thing to say in principle women should be independent, and should have jobs, but in a climate where women aren't encouraged to have jobs, where you suffer in your career if you do have breaks to look after children, where there isn't well-paid part-time work, and in a shrinking job market, then it's bad news for a woman whose standard of living suffers drastically if she's been dependent on the marriage.

[PSA, 3 5–17 years, public school]

At the following meeting with this public-school group, I asked them more about feminism, specifically why Clare had said 'Careful though, this is getting a bit feminist'. (I gave them copies of the previous week's transcript so they knew exactly how the discussion had gone.) Here is an extract from the talk that followed:

Extract 7

Clare: But they're so annoying, saying men are terrible.

Candida: Sometimes they really are annoying.

Clare: Yeah, they are, sometimes stupidly so, saying you know like, oh women could work down the mines, you know they go so far.

Candida: What woman wants to work down the mine?

Cressida: But that's not every feminist.

Jemima: The thing that annoys me is that people who aren't feminist, women who aren't feminist – I was watching tele, we were watching a television programme about feminists – and they were just saying 'oh stupid feminists, they don't know what they're going on about', but actually these feminist women who were talking did have quite good points, and I do feel that when people think about feminists they think about lesbians and CND, but they don't actually think about other feminism.

Clare: I think a lot of it's true, but I think there are a lot of cases where some of them do just go on and on about it.

E.F.: Is this stuff you read or programmes on TV? I mean, where does this come from, this acquaintance with feminists who go on and on?

Candida: I think books and television, well, not soap operas, but films and things.

Harriet: It comes from the news when you watch CND being really masculine, quite repugnant in fact.

[PSA, 4 4]

The first and most obvious point to note is that discussion about gender relations and girlhood for the public-school girls is problematic, because talking about these things is entwined with feminism, and feminism is constructed, by most of them, as an object of disapprobation, disdain, and even disgust. The power of these affective attitudes put Jemima (and also Fiona, although this is not clear in this extract) in a very difficult position as they try to negotiate an alternative stance. Notably too, they construct 'feminists' as a unified group of which they are not members; and identify me as belonging to that group. The comprehensive-school girls do not construct feminism in this way – analysis of the transcripts shows that they used feminist discourse constantly, but never constructed feminism itself as a problematic object for discussion, and never asked me direct questions – like Jemima's about what feminists think.

A second contrast is in the kind of feminist discourse employed. The public-school girls, like all the others, discuss concrete problems of femininity: the sexual double standard, the situation of divorced women, tensions between femininity and paid work. But the comprehensive-school girls also discuss how and why these problems are constituted and perpetuated. In Extract 7 they consider representation, media images, sexual discrimination in the job market, meanings of femininity, male violence against women: in short, social forces and social structures. As we have seen, the difference is certainly not that the public-school girls don't employ theoretical discourse at all. But, in talking about gender relations, the available theory – feminism – is unacceptable, and, in rejecting this, they fall back on an untheorized discontent with how things are. The question obviously arises: why is feminism so rebarbative to the public-school girls?

CLASS

Whatever we talked about in the public-school groups, categories of class and preoccupation with class difference shaped the discussion. All the groups spent one session reading and talking about a romantic photo-story in *Jackie*, a British weekly magazine for girls. (A full discussion of this part of the project is given in Frazer, 1987.) There is insufficient space here to reproduce the complete discussion of this, but the distinctive flavour of the 13-year-old public-school girls' response is clear:

Extract 8

Clara: I like his jersey.
            [laughter]
Samantha: I've been looking at his jumper.
            [laughter]
E.F.:   Do you know boys who wear jumpers like that?
Several: Yes.
Clara: I'd say most of Eton ...
E.F.:   So you like the way he dresses, right?
Clara: I don't know what he's got on his feet, though.
            [laughter]
Clara: It's really annoying, you know.
Samantha: Probably Adidas trainers or something.
Clara: I wouldn't go out with him if he was wearing those
            ...
Samantha: And then, you know, trousers that, you know, only
            come to about here, then long white socks under
            ...
Clara: Oh, long *white* socks ...
E.F.:   What, whether you'd like him or not?
Clara: Well, it depends what kind of school he goes to, I
            mean that sounds really awful, but —
Louisa: His classical background. *[laughs]*
Clara: Yes, no.
Louisa: Yes, but Latin and classical background
            [laughter]
            ...
Clara: I don't like the jeans, I don't like the way she
            dresses, so if he goes with people like her, then I
            mean ...

[PSC, 6 3–5–13 years, public school]

Their response to the hero of the photo-story is constructed entirely as a class response – in short, they only fancy him because he wears the sort of jumper that their friends (and potential boyfriends and husbands) at Eton wear, and they would cease to fancy him if it were revealed that he was wearing footwear and jeans of the sort that mark working-class membership, and/or if he didn't go to one of the major English public schools. (So much for love conquering all!) In any case, his romantic interest in the heroine of the story, whose class identity is quite unambiguous (her sartorial style is unmistakable), in the end makes him undesirable.

There is, though, more to the public-school girls' class consciousness than acquired distinction of taste. Also at stake is their experience of class hostility and violence. The conversation about the *Jackie* story (Extract 8) continued like this:

Extract 9

Clara: Yes, 'cos you see we all speak quite well and it's quite embarrassing when you go to some places.

Louisa: They all go 'Oh' [*an exaggerated upper-class accent*]

Clara: 'Oh'

Louisa: 'OK, yah, Henrietta'

Samantha: But we're not conscious of speaking —

Clara: My parents speak like that, and everyone does at home, so you're really brought up to know —

Samantha: Brought up speaking the King's English.

E.F.:   Do you call it that?

Samantha: Yes, they get at us for having a normal English accent, you know.

           ...

Samantha: And I was riding down the road back towards the trailer and, um, Echo was really walking out, and seemed to be quite proud of himself 'cos he'd done well, and there were these two girls on tiny little shaggy ponies and they were about 15 and really fat, and the poor ponies' backs were like this [*draws picture in air with her hand*] and they said 'Oh, inne snobby?' [*exaggerated 'Cockney' accent*] and they looked at me, and then they were determined to make him canter and for me to be taken off him, and I was just sitting there and I didn't know what to do, and I was going 'Echo, just for goodness sake keep walking', and they kept on galloping past me on their ponies, and they were just so awful about the whole thing.

Clara: Yes, 'cos people like that, they always get at you at point-to-points and things.

Louisa: They always seem to tease us more than we do them.

Clara: I mean we'd never go up to someone and say 'God, you're such a pleb', 'cos, I mean, mostly if you're a pleb it's not your fault.

[PSC, 6 10]

And later in the session from which Extract 1 is taken, the lower sixth discussed their experience of conflict:

Extract 10

Arabella: But the bottom of the lower class, oh —

Kate: Most of the people down in the working, well —

Sara: Why, just when we walk in just because we're [*name of school*] girls if we walk into [*name of town*] when we're in uniform, and —

Annabel: They're spitting.

Sara: Tripping us up.

Kate: We've got these people with milk bottles, threatening to smash them in our faces.

. . .

Annabel: What do you do if someone spits in your face, you say 'right, well, fine, it doesn't actually matter'?

Kate: They throw stones at your horse when you're riding past.

Arabella: Throw stones at your bike . . .

Kate: I don't know if the snobs' views of the lower class are as bad as the lower-class views of the snobs.

[PSB, 5 14, 15]

These experiences of class hostility from 'the lower classes' validate the girls' class categories for them, as do other cultural differences:

Extract 11

Candida: I hate the nouveaux riches *far more* than I hate the middle classes.
            [*Laughter*]
Candida: They look down on the lower classes much more than we do, I mean the character of a person isn't to do with class, it's to do with upbringing; the nouveaux people are such snobs.
E.F.:   How do you define a nouveau person?
Candida: They go to Tunisia for their holidays, they're really pretentious, we hate pretension – they buy all their furniture new, from Harrods; they don't own land.

[PSA, 6 2–17 years, public school]

However, in this connection too, questions of the *status* of their experience, the categories they employ to understand the world, and the construction of social life, are also at the forefront of their minds:

Extract 12

Caroline: Well, it's money that makes you upper-class.
Jemima: No, I think upbringing.
Fiona: Or mixing with rich people.
Jemima: Yes, but look how we look down on people with new money, nouveaux people —
            . . .
Jemima: Well, it is to do with us going to public school, that's why Labour would abolish public schools.
Caroline: But in France there aren't any public schools, they've still got social class divisions though. I think it's the family, the family is the hugest part.
Candida: But think, if we all went to comprehensive schools, you'd have to go to school where you live, you'd have to mix with people of a lower class, friend-

138

ships would be based on where you live, there would be a mix of classes, so the high class society wouldn't exist – at the moment we all go up to London, but we wouldn't.

...

Caroline:	But *is it* that bad? Is there any need to reduce the classes?
Candida:	Of course it's bad.
Cressida:	Look at how we patronize them, they resent us.
Caroline:	I think they're jealous, they want our money.
Candida:	Of course they resent, their families were our grandparents' servants, of course they resent ...
Caroline:	They wouldn't say that, though, would they? They'd say it's because we're rich.

[PSA, 6 1]

The lower-sixth group spent much time and emotion discussing their contradictory understandings and experiences of class relations: they wanted to distance themselves from what they understood to be the 'stupid prejudices' of other girls in the school (Extract 1), yet they too feared and disliked the 'lower classes' who are the wearers of the white socks constantly picked out and remarked on by the very class-conscious girls (Extract 10). One member of this group was very challenging and scathing.

Extract 13

Amy:	I do hate Sloanes, I still hate them.
Annabel:	You can still hate them, but you can't hate the individual people. I mean, do you remember in [*name of school house*] you put up this big argument, 'I hate Sloanes', but you see the thing is here, horrible as it may be, this is a Sloane school. There are Sloane people and you cannot make a wide —
Amy:	Well, I don't know, that's not true.
Annabel:	You can hate the attitude, but you can't hate the people —
Kate:	You can't hate the people underneath the Barbours and the Hunter wellies.

[PSB, 5 11]

139

They were caught between a naturalistic and categorical analysis and theory of class ('nouveaux' people are snobby and vulgar, the 'lower classes' are violent); an understanding of (and a measure of guilt about) inequality and relations of exploitation – a perception of class as a construct based on antagonistic interests; and a denial of the significance and reality of class at all – 'I don't like white socks, but that's only because they're not practical' as Annabel said. Or: One has to take people as they come, some are nice and some are nasty, and some are unfortunate enough to be ignorant and not know that people from other classes can be perfectly pleasant.

By contrast, while a class standpoint is clear in the comprehensive – school girls' discourse, it is striking that they never steered the conversation round to the subject of class, or invoked class distinctions in their discussions of other topics. Having observed this, I raised the subject myself – asking them to draw a diagram of the class structure of Britain, and then asking them to talk about their diagrams, and their own class identity. (Here I was following the method of one element of the research in Goldthorpe *et al.*, 1969.) They hated doing this, and the discussions were marked by a hesitancy and a reluctance to speak that I was quite unused to. Here, the difference in their garrulity is marked by the number of utterances and prompts from me; phonetic transcription would show that there were many long pauses in the girls' speech.

Extract 14

Heather:	[*Whispers*] What's the difference between middle class and lower class?
Linda:	Lower class don't work.
Sarah:	Middle class are lower than working class.
Suzanne:	No, working class are lower.
Heather:	What is the lower class?
E.F.:	Well —
Heather:	I think it is the working — ( )
	...
Heather:	Well, I think, I've always accepted, because I've worked and my family's working, that I've been in the working — ( )
E.F.:	Yeah

Heather:	But now when you start getting older, I think why should I be branded as part of the lower, the working, I mean what is —
Linda:	I think it's judged, well, on what you own and ( )
Suzanne:	I don't know where I am.

[CS6, 4 2 – 17 years, comprehensive]

Extract 15

Jen:	I see myself as quite middle-class ( )
E.F.:	And why's that?
Jen:	Well, because of the way I've been brought up ( )
	...
E.F.:	Has anybody put they're working-class?
Amanda:	Me.
Annette:	I s'pose I do ( )
E.F.:	And why?
Amanda:	I don't know ( )
Jen:	I'm somewhere in between those two.
Annette:	Yeah, I reckon we're there as well ( )
Jen:	I reckon we're middle.
E.F.:	Why?
Jen	I don't know, I can't think of —

[CSF, 4 2 – 14 years, comprehensive]

The sixth-formers were on firmer ground later on in the session when they got to talk about the occupants of the upper echelons of the class structure ('upper-class hooligans' from Oxford University had received a great deal of publicity in the local press that year):

Extract 16

Sarah:	Then you get the people who're sort of, oh 'Daddy owns a farm' and the real, you know, aristocrats, people who, well, you see as wasters really.
Linda:	Wasters.
Sarah:	You know, like they're going on at the moment about Oxford and about a lot of students who come from the upper classes.

141

Linda: Champagne Charlies.

Sarah: Yeah, and they're cleaning up their image and stop mucking about because they're saying a lot of these people only got in because of who they are.

Linda: That's true.

Suzanne: Mm.

Linnie: It's like when Prince Charles went to Cambridge, isn't it?

Suzanne: Yeah, I mean, on his grades he would never ever have got in and they arranged it.

. . .

Heather: It's not what you know, it's who you know.

E.F.:   The old school tie.

Linnie: Judges, civil service and things like that, it's all what school you went to.

[CS6, 4 3, 4]

But the fourth-formers were never happy talking about class and the discussion from which Extract 15 comes did not last long. It was as though I had touched on a topic that was taboo to girls who would happily talk without pause about menstruation and sexuality.

The contrasts between the comprehensive and public-school groups' discourse about class are striking. To begin with, there is the clear difference in the complexity of class stratification constructed by their respective sets of categories. The public-school girls understand the class structure to have fine gradations, with distinctions between old and new money, the respectable and the 'lower' working classes, and so on. By contrast, the only categories I elicited from the comprehensive fourth-years were 'working' and 'middle', while one of the sixth-formers was confused about the distinction between 'working' and 'lower'; and, as we have seen, they had great difficulty in giving any clear content to any of the categories they produced. Secondly, the public-school groups have a clear consciousness of their own class position. Many of them understand themselves to be upper-class (although many of them would be designated middle-class by a sociologist – a categorization that would be offensive to the girls themselves). Thirdly, the sixth-formers immediately embark on an enthusiastic theoretical discussion about the social structure of class division. The comprehensive-school fourth-formers produced no theory of class at all; the sixth-formers finally (after 15 minutes of prodding from me) grasped the topic of upper-class hooligans, and produced a theorized discourse of privileged access to education and the professions.

This raises a third contrast: the public-school girls' theory is unstable and unsatisfactory, a matter for debate and dispute. This surely, though, is a function of their wider repertoire of conceptualizations of class, and experience of class relations, than it is of the comprehensive girls' greater analytic clarity.

RACE

The comprehensive-school girls were much more at home discussing racial and ethnic relations:

Extract 17

E.F.:   Has anybody divided up along any other lines, not class?
Natalie: I've got religion.
Amanda: Yeah.
Natalie: People like Pakistanis.
             (*Here Natalie tells a long story about a friend who had an unwanted arranged marriage.*)
Jen: And no Asian girls could come to this group, because it's staying after school, innit? They all get picked up usually, they're not allowed to walk.

[CS4F, 4 3 – 14 years, comprehensive]

Extract 18

Sarah: But that hasn't worked in this school, you can walk about and I don't think it has mixed everybody up, the Asians and the different races, it just hasn't.
Heather: I think it's alienated them even more.
Suzanne: But it works two ways I think, though.
Linda: They've alienated themselves.
Sarah: I mean, in the sixth form, we mix more, I think, but lower down the school I don't think it happens at all, I mean I see groups of Asian girls walking around speaking their native language, and in groups, I mean you see them all over the place.

Heather: And Chinese, there are a lot of Chinese round here.

Sarah: And they don't, well, most of them, well not most of them, I won't say that, but a certain percentage of them make no effort to mix whatsoever, it's not all one-sided at all.

Heather: And they've got an advantage 'cos they can speak, what is it, Urdu, Asian and English and if they don't want us to hear they go straight into Asian, or it's like the Chinese, they go straight into Chinese when they talk among themselves.

Suzanne: But you could learn Asian.

Heather: Why should you?

Linnie: I mean, if you wanted to make a real effort then you would, I suppose.

Suzanne: Quite a few people do.

Linnie: Yes, that's true.

[CS6, 4 10 – 17 years, comprehensive]

The most striking contrast here is with the comprehensive-school girls' own discussion of gender. Here, with gender, their talk is theoretical – but the theory is of a very different kind. In the case of gender, they talk about cultural representations, interest and power. But their discussion of race and ethnicity is theoretically confined to what they understand to be non-English ethnic groups' wilful reluctance to integrate. Their failure to discuss racial difference in terms of power is glaring, and raises serious issues about the school's management of ethnic relations. But for the purpose of this chapter, the important contrast is between the comprehensive and public-schools' groups – while the public-school girls embed their experience and understanding of racial difference in their experience and understanding of class difference, the comprehensive-school girls move into the discussion of race and ethnicity with relief, as a *substitute* for discussing class.

III

In this section I want to consider further this imbrication of race, class and gender for the public-school groups. As we have seen, for them the experience and understanding of femininity *is* the experience and understanding of class. This is especially clear when their talk about these topics is contrasted with that produced by the comprehensive-school girls. When discussing the *Jackie* story, when talking about how girls are expected to behave at parties or in school, when talking about marriage and jobs, the public-school girls always invoke gender categories that are class-specific, and are articulated as such. If this is taken as a mark or measure of class-consciousness, then these girls are far more class-conscious than the comprehensive-school girls. Furthermore, their class identity is an explicitly racial identity.

This is illustrated particularly vividly by looking at some extracts from sessions in which we talked about their envisaged future careers. In these discussions they construct their idealized conception of marriage as entailing distinct spheres for husband and wife. Running a country house is not an occupation that can be skimped.

Extract 19

Annabel: [*In ten years*] Um, I'll probably be starting my own household.
. . .

Arabella: Sometimes I think it's such a waste of time going to university because you go there for three years when you're 18 till you're 21, be just beginning to start something and then you'll get married, OK, and not much point doing it if you can't carry it on.
. . .

Sara: Well, why can't you get married and still carry on having your job and everything?

Annabel: Because if I'm having a family, then children come first, that's what I think, rather than put them in someone else's care. My mother was saying about a friend who has a job and they were all in the nanny's care and the mother does very much what she wants, and that's all very well, but Mummy said the children looked so unloved and that, 'cos they're only small; I think for the first, what, however many, years till they go away to school, I think for that time, anyway, being with them's very very important.

E.F.: Mm, why would you send children away to school?

Annabel: Probably because I found it was so character-building, because before I went away I think I was probably very much a Mummy's girl because my brothers went away before me, so being alone at home —

[PSB, 1 6, 71]

Extract 20

Candida: [*invited to think about her life in her late twenties – E.F.*] I'll be living in the country, and I think I'd have a job, but in the local town or something ... like running a shop, or having something ... I'd prefer if he wasn't in the army, or he wasn't in the sort of job where he'd be up in London all week ... [*About her mother – E.F.*]: She doesn't do anything all day, she's very much run by my father ... like she doesn't have her own diary, she works off Daddy's diary ...

E.F.: When you say she doesn't do anything all day, what actually does she do all day?

Candida: Oh, well, she cooks, and she gets ready for it if we're going down at the weekend, the children, in the morning, 'cos, Daddy's the Master of Hounds so we have all the kennels and we've got ten horses which we look after, and we've only got two girl grooms, which they can't do it all, so Mummy goes down and does the horses, so that takes up most of the morning, and we don't have lunch, just bread, soup, so in the afternoon, she just sort of does things round the house, and she goes and does the shopping —

[PSA, 5/2/86]

Candida wants a degree of economic independence that her mother doesn't have, but having a shop (an antiques shop was favourite) 'in the local town' evokes a very traditional marriage, and class-specific social and economic relations in countryside and community. Annabel says that at 26 she will be 'starting her own household'. This is an almost Victorian locution, which actually sounds very anachronistic. Again, it conjures up a very traditional picture of family life and marriage, in which women's work is at the service of their men and in which they take up housekeeping almost as a profession; and yet, of course, not quite a profession – as an occupation it can still count as 'not doing anything all day'! The conceptions of 'wife' and family life Candida and Annabel are employing here, and the accompanying theorization as to why family life should be so, is inextricably bound up with a particular class, race and gender identity.

IV

These contrasts between the comprehensive- and the public-school girls are so marked that it is tempting to 'let the data speak for themselves'. However, data never do simply speak for themselves, so I want now to consider what conclusions we might draw about the significance of this material. First, I must make some brief remarks about the effect of method and context on data construction.

Recording talk in a discussion group, as opposed to interviewing individuals, or asking them to fill in a questionnaire, is clearly a method that focuses attention at the inter-subjective, social level. To look at this from another angle, it may be feared that individuals' responses and attitudes in a group might differ from their responses and attitudes in a one-to-one interview. This, however, can be construed as a positive advantage of the group method over the interview or questionnaire. People's racial, class or other attitudes and experience are, after all, usually manifested in social situations. Where a questionnaire elicits an 'opinion' or 'attitude' as a discrete datum, this kind of talk reveals to some extent the negotiation and reasoning that constructs it.

The norms of the discussion group constitute a specific context, in the framework of which the data must be interpreted. The groups were stable and closed, confidential, and met regularly. Norms include the obligation to participate, to listen, to be supportive and co-operative in discussion (rather than competitive, as in debate), and to be truthful. In this context, participants can afford to change their minds, say things they really don't mean, clarify what they did mean, and so on. That is, the discussion group is marked by a specific discourse *register* which has its own effect on what it is possible to say. In this context, firm conclusions about comparative *attitudes* among the girls are less easy to establish than findings about the differences between their respective *repertoires* of discourse.

To sum up, for the purposes of this chapter, the data can be analysed under three main headings. First there is the distribution, or comparative repertoires, of discourse. Girls from the two schools share a basically feminist way of talking about their gender experience; but the public-school girls also revealed a conservative understanding of gender relations, which was in tension with their feminism. Second, the public-school girls were highly conscious of their upper-class identity, and talked very fluently about it; in contrast, talk of class division was an embarrassment for the comprehensive-school girls. Third, both groups' discussion of identity and experience revealed a clear ethnic identity; but again there were differences between them. The public-school girls' talk articulated the racial specificity of their class position. For the comprehensive-school girls, ethnicity was a major line of social stratification, a division lived out in daily life in school. Neither of the groups, however, employed any critical discourse about race – although one might expect to find anti-racism in the comprehensive-school girls' discursive repertoire. Fourth, while the comprehensive groups (especially the sixth-formers) were interested in theorizing gender relations, and enquiring into competing accounts of gender inequality, the public-school sixth-formers' conversation invariably turned from gender inequality to class inequality.

The next major category of analysis is that of moments of ambiguity, contradiction and uncertainty. I have referred to the public-school girls' 'upper-class' identity and the fact that their conceptualization of class relations was not quite secure – their conventionally naturalistic analysis of class differences and inequality was challenged by their own understanding of class dominance and power. Their feminist understanding of the sexual double standard, the problems of gender that, as teenagers, they were dealing with daily, clashed with gender norms specific to their class position.

The third major category of analysis picks out the moments of tension, which are the most interesting data the project produced. The comprehensive-school girls' inarticulacy and embarrassment on the subject of class produced silences and hesitations, awkward moments in the otherwise relaxed and fluent conversation. In the public school, the subject of class also caused clashes, both within and between members of the group, and, in what was otherwise a relaxed atmosphere, emotional feelings ran high.

For the purposes of this book, one major question is raised. What is the role of the respective schools – formal teaching, the pupils' sub-culture, informal teacher–pupil interaction – in this distribution, as it were, of discourses of class, and, derivatively, the formation of class-consciousness? Unfortunately when this question is posed, the limitations of the project are plainly exposed. Interviews and discussions with teachers and other staff are needed, at the very least; and also participant observation and recording of data in the classroom and settings other than this type of formally structured discussion group. For myself, as the fieldworker, I am left with the impression of general worry about ethnicity on the part of the staff at the comprehensive school – and the complete absence there of any preoccupation with class as a social division; and, by contrast, an all-pervading and insistent preoccupation with class throughout the public school.

I made some notes of conversations and events outside the discussion groups themselves, but not systematically. So the evidence I have for the analysis that follows is only anecdotal (although they are my anecdotes). There are three motifs under which the teachers' preoccupation with class was articulated. First, in talk about girls' family backgrounds and 'family problems'; second, in discussion of their 'sheltered lives'; third, in the girls' television viewing and reading.

Teachers acted as intermediaries for me when the groups were forming, giving me the names of girls who were interested, organizing the allocation of a room to meet in, helping to negotiate a time. In this process, staff frequently gave me background information about individual would-be group members. At that early stage I was struck by the frequency of comments like, 'Oh, Alicia, yes, she's very nice – and a real "Honourable", you know.' As at the comprehensive school, I was sometimes offered confidential information about family 'problems'. A main staff worry was the way some girls seemed to be neglected by their parents; and this connected with the pre-occupation about the unsatisfactoriness of aspects of the boarding-school regime and a worry about the girls' 'sheltered lives', which I shall discuss next. For the moment, though, talk about parents' social status was invariably imbricated with talk about individual girls' unhappiness and so forth: and without really trying, I soon came to know the exact social status of each group member. I had to ask for guidance from one teacher about the relative status of earls, barons and so on before I could really understand the hierarchy. The girls, too, seemed very conscious of the fine gradations among them. On more than one occasion, seeing a car outside, someone remarked something like, 'Oh, it's Lady X' – although they were not in the habit of remarking on the occupants of every car that drew up.

That the girls were thought to have over-'sheltered lives' was made clear in the first instance by the open arms with which I was welcomed into the school and given access and resources. Later, in discussions about the school's relations with the town, and about the girls' fortunes at interviews for university, the term continually cropped up. It seems to me that 'sheltered lives' is more or less a code for the terms 'upper' and 'upper middle class', expressive of anxiety about class hostility and guilt. That is, the staff's view was that the girls' school and home situation meant it was inevitable that they would feel beleaguered in their class position. It is not clear from my notes what the teachers' expressed or tacit reactions were to the frequent, unpleasantly snobbish and racist expression and policing of class identity, described in Extract 1 and discussed by the lower-sixth.

The main point I wish to make is that when I think back to what was actually said about class, what conversations contributed to my impression that members of the school harped on it endlessly, I realize that class as such was rarely explicitly mentioned; but that talk about class was encoded in talk about family problems, sheltered lives, and the like. Obviously, this interpretation should be tested against analysis of recorded talk, which we are not in a position to do.

I had several conversations about television and books with staff members. Popular culture was a category that I had designated a significant area for exploration at the first stage of research design. The school's articulated policy was that, in reading romantic fiction, girls at least were reading something, which is better than nothing. Again, it is arguable that issues about class were close to the surface in this connection. I have already briefly discussed the process by which the girls took up an explicitly articulated class stance when reading (cf. also Frazer, 1987). In the conversation about the *Jackie* story, the 13-year-olds considered further the role of this kind of fiction in their lives:

Extract 21

Sara: ... because we're sort of shut up here we'd get to know about outside life.

E.F.:   Sorry?

Sara: That sort of thing, because we're –
             [*laughter*]
Sara: Not that, well, I don't know, we're all prisonized
             here.
E.F.:   Yes, because you're shut in school.
Sara: You know, we're all just shut up, we've got to get
             in the towns and everything.
Clara: 'Cos we're not allowed to go to [*nearest town*] even.

[PSC – 13 years public school,]

In other words, Sara considers photo-stories to be a significant substitute for her own first-hand experience of 'life in the towns'. But as photo-stories are neither addressed to Sara, nor about girls like her or her friends, so 'life in the towns' is, it is implied, not for her. The implied viewer or reader in the TV soaps and comedy programmes does not share her class; in romantic fiction, the female reader is asked to identify with a heroine who is usually of a lower-class position than the hero.

One teacher pointed out to me that this can be understood as the fact that the girls are routinely marginalized by popular culture. This is an area for further research: the way class positioning is negotiated when readers of different classes read Mills and Boon romances, *Harpers* and *Vogue*, and Jane Austen, the Brontës and other staples of secondary-school English literature.

V

The inescapable impression I have from these data is of a continual current of anxiety about class among the girls and teachers of the public school. Feelings of guilt at class inequality are mixed with contempt for and fear of the 'lower classes'. The girls' thoughts, feelings and talk about every topic from TV soap operas, their relations with the local town, to their ambitions for the future, and their sexuality, are inextricably bound up with feelings about their class position, and the class structure of the society in which they live. In their professional capacities, their teachers seem to consider that every aspect of their pupils' welfare and progress is to some degree conditioned by their class.

Perhaps these observations about this school are less notable than the contrasting evidence from the comprehensive school in the study: where the girls and teachers seemingly inhabit a classless society (not, though, where class is neutrally absent, but seems to be taboo). The question there perhaps is, why is there no civic, political or socio-logical education in the curriculum? (And my feeling is, that this is an important and urgent question.) However, it is not that the public-school official curriculum features an unusual amount of civics, political studies or sociology – as far as I know, they don't figure much at all. Of course, in the absence of classroom study, I am not in a position to speculate about the treatment of these questions in an academic context. But the motif of class seems to be tightly and repetitively woven into other layers of the school's culture.

NOTES

1. Key to symbols used in the extracts:
   ( ) = a pause or silence in the talk; ... = material from the transcript has been omitted;
   —(at the end of an utterance) = utterance trailing off and/or an interruption by the next speaker.
2. The letters and numbers in brackets are references to the transcripts:

PSA = public-school upper sixth; PSB = public-school lower sixth; PSC = public-school third form; CST = comprehensive-school fourth-form Tuesday group; CSF = compre-hensive-school fourth-form Friday group; CS6 = comprehensive-school upper sixth. The subsequent numbers refer to the date or number of the meeting, and the page number in the transcript.

REFERENCES

Frazer, E. (1987) 'Teenage Girls Reading *Jackie*', *Media, Culture and Society*, 9: 407–25.
Frazer, E. (1988) 'Teenage Girls Talking about Class', *Sociology*, 22: 343–58.
Goldthorpe, J., Bechhofer, F., and Platt, J. (1969) *The Affluent Worker in the Class Structure*. Cambridge: Cambridge University Press.
Marsh, P., Rosser, E., and Harré, R. (1978) *The Rules of Disorder*. London: Routledge & Kegan Paul.

7

'We're just here to make up the numbers really.'

The Experience of Girls in Boys' Public Schools

JENN PRICE

The first female sixth-formers within the formerly boys-only Head-masters' Conference schools appeared at Marlborough College in 1968, and by 1980 over 100 of these establishments had girl pupils, at least in the upper forms (Walford, 1986). Currently many such schools are extending their welcome to girls of 13 and upwards so that more than half now have girls.

Why did these schools, some of which had been 'bastions of sexual apartheid' (Rae, 1981) for hundreds of years, open their doors to girls? Research conducted by Walford in 1981 investigated staff opinion in a school that was considering becoming co-educational. He concluded that many saw single-sex education as advantageous for boys, but were worried about it encouraging homosexuality and making its pupils uncomfortable with girls. The presence of girls would, it was thought, improve boys' behaviour, give them more ease in interacting with the opposite sex, and provide 'more acceptable sexual partners'. In short, girls would broaden the boys' general education. No one suggested how the girls themselves might benefit. If this can be taken as typical of thinking within schools, it may not constitute enough reason for change, so other factors must be taken into account.

The early 1970s saw unprecedented inflation and, together with the substantial Houghton pay award to teachers, private schools were hit hard. Drastic measures were required for their survival and between 1966 and 1980 major boarding schools were obliged to increase their fees by about 400 per cent (Rae, 1981). This was a critical time. 'Independent education is a service industry: if a school cannot attract

153

customers it will go out of business' (Rae, 1981). In order to keep the fees down, schools had to become more cost-efficient. Many of them saw that a small expansion, particularly of the sixth form, would help. But the combination of increased fees and the introduction of more attractive state provision, especially in the case of sixth-form colleges, was losing them pupils.

A particular problem that many schools faced was the need to attract more boarders as these numbers were falling. There were two possible new markets: foreign males or British females. Some schools began recruitment in the Middle East, Malaysia and Hong Kong, and by 1978 foreign nationals made up 4.72 per cent of the pupils (Rae, 1981). Other schools decided on girls. Where the school was of a strong Christian persuasion, foreigners with different religions would be unsuitable. Girls, on the other hand, might usefully fill places in the under-subscribed subjects – for example, the Arts – which were less popular with boys.

Other events were threatening the existence of the public schools as well. In the 1960s, secondary schools were being reorganized into comprehensives and the Labour government was pushing for integration of public schools into the state system, in order to 'bring about a socially mixed entry into the schools'. In 1975, financial support was withdrawn from the direct-grant grammar schools and two-thirds of them entered the private sector (Johnson, 1987).

The government also threatened to remove the charitable status of public schools if they resisted co-operation with the state system. But Labour lost the 1979 election and Thatcherism arrived. Government-funded assisted places were introduced in 1980 and, along with its ideology of 'parental choice', the Conservatives guaranteed the continuing existence of private schooling.

Some middle-class parents who had enjoyed the benefits of the grammar schools were distrustful of the standards in the comprehensive schools. They looked to the independent sector for academic excellence and they wanted the same opportunities for their daughters as for their sons. Thus the numbers in the HMC schools rose steadily, and by 1989 there were 151,700 pupils, 24,400 of which were female (ISIS Annual Census, 1989).

But what about the girls? What was it like to be in a boys' school? Were they doing better than they would have done in other schools? Were they changing the male character of these institutions, or were they submerged and stereotyped by it?

By appeals in the Press and to the Girls' Schools Association, I located 15 women who had attended HMC schools in the years between 1970 and 1986. Most had transferred from girls' schools into the sixth form. Of these, two had fond memories and spoke enthusiatically of their time there, but the rest had mixed feelings about it:

> I'm really glad I did it, but it was hell at the time (31-year-old).

> Educationally it was OK.... Emotionally it was a really bad move ... it was just at the stage when I was getting ready to grow up and it pulled the carpet from under my feet (35-year-old).

> I found the whole environment very hostile, [the boys] were extremely critical, very happy to rip people apart (24-year-old).

> I remember feeling constantly anxious, scared, unconfident, ugly, and I hated it (27-year-old).

> It is easy to paint the whole experience black and I often did so. It is not right to superimpose girls on a school designed for boys (21-year-old).

> If you can survive in a boys' public school, you can survive anywhere (20-year-old).

Clearly, most had found the experience less than pleasant. But the sample was small and self-selected, so their views cannot be taken as representative. Some were pioneers in establishments that had not yet fully catered for girls or identified their needs; females were likely to have been a small minority in the school, which in itself could have increased their problems. It would be interesting to compare them with present-day sixth-formers and find out how conditions have changed.

METHODOLOGY

In 1988, I spent a short period observing school life and talking to staff and pupils in a minor public school which I shall call St. Bee's. The college had about 450 pupils aged 13 and above, with 45 girls in the sixth form. There were eight Houses, two for boy boarders, five for day boys and one for girls, almost all of whom boarded. The boys' Houses had about 60 pupils, each with a housemaster and two male tutors; the girls' House had female staff.

Also, to broaden my study, I visited two major schools of the Eton group (St. Sea's and St. Dee's), observing lessons and conducting interviews. All three schools had had girls in their sixth forms for many years and were planning to take younger ones in the future in order to become fully co-educational.

Additionally, as a result of a chance meeting with a fellow science teacher, I managed to gain admittance to a well-known girls' school (St. Kay's), to talk to a small group of leaving fifth-formers, some of whom had chosen to go to the sixth forms of boys' public schools.

I set out to do non-participant observation, where the observer 'stands aloof from the group activities (s)he is investigating and eschews group membership' (Cohen and Manion, 1985). Most of the lessons I observed were of the 'chalk and talk' type and, like Delamont (1984), I 'lurked' at the back 'and watched'. Although I wanted to be invisible, I was not ignored. Some teachers tried to include me, lending me textbooks or explaining what they had been doing previously; some boys asked me what I was doing there. Inevitably, my presence affected proceedings and changed behaviour. On two occasions I joined in, singing with the choir and helping in a physics practical session.

In each class I noted numbers of girls and boys and how they seated themselves in the rooms. I recorded the lesson format – for example, lecture, question and answer, etc., and its content, who spoke, and how often – and also any interesting exchanges. I did not use a structured proforma for classroom observation.

I aimed to observe equal numbers of lower- and upper-sixth classes and to try to see a variety of subjects. I realized after my first day at St. Bee's that I would have difficulty finding my way around, so I instituted a system of 'native guides' to take me from one location to another. I attended the girls' roll-call every morning, and organized my timetable for the day with their help. Thus Sarah would know to ferry me to lower-sixth English and Kate would be instructed to collect me afterwards for an economics lesson.

Being unfamiliar with public-school routine, I was surprised by the length of the day. It began with a roll-call and chapel service before 9.00 a.m. There were eight 40-minute teaching periods on Monday, Wednesday and Friday, and five on Tuesday, Thursday and Saturday. The latter were termed 'half-days', but there was compulsory sport until 4.00 p.m. On Monday, the early afternoon was taken up with the Combined Cadet Force, so the last lesson did not end until 5.30 p.m. and, on the other full days, societies and other activities in a long lunch-break brought the end of the day to 5 o'clock.

Outside lessons, there was plenty of opportunity for me to absorb the atmosphere of the school. I spent time chatting in the staff-room and the girls' common room, ate school meals, and attended clubs and hockey matches. I was invited to supper by women teachers and, on one occasion, drank in the staff bar with the men. Also, at St. Bee's, I spent a lot of time in the girls' toilets (there was no separate provision for female staff), the only place I could find where I could write notes undisturbed.

I managed to interview 54 girls in the three schools and ten boys at St. Bee's. When interviewing I used a schedule in order to make sure that the same ground was covered each time. With teachers I did short informal interviews (or formal ones with headmasters), and wrote down what they said. With pupils I used a tape-recorder and transcribed the recordings later. These interviews lasting about 30 minutes took place in groups of about four or five because I thought pupils would feel more relaxed like this. I decided to keep the groups single-sex because I wanted the girls to talk about their experience of the boys and vice versa.

These interviews were more like open-ended conversations. I first assured pupils of confidentiality and said that no one but me would listen to their tapes. I emphasized that I would not tell the teachers what they said. This helped them to talk freely. I did not act in an aloof and formal manner, and, like Oakley (1981) and Lees (1986), if anyone asked me for personal details or opinions I would answer. This again served to enhance rapport between us. I wanted to learn about pupils' experiences and feelings; I did not want them to try to be 'objective'. The notion of objectivity is a nonsense; as Adrienne Rich (1979) has commented, 'Objectivity is the name we give to male subjectivity'.

THE GIRLS

More than three-quarters of all the sixth-form girls that I met in the three schools had previously been to single-sex schools, and almost two-thirds had changed from day to boarding. They considered mixed classes to be advantageous for various reasons. Some thought it was more natural, a good preparation for mixing with men in university and the world of work; and some thought it would just be more fun.

Eighty per cent of them were intending to go to university. They felt that their old schools were inferior:

157

I wanted the increased opportunities which are available to the boys – the better standard of teaching, the wider range of activities' (d2).*

Their selection at 16 by O-level results, interview and possibly an examination, coupled with their small numbers in the schools, meant that, on the whole, the girls were more intelligent than their male classmates.

The views of the ten leaving fifth-formers at St. Kay's were illuminating as to why the sixth forms of boys' schools were thought superior to their own. They assumed that because girls were in the minority, facilities such as those for boarding and sports would be newer and better. They thought lessons would be stricter, the general attitude towards work more serious, and the teaching of science and maths would be superior. They also felt that out of lesson time they would have more freedom and more fun.

IN SCHOOL AND CLASSROOMS

After a preliminary visit to St. Bee's to explain the nature of my research, I decided to attend the annual House Music Competition. It would provide a good opportunity for me to absorb the atmosphere of the place and meet some of the staff. During the evening, soloists, small groups and choirs performed for each House and every pupil had to take part. It was a good introduction for me because it illustrated vividly the extent to which females were in the minority – four or five teachers only and one girls' House out of eight. The musical offerings varied within the chosen theme, 'The Twentieth Century'. There were several popular songs sung. Cole Porter's 'Brush Up Your Shakespeare' was performed with excellent diction by some of the boys. This contained advice to men on how to use a knowledge of the Bard's words to make dainty 'debbies' and 'blond(es)' 'kow-tow' to them. Another House choir sang a song entitled 'Fat-bottomed Girls'.

The girls had drawn the final performance slot and their house-mistress said they ought to do well. They were very good at singing. They had several accomplished instrumentalists too, but unfortu-

---

* A letter is used to denote the school of the speaker; b is St. Bee's, c is St. Sea's and d is St. Dee's. The numbers refer to the interviews, in chronological order: they identify small groups of girls.

nately some of them had refused to perform solo infront of the boys, because it was too nerve-racking.

Indeed, their choir was excellent and received enthusiastic applause. Next in their programme was a piano piece and the schoolgirl announcer introduced the soloist with the words, 'She had been known to have a talent from an early age ...'. At this point the hall erupted. Braying male adolescent voices made it plain that they had detected a sexual innuendo. The blushing announcer struggled to carry on and the piece was played when the din subsided. There was no attempt by the teachers to reprimand the boys for their loutish behaviour.

The first lesson I observed was biology, taught in an ancient, cold and musty laboratory. The stuffed dodo on one of the display shelves enhanced the feeling of obsolescence. There were seven pupils. The front row contained the boys and the two girls sat behind them. I was to find this voluntary segregation universal throughout.

The teaching styles that I saw were diverse, and I was successively fascinated, bored, enthralled or merely kept awake by the lessons. Groups were small and discipline was tight, and at first I saw little of the sort of disruptives male behaviour noted by Mahony (1985), Spender (1982) and others. Teachers seemed to treat boys and girls fairly, addressing questions to them equally, and I saw only two instances of adverse comments by males when females did exceptionally well – and even these seemed good-natured enough. Were they behaving normally, I wondered?

At break one day in the masters' common room (its name unchanged despite having had female teachers for years), Mr C, who taught economics, confided to me that he was appalled by the sexist attitudes of some of the lower-sixth boys. I decided to go and watch one of their lessons. The group was large by public-school standards; five girls and ten boys in a small room. The girls sat in the second row with boys both in front and behind. It was the most boisterous group I had seen and Mr C was having a struggle to control them. He was addressing questions to everyone in turn, but the boys frequently butted in when girls were trying to give their answers. Two lads kept turning round to the girls behind them to borrow pens or snatch the notes they were writing. Many boys were disruptive – joking, chatting and calling out. The teacher had to call them to order and stop girls being interrupted on several occasions. At one point, a female gave a perfect answer. This was greeted by praise from the teacher and groans from some of the boys.

As we walked back to the common room Mr C said that they had been better behaved than usual, and some of the girls verified this later. The problem was that half the lads in the group were in the school rugby team and had what he termed 'a Rambo mentality'. He had reported several of them to their housemasters, but there seemed to be little that could be done because they were not actually behind in their work.

Doing an A-level course, pupils came into contact with only a handful of teachers during the two years. Thus their experience depended upon the personalities with which they interacted. Some girls had no complaints, but others expressed various difficulties. The schools had a proportion of their staff of the 'old school' type; men who had been boarders at boys' schools, gone to single-sex Oxbridge colleges, then, perhaps, into the Forces, before returning, sometimes to the same school, to teach and live among the boys. In short, they had had little experience of girls and exhibited sexist attitudes:

> The married males are fine, especially ones with children. It's the bachelors who are the problem (Head boy, St. Bee's).

The girls felt that a few teachers ignored them completely:

> In class they tend to talk to the boys. It's like we're not in the room, and even the subject of the sentence – 'he', never 'she'; 'Gentlemen' never 'Ladies'; or 'Chaps'...(b2).

Some girls felt intimidated by masters:

> Mr W makes fun of you, so I don't bother to speak (b2).

> Mr G ... will always ask the girls specially if they understand, in a condescending way (b4).

If they were the lone female in the group it was particularly unpleasant:

> Right from the beginning I've felt that he'd rather I wasn't there. He makes me feel stupid when I ask questions if I don't understand. I don't feel comfortable (c3).

I was especially interested to observe classes where there was only one female pupil. Karen of St. Bee's was finding this experience very unnerving. She told me:

> When I walk into my geography class, the only girl in the group, every time before I walk in there – I know I shouldn't – but I

actually brace myself and I feel inferior before I've even walked in.

I decided to attend one of the lessons and at the appointed time she arrived to take me to the correct place. She told me, 'You don't know how good it feels to be walking into that room with another woman.' As it was, we arrived a little late and Karen was immediately reprimanded by the teacher. Feeling it was probably my fault, I stepped forward to apologise and introduce myself. At the words 'researcher from Sussex University', the whole class stood up. 'Oh, please don't bother to stand,' I said graciously. 'They were not standing up for you, they were standing up for Karen,' quipped Mr S, precipitating much laughter. Feeling slightly uncomfortable, I seated myself at the back of the room.

Then another pupil walked through the door. The conversation was as follows:

'Why are you late, lad?'

'She wouldn't let me out, sir,' came the reply.

'Who do you mean – Karen?' And again gales of male laughter. Karen shot me a look.

The lesson finally got under way and towards the end someone asked if their essays had been marked.

'Yes, I've marked them all, except Karen's,' said Mr S.

As we left the room Karen said she thought the remark had been really unfair. She had handed it in late, but so had two of the boys.

Other girls complained of similar experiences:

Certain teachers make it known that you're the only girl and treat you differently. It's not nice (b5).

I was always at the end of his jokes and it was really awful – sat there, and all the boys laughing. To begin with I didn't know how to cope with it – pulling all these gags and me sitting there thinking, 'These aren't funny ...' (d2).

But it was recognized that sometimes the intimidation it produced was unintentional. A boy explained:

Many of them do it to develop a relationship. It's the only way they know to try to get to know the girls. It just happens to come out the wrong way.

Perhaps some masters were trying to cover up their gaucheness:

161

> When they make a joke, they look to see if the girls are laughing. Yes, they're just grown-up schoolboys really (d1).

On the other hand:

> There are teachers who think females are not as good as males. It's very subtle, they never openly admit it. You might be accused of being 'girlie' in a lesson. I'm a girl and I would think it was very natural, but they imply it's a bad thing (b8).

Some teachers openly admitted it:

> Mr P ... he *says* he's an m.c.p. He treats us with indifference (b6).

There was a general opinion, however, that men were more lenient with girls.

> I think he's afraid I might cry if he's too nasty. ...if a boy gets a bad mark he'll be angry about it and the teacher knows how to relate to that, but, with girls, he's on uncertain emotional ground (c1).

For the majority of the girls, learning in a mixed-sex class was a new experience. Many found it very difficult at first. Apart from being shy with new classmates and teachers, they were usually in the minority. For some this resulted in nervousness about making contributions:

> If you say something and it's wrong, you've had it. As long as you're 100 per cent positive you are going to be right, you just timidly put your hand up and offer the answer tentatively (b1).

Being the only girl in the group made it worse:

> I'm absolutely terrified they're going to ask me a question. When they start a discussion, then I get in there as soon as possible, because that breaks the ice. If I leave it and leave it I'll never say anything (b1).

Girls who did speak up in the normal way found that there was opposition. There were many way that boys tried to silence them:

> They turn round and snigger (b1)

> They laugh at us if we get the answer wrong, yawn because we're going slowly (d2).

> Jeering – they do it to everyone, but they do it in a high voice for a girl (d1).

162

The boys used to gang up and talk all the time and put forward the most ridiculously chauvinistic points they could (c1).

Everyone agreed that it was a rare teacher who objected to sexist comments by boys, and that they themselves were quite likely to be the ones to make them:

Some men seem to be deliberately sexist to provoke the girls to defend themselves or say something (c1).

Some think sexism promotes healthy discussion (b9).

Devices for male domination were not employed, however, if the boys were in the minority:

In English there are two more girls than boys, they can't say a thing. It's brilliant! (b1).

There's one set where we have five girls and two boys and I do enjoy it. I say, 'Come and sit next to us, we won't bite you', and they get really agitated. It's quite funny because that's what they do to us (d2).

Because the dominant voices in the classrooms were always male ones, this gave some girls a mistaken impression:

I thought the boys were much more intelligent than the girls, even though I'd been warned before I came that the girls would be more intelligent than the boys. I thought [my parents] must have not known what they were taking about. The boys were so confident, I thought they had it up top as well, and it wasn't until I saw the results of the exams, where all the top places were taken by girls, that I thought, 'Wow, we are more intelligent than them!' (c1).

Girls who excelled invited comment from the boys. 'Girlie swot' was a common rejoinder, but remarks were not always good-natured:

If you beat them they might say, 'You cheated', or, 'Who did you copy it off?'(b2).

Boys seemed to want to give the impression that they did not care about academic achievement. A St. Bee's girl said:

I don't understand why boys won't admit that they're hard workers. Why do they have to pretend that they're just intellectual? (b9).

163

Some boys negated girls' achievements. A girl who came top in an exam was told:

You're a girlie, you don't count – girls always revise (d2).

This made some girls work harder in order to prove themselves, but others hid their talents to avoid comment and notice:

A lot of the girls want to seem like dumb blondes, but they're not dumb really. God, no! Sometimes they come out with intelligent things, but they don't in front of the boys (c7).

A teacher at St. Sea's confirmed this. In her English set, at first, the girls outshone the boys and always beat them. One girl was so embarrassed by this that she began to underachieve markedly until she was moved to a faster group.

BOYS' SPORT AND GIRLS' SPORT

Historically, games have always been important in boys' public schools. They began as competitions within the establishment, and by the end of the nineteenth century they had developed into the inter-school contests that are still an essential feature today.

The possible reasons for this continuing obsession are myriad. Games are not just exciting and fitness-promoting; they require good interpersonal co-operation and engender a strong team spirit. Belonging to an institution whose teams beat others increases the individual's sense of the school's worth. Another popular notion is that games, like cold showers, curb the adolescent sex drive, a desired feature in a single-sex institution. On the other hand, success in 'macho' sports like rugby is seen to confer manliness on the player. Also, sports are deemed to be character-building, the successful player denying individual worth, being brave in the face of adversity, and obeying a leader. Or, as *The Marlburian* put it in 1867, '... a truly chivalrous football player' would be 'never yet guilty of lying, or deceit, or meaness, whether of word or action' (Gathorne-Hardy, 1977).

According to McCrone (1988), this belief in the intimate connection between intellectual and physical health was also held by some of the Victorian reformers of female education. By the late nineteenth century the boarding-schools emulated the male models particularly closely, introducing team games like cricket and hockey alongside the more sedately feminine activities like Swedish drill. In day schools, too, sport became an essential part of the curriculum.

At St. Bee's in 1988, the provision for sport was impressive. There were two afternoons of games per week and inter-school matches on Saturday. As well as the boys' major team games of rugby, hockey and cricket, 13 minor sports were offered, including swimming, sailing, judo, tennis and fencing. An indication of the scale of these activities came from the current school magazine; this had more than one-third of its pages devoted to closely written accounts of teams' successes. But how did the girls feel about it?

> Girls' sport is nothing. It doesn't mean anything to anyone (b7).

> If you're a boy, it's important. If you're a girl, it's just tedious (b2).

They explained:

> Girls don't have a full netball team because there are so few females. Hockey – there's not enough choice out of 45 girls. We need every single fit girl. Most of the time we lose (b1).

Lack of bodies was not the only problem. As in most public schools, the coaching of teams was largely the responsibility of staff employed primarily to teach academic subjects. With the small number of women teachers, expertise in girls' games might have been lacking:

> If we were taught something about tactics we might actually stand a chance. Mrs T [a physics teacher] doesn't really know [enough about it] (b4).

This hampered progress and caused resentment:

> Some of us have been playing hockey for a long time. Clare is an ex-county player, I've played for Crawley. It's quite frustrating when we lose all the time (b4). Our games captain is very good at netball, she was so disheartened at being publicly humiliated by losing, she refused to play and now plays squash instead (b1).

St. Bee's had no changing rooms for females and there were other complaints:

> Girls never use the home pitch. Never. [We have] a half-mile hike down to the council pitches (b2). [The boys] always get the coaches whether it's a major or minor match. We never do. We get a cranky minibus (b1).

They sometimes felt ridiculed.

If someone has to leave a lesson early because of sports, the girls always get laughed at. Boys – it's just accepted it's important. Jokes are always made about girls' sport (b7).

Perhaps there was a better chance of success in individual or small-team games. But participating in these activities was not without its problems. At St. Sea's, a would-be rower told me:

If the girls want a couple of double sculls, we've got to wait until all the boys have come down and the masters have chosen what they want to take out. Then we get what we want, if it's left (c1).

This school also provided a multi-gym for mixed use, but a girl found that:

One ends up treating it as a joke, putting oneself down and getting off apparatus as soon as boys are waiting to use it, even if you've waited ages yourself (c1).

There seemed to be confusion as to whether it was desirable for girls to be sporty. The qualities required, 'competitiveness, aggression and instrumentality', could have been seen as masculine ones (Graydon, 1983) reflecting on the girls' feminity. A girl explained:

In rowing, they like the girls to be slightly refined, but muscley as well. It's a difficult path to tread (c1).

At St. Bee's, if girls did do well, the rewards were minor compared with those for boys; there were no 'colours' awarded to females. The school magazine, with 20 pages of sports' reports, devoted only seven column-inches to girls' achievements. Also, the girls said:

It never gets mentioned in assembly – ten minutes' worth of rugby, hockey, whatever – all boys (b2).

At St. Sea's, however, 'colours' were awarded and they had stopped the traditional cheering in of the first rugby XV to assembly. Nevertheless, inequality was perceived:

They're little things – boys' sport gets into the papers; the cricket results are in the *Telegraph* (c1).

At St. Dee's, during dinner with the female staff, a heated discussion had ensued. The PE teacher was lamenting the girls' lack of motivation and seemed to see it as an inevitable attribute of females of their age. This infuriated one of the other women who rounded on her, waving a wine glass saying, 'If the girls win they get something this size. If the boys win they get one of those...' and she pointed to the massive silver rose bowl in the centre of the table.

PUBLIC-SCHOOL CULTURE

Many girls found the general behaviour of the boys puzzling and difficult to take:

> I went to an all-girls school and I knew a lot of boys outside school and knew how to cope with them. But here the boys are different; emotionally they're different, intellectually they're different, their whole minds are different (c1).

> Coming from a co-ed. school, I've worked with boys before. You might think, 'I've had experience with boys,' but you haven't, not with boys like this (c1).

The boarding life was blamed:

> They can't express their emotions. They have to be tough and 'laddie'. So, [they] can't cry and [they] can't complain, they've got to be good at sport. They're emotionally crippled (c1).

Their relationship with those in power was considered rather unsavoury:

> The boys will do anything to suck up to the staff. I don't think the boys value friendship with [other] boys as much as they do with the staff. They'll 'grass up' [tell tales about] anybody just to get right with that member of staff (c2).

Another St. Sea's pupil put it more succinctly:

> Sport matters, work matters, drama matters: excellence in all things. But people don't, friendships don't (c1).

The boys had a very strict social hierarchy which the girls automatically joined:

> It's hard to define what constitutes a 'lad' or a 'lass'. It's all a question of image, which is absurdly important here, activities, looks, clothes and speech are all under scrutiny. Those from groups considered 'laddish' will not talk to people who are less [socially acceptable] as it is not good for their image. Having

been rejected, these less acceptable people, generally known as 'losers', dissociate themselves from the others.

This had made her life very miserable:

> I couldn't see why I shouldn't fit in as I'd had no problems before. I was shocked at the superficiality and the hypocritical attitudes (c1).

In the first term or so, concern about work took second place to the business of getting to know the opposite sex. The headmaster of St. Bee's described the pupils' behaviour at this time as like that of 'young puppies'. One of his pupils described it differently, however:

> It was like a cattle market. They were all after somebody, each and every one of them (b4).

Many of the pupils were socially inept with the opposite sex. Some boys confided:

> I was really shy ... used to ask really stupid questions like, 'How many O-levels did you get?' It was totally ridiculous. I tried to show off. I was embarrassed.

Girls, too, expressed their insecurities:

> I thought we were really ugly because we didn't get asked out by a million boys. I thought there was something wrong with me, I got such an inferiority complex (b7).

But the girls were not welcomed by all the boys. Their arrival caused disruption to the status quo. A boy said:

> You lose friends. A boy is attracted to a girl and moves towards them and you get left out.

This caused problems for the girls too:

> Before the girls arrive the boys make pacts with each other that they're not going to let the girls break up their friendships. There is a sect of boys like this and they're the most difficult to cope with (c1).

A few months before I visited St. Dee's, a group who called themselves 'The Bugger Off Women Club' had caused some very nasty incidents and, eventually, their activities had been banned by the staff.

All of the girls complained about cruel comments and loutish behaviour from the boys. There were many examples of sexual harassment mentioned to me:

There's some quite physical stuff – like pinging your bra, pulling your skirt down, taking your hair down (d1).

Some boys touch you up every time you walk past, feeling your legs – 'Have you shaved today?' – Some of them put their hand up your skirt (b7).

Boys pour water over girls from the upper windows (Teacher, St. Dee's).

At St. Dee's, verbal abuse was given frequently during 'grief sessions' in the large dining-hall. The girls told me:

You'd get shouted at. Sometimes the entire hall shouting at you, banging their trays on the table. Made you feel sick with nervous apprehension. Some people missed meals because of it (d2).

The perceived beauty of the girls received much attention in the schools:

They judge you by the way you look. They mark you out of ten (C1).

We all get branded 'good-looking' or 'not good-looking'. They class people in the first week and it sticks for two years (d1).

So, popularity revolved around a girl's looks. A St. Sea's girl summed it up most eloquently:

If you're good-looking, then the boys will talk to you. If you're good-looking and haven't got much to say for yourself, or are a bit dim, then you're enigmatic and exciting. If you're not good-looking and you haven't got much to say for yourself, then who the hell are you anyway, and why are you in this school?

But popularity of this type could be ephemeral:

Suddenly she's the centre of attention; all the boys are flocking round her for a whole week. Then, the next week, she'll have done something wrong, some big scandal's going round, and immediately she's a 'cow' and a 'slag' and 'ugly' and no one likes her (c1).

Many girls had found it difficult to have platonic friendships with the boys:

> I've got a friend in the Fifth Form, they think he must be my toy boy and I'm screwing him every weekend. He's one or two years younger than me. Why can't I have a friend? They've been so ... vicious and horrible about the whole thing ... I can't speak to him when I'm in school (b1).

Some boys saw girls as mother-figures, a shoulder to cry on. They wanted sympathy but gave nothing in return:

> Sometimes boys tell you their problems, but not in front of their friends. It's very frustrating. When you think you're getting somewhere you find you're just an emotional buffer. When their friends come in they ignore you (c1).

In the closed community of the boarding school, sexual relationships were always subjected to public scrutiny. Gossip and rumour were rife. A boy explained:

> Girls are very worried about getting a bad reputation, much more than the boys. Boys just get called a 'stud' (b10).

CONCLUSION

The permissive attitudes of the 1960s and the economic climate of the 1970s paved the way for the admittance of girls into boys' public schools. Their presence, particularly in the sixth form, is seen to improve the schools. First they have a civilizing influence:

> Girls are good for boys. They are badly behaved in the fifth form. It makes them grow up (Male teacher, St. Bee's).

> The boarding houses have a better atmosphere because the younger boys can relate to the young mother-figures (Headmaster, St. Dee's).

And, as a consequence, bullying is reduced because, 'As girls are incipient mothers they are protective towards small boys' (Headmaster, St. Sea's).

In many cases, girls raise the academic standard of the school, they increase competition and add to the number of Oxbridge successes.

They broaden discussions by giving 'the woman's view' and improve drama productions, boys no longer having to act the female roles. The girls also provide a more acceptable outlet for male sexuality. Whether this curbs homosexual activity or increases it by stimulating erotic feelings which, for most boys, cannot be assuaged hetero-sexually, it is difficult to say.

But how do the girls benefit? First it is assumed universally that they gain both academically and culturally from the superior facilities and teaching. A study by Fox and Cresser (1987) concluded that girls with good O-level results do well irrespective of the type of sixth form: whether girls', co-educational or mainly boys'. Boys' schools seemed to be attracting girls with slightly better O-level results and encourag-ing them to take more public exams. But, despite the alleged super-iority of facilities, girls' schools retain and encourage the best female scientists and teach mathematics more successfully.

On the other hand, being a girl in a boys' sixth form certainly develops a valuable understanding of the opposite sex:

> I think I now know about the men I may come across as a career woman. I understand men's characters a lot more ... now I'm not going to be daunted by public-school people and I'll be able to give as good as I get (c1).

But, for many girls, this learning experience is a traumatic one:

> It's hardened me up through this gossip ... and nastiness. I've learnt my faults ... because it's been so vicious (b1).

> I have a complete inferiority complex now, since I've been here. I used to be really outgoing and now I'm not at all. It's really sad (b7).

At St. Dee's, an ex-girls' school pupil said:

> If you get through this place sane, you'll get through a lot of situations.... You're put through unnecessary pressure, things you wouldn't normally find at a girls' day school – You don't have to worry about [having your] skirt whipped down to your ankles [for instance]! (d1).

The public schools I studied differed from truly co-educational schools because of the unequal numbers of the sexes. They were 'boys' schools with girls', and the experience of their female pupils was modified by this. The current movement to have girls throughout the school, not just in the sixth form, could be seen as an improvement, but, I discovered, each school was aiming eventually to have boys and girls in the ratio of two to one.

The reasons given for this by the three headmasters were, to me, astounding:

> We cannot have 50 per cent girls because the character of the school is boys' sport, and if we had too few boys the standard of rugby would suffer (St. Bee's).

> Two boys to every one girl reflects the ratio in the universities (St. Sea's).

And from St. Dee's, which has had girls in the sixth form for nearly 20 years: 'You can't change a traditional boys' school too quickly.' It seems that a female presence is acceptable only if it is small. Girls may adorn the school, but must not alter it. Equal numbers are considered undesirable because it is felt that girls will dominate. It is considered important to maintain the status quo.

As the minority, girls are subjected to 'stereotyping, mistaken assumptions and biased judgements which tend to force [them] into playing limited and caricatured roles' (Kanter, 1977). They find themselves under scrutiny at all times. Whether it is their perceived beauty, the clothes they wear, or the loudness of their voices, they are expected to conform to a restricted notion of femininity. As one girl put it: 'You do better in a school like this if you're a "girlie-girlie" girl' (c1).

Girls who do conform are beatified. Should they reveal their fallibility by erring, then they are likely to experience the uncomfortable effects of disapproval by the male majority. It is the madonna/whore dichotomy. The sexual double standard prevails. With the boys, sexual adventuring is admired and encouraged, but females, while doing all they can to attract, must guard their reputations, because they are vulnerable to coercion, exploitation and, of course, pregnancy.

Being in the minority makes it difficult to alter sexist practices that make life uncomfortable for girls. An ex-pupil explained why she had never complained:

> for fear of retaliation from the boys and an unsympathetic response from the teachers.... As long as one remained within certain boundaries one was treated well. To step outside was to invite the full weight of a chauvinistic institution upon one's self.

172

This feeling of powerlessness and isolation within the institution was compounded by the very small number of possible allies in authority – that is, adult women.

The traditional role of the public school is to teach boys to rule:

School fees buy far more than exam success. They are the admission charge for a ruling elite whose wealth gives power and whose power gives wealth (Labour Party, 1980).

This elite is largely male. Girls of the upper classes enter it usually by a 'good' marriage. Many public-school boys see females as non-working wives, and the paucity of women on the staff does nothing to contradict that notion. There is no place within this milieu for strong, independent women. Girls who show these traits are at risk of being thought deviant. The words 'feminist' and 'lesbian' were used as terms of abuse towards them.

What schoolgirls need is to be able to learn and develop in a sympathetic atmosphere, in which the interests and aspirations of women are considered paramount. Boys' public schools do not provide this.

REFERENCES

Cohen, L., and Manion, L. (1985) *Research Methods in Education*. Beckenham: Croom Helm.

Delamont, S. (1984) 'The Old Girl Network: Reflections on the Fieldwork at St Luke's', in R.G. Burgess (ed.), *The Research Process in Educational Settings: Ten Case Studies*. Lewes: Falmer.

Fox, I., and Cresser, R. (1987) *Girls in the Boys' Public Schools*. Girls' Schools Association.

Gathorne–Hardy, J. (1977) *The Public School Phenomenon*. London: Hodder & Stoughton.

Graydon, J. (1983) ' "But it's more than a game. It's an institution." Feminist Perspectives on Sport', *Feminist Review*, 13: 5–18.

Independent Schools Information Service (1989) *Annual Census*. London: ISIS.

Johnson, D. (1987) *Private Schools and State Schools. Two Systems or One?* Milton Keynes: Open University Press.

Kanter, R.M. (1977) *Men and Women of the Corporation*. New York: Basic Books.

Labour Party (1980) *Private Schools. A Labour Party Discussion Document*. London: Labour Party.

Lees, S. (1986) *Losing Out. Sexuality and Adolescent Girls*. London: Hutchinson.

Mahony, P. (1985) *Schools for the Boys?* London: Hutchinson.

McCrone, K.E. (1988) *Sport and the Physical Emancipation of English Women 1870–1914*. London: Routledge.

Oakley, A. (1981) 'Interviewing Women: A Contradiction in Terms', in H. Roberts (ed.), *Doing Feminist Research*. London: Routledge & Kegan Paul.

Rae, J. (1981) *The Public School Revolution*. London: Faber & Faber.

Rich, A. (1979) *On Lies, Secrets and Silence*. London: Virago.

Spender, D. (1982) *Invisible Women. The Schooling Scandal*. London: Writers and Readers.

Walford, G. (1986) *Life in Public Schools*. London: Methuen.

8

Take Three Girls:
A Comparison of Girls' A-level Achievement in Three Types of Sixth Form within the Independent Sector

ROSEMARY CRESSER

In seeking to explain the motives for the research that forms the basis of this chapter, various factors vie for prominence. However, the overriding motive must be seen as a concern on behalf of the Girls' Schools Association (GSA) regarding the increasing numbers of girls leaving girls-only schools post-16, at the end of the fifth year, to take up a sixth-form place in one of the former boys-only schools.

Since the early 1970s this phenomenon has been gaining momentum. The movement is virtually in one direction and represents a serious loss in the number of girls attending girls-only schools. The girls' schools have neither the resources nor the will to accept boys into their schools. Walford (1986) reports that while the boys-only schools increased in size, the number of girls aged 11 and over in GSA/GBGSA schools fell significantly between the mid-1970s and mid-1980s.

At the onset of the research it was felt that changes in the admission policies of many of the former boys-only schools had been prompted more by a need to restore diminishing school rolls than by a deep-seated belief in the education of girls. Walford (1983) has already suggested, in an earlier small-scale study of staff working in a boys-only school within the independent sector, that the schools saw two clear alternatives to the problem of diminishing school rolls. According to a school's particular needs, this could be to encourage more foreign entrants, or to offer sixth-form places to girls. Several of the staff who were interviewed saw the introduction of girls at sixth-form level as preferable, because of the problems associated with introducing foreign entrants at a time when students are expected to play an important part in the smooth running of the school.

This concern over the increasing number of girls choosing to complete their studies in the sixth form of a former boys-only school was accompanied by a renewed interest in girls' educational experiences in general and in their academic achievement in particular. The acquisition of academic qualifications is now essential to enter universities and other higher-education establishments, the professions and the world of work. If girls are to be able to compete, then they need to be able to obtain the academic qualifications that represent the passport to entry to each of these spheres. In particular, they need to achieve academic success in the sciences, where they are at present grossly under-represented.

Within the maintained sector, the DES Circular 10/65 spurred the move towards secondary schools modelled along comprehensive lines. This was accompanied by the move towards co-education. Both of these changes were welcomed, for it was believed that they would lead to greater equality of opportunity, both between the social classes and the sexes. From its onset, researchers have sought to compare the effects of single-sex as opposed to co-educational schooling on girls' academic achievement.

Reginald Dale's work for the DES, carried out between 1969 and 1974, may be seen as one of the earliest attempts to assess the effects of the demise of single-sex education within the maintained sector. From this, Dale (1969 and 1974) concluded that the segregation of the sexes for the purpose of education was an artificial one and that the average co-educational grammar school was a happier place, for both staff and students, than the average single-sex school. Dale claimed to have demonstrated that this happiness was not at the expense of academic success. However, this is not altogether convincing and it is possible that the effects of co-education on girls' academic achievement were neglected in Dale's desire to pursue other issues.

More recently, Bone (1983) carried out a review of the various research reports published since the move away from single-sex schooling. Data from the report were used to assess whether girls in single-sex schools achieved better academic results and to what extent they have greater freedom to pursue courses, and therefore careers, that do not conform to sex-stereotypes. Although in general the evidence was confirmatory, it is difficult on the basis of the data to disentangle the effects of single-sex education from those of selective education. (The review identified that single-sex education was more commonly concentrated within selective grammar, direct grant and independent schools.) It is possible that the improved academic results that the review identified were associated more with the

175

school's academic tradition and the ability of such schools to recruit pupils of a higher academic calibre, than the fact that pupils are educated in a single-sex environment.

Shortly after this, Steedman (1983) published the results of research using the National Child Development Study (NCDS), a national cohort study of all individuals born in Great Britain in one week in 1958. The research, which was based on the examination results of over 7,500 16-year-olds, controlled for a number of factors – including the student's home background, the type of school attended, and a measure of the student's ability at age 11. The work showed that controlling for these factors resulted in a reduction in many of the differences between the examination results obtained in mixed and single-sex schools. A particular interest in the girls' O-level science results led Steedman to discover that as far as their performance in chemistry and physics was concerned, there appeared to be little advantage in girls-only as opposed to co-educational schools.

ILEA (1982) have also published research, focusing on the academic performance of a cohort of 16-year-olds in mixed and single-sex schools. This showed that, without controlling for the child's ability at intake, results were higher for both boys and girls who attended single-sex schools. However, an adjustment for the child's ability at intake caused some divergence in the results – differences between the academic performance of boys in co-educational and single-sex schools were reduced, whereas those between the girls remained.

The work of Steedman and the Research and Statistics Branch of the now demised ILEA have made a considerable contribution to the debate focusing on the effects of single-sex as opposed to co-education. By taking into account the child's ability at intake, both studies were able to go some way towards assessing the extent to which the superior academic performance of girls in single-sex schools is the result of their recruitment policies. By choosing to focus on 16-year-olds, both of the reports are limited, in the sense that they neglected the academic achievements obtained post-16 which are so crucial for higher study and entry to the professions. Furthermore, although Steedman's report covered children in the independent sector, the numbers of such children, even from a sample of over 7,500, were small.

Concern over the increasing numbers of girls leaving girls-only schools post-16 was important in influencing the GSA's final decision to fund a researcher to evaluate the effects on girls' academic achievement of completing their studies in different types of sixth form (Fox and Cresser, 1986). In order to assess these effects, we chose to set up a research study focusing on the quantitative aspects of academic achievement. The findings of this study, which are of a preliminary nature, form the basis of this chapter.

THE OBJECTIVES OF THE STUDY

A combination of the factors outlined above provided the researchers with a main objective – to assess to what extent the type of sixth form attended affected the overall A-level results of girls educated within the independent sector.

The study provided an additional opportunity to assess the effects of type of sixth form in relation to the number of 'B' grades and above achieved by pupils at A-level and, within this group, the effects of type of sixth form on the results of the small sub-group of pupils who obtained at least three 'B' grades. The rationale behind this was to determine the extent to which the type of sixth form attended was significant in explaining the academic achievement of pupils whose A-level grades fulfilled the minimum-entry requirements of the more prestigious universities.

Within the school curriculum, the subjects in which girls' examination performance has generated the most concern are those comprising the hard sciences: namely mathematics, physics and chemistry. Those advocating single-sex education for girls have suggested that their biggest contribution may be in the teaching of these subjects. It is suggested that girls are freer in a girls-only school to pursue those subjects that do not conform to a feminine stereotype, and where they are not exposed to the teasing and innuendo from male classmates that have been identified by Kelly (1981) and DES/HMI (1980). However, Walford (1986) found that in 1984 the proportion of girls in HMC schools who took only maths and science A-levels was far less than among their male counterparts, and slightly less than the proportion of girls who studied these subjects in girls-only schools.

The final objective of the present study was therefore to assess the effects of school type on girls' sixth-form performance in the hard sciences. Within this small group of subjects, Bone (1983) identified physics as the subject that girls are least likely even to attempt. While Bone's work identified an improvement in physics performance in some girls-only schools within the maintained sector, the evidence was not conclusive. This provided one final objective – to explore the effect of school type on girls' A-level performance in physics, while controlling for prior achievement in the subject.

177

A NOTE ON METHODOLOGY

Information was obtained from a random sample of schools which were stratified according to the following factors: school type (girls-only, fully co-educational, co-educational sixth form within a former boys-only establishment); sixth-form size (expressed as a proportion of the total school size; day or boarding status; and the association to which the head belonged. Although the Independent Schools Information Service (ISIS) was able to provide information on sixth-form size, the number of girls who had attempted A-level examinations in 1983 was unknown. For this reason, the research made use of a multi-stage sampling method that sampled schools with probability proportional to a 'measure of size' – in this case, the number of girls in the sixth form.

The following sampling formula was used in each stratum:

Cumulative total in the sixth form divided by the number required in stratum = X

Take a random number between 1 and X, e.g. Y

First selection = Y

Second selection = $Y + X$, etc.

The method yielded 47 girls-only, 27 fully co-educational and 30 former boys-only schools. Of the 104 schools selected, 78 returned questionnaires providing information from existing school records on those girls who had taken A-levels in the summer of 1983. For both the fully co-educational and former boys-only schools, the most important reason for non-response was the incorrect inclusion of schools with no female A-level candidates in 1983. The questionnaires generated data for a total of 2,385 girls. Of these, 1,623 had attempted A-levels in a girls-only school, 325 in a fully co-educational school, and 436 in the co-educational sixth form of a former boys-only school.

To explore the effects of the type of sixth form attended on the girls' academic performance, analysis of covariance was used. An explanation of this method may be found in Ferguson (1966). This involved a regression of various measures of A-level performance on the type of sixth form attended, while controlling for academic achievement before sixth-form entry and the number of A-levels attempted. The need to control for the number of A-levels attempted arose because of differences between the numbers of A-levels undertaken by pupils in the three types of schools. Inclusion of the number of A-levels as an additional control ensured that any observed differences, between the three types of school, in the measures of A-level academic achievement, may be attributed to the type of sixth form attended, rather than to differences in the number of A-levels for which pupils were entered.

Given that over 70 per cent of the girls had fathers whose occupation may be included in social class I of Goldthorpe's class scheme (Goldthorpe, 1980), it was decided not to control for social-class background.

Measures of A-level academic achievement were constructed by assigning a score ranging from 13 to 17 to each of the A-level grades and a score of 7 for each A-level that resulted in an O-level pass. The scale 13–17 may be thought of as an extension of the scale developed by the ILEA Research and Statistics Branch to quantify O-level

TABLE 8.1

A COMPARISON OF THE ACADEMIC ACHIEVEMENT OF GIRLS WHO
TOOK A-LEVELS IN 1983

Type of school	Girls-only	Co-ed.	Boys
No. of O-levels achieved	8.00	7.48	8.18
No. of A-levels attempted	3.06	3.04	3.23
No. of A-levels achieved	2.70	2.50	2.95
A-level success rate (%)	88.0	82.0	91.0
Total A-level score	42.95	40.42	46.45
No. of grade A/B A-levels	2.08	1.82	2.04
Hard sciences			
Total A-level score	28.01	23.68	26.89
No. of grade A/B A-levels	0.90	0.69	0.74
% of all A-level attempts in the hard sciences	26.9	25.3	24.0

achievement. To produce a measure of total academic achievement at A-level, all of these scores were summed; a measure of A-level achievement in the hard sciences was obtained by including only those scores relating to the appropriate A-level subjects.

RESULTS

Results are presented in the form of 'school sector' means both before and after controlling for prior academic achievement, and in the form of significance tests.

The results of the preliminary analyses included in Table 8.1 show that girls entering the co-educational sixth forms of boys-only schools did so with a higher mean number of O-levels than either those who remained in their own sixth forms or those who chose to complete their secondary education in a fully co-educational school.

It appears that this pattern is also reflected in the variation between

179

the raw scores of many of the measures of total A-level achievement included in Table 8.1. However, this pattern is partially reversed for girls' performance in the hard sciences. While those girls educated in fully co-educational schools retain their position at the bottom of the ranking, girls in the girls-only schools appear to obtain higher results in these subjects than their counterparts who chose to take A-levels in the co-educational sixth form of a former boys-only school. Further-more, it appears that girls who remained in girls-only schools are most likely to have attempted a hard science.

TABLE 8.2
A COMPARISON OF THE A-LEVEL RESULTS ACHIEVED
BY GIRLS IN 1983

Measure of academic achievement	Before		After	Significance level
NO. OF A-LEVELS				
1. Controlling for number of O-levels obtained				
All pupils	2.70	G	2.69	
	2.50	C	2.62	
	2.95	B	2.90	.001
Single-sex only	2.70	G	2.71	
	2.95	B	2.91	.001
2. Controlling for number of O-levels and number of A-levels attempted				
All pupils	2.70	G	2.72	
	2.50	C	2.61	
	2.95	B	2.79	.001
Single-sex only	2.70	G	2.74	
	2.95	B	2.80	Not significant
TOTAL A-LEVEL SCORE				
1. Controlling for O-level score				
All pupils	42.94	G	42.78	
	40.42	C	42.56	
	46.45	B	45.47	.001
Single-sex only	42.95	G	43.13	
	46.45	B	45.79	.001
2. Controlling for O-level score and the number of A-levels attempted				
All pupils	42.94	G	43.27	
	40.42	C	42.31	
	46.45	B	43.82	.025
Single-sex only	42.95	G	43.57	
	46.45	B	44.14	Not significant

Note: G = girls-only schools
C = fully co-educational schools
B = former boys-only schools with a co-educational sixth form

The results of these preliminary analyses showed that there was a difference between the schools, not only with respect to the number of O-levels that the girls were bringing with them, but also with regard to the number of A-levels for which the girls were entered. Table 8.2 shows the results after controlling for both of these variables. The results of analyses focusing on all three types of school and those restricted to single-sex schools are reported separately.

Table 8.2 shows that the number of A-levels obtained is significantly greater in the former boys-only schools than in either the girls-only or co-educational schools, even after allowing for previous academic achievement. Examination of the results reveals that this is largely explained by the greater number of A-levels for which girls in boys-only schools were entered, and that once an allowance had been made for this the difference between the results in the girls-only and

TABLE 8.3

A COMPARISON OF THE A-LEVEL RESULTS, AT B GRADE AND
ABOVE, ACHIEVED BY GIRLS IN 1983

Measure of analysis	Before		After	Significance level
NO. OF GRADE A/BS				
1. Controlling for number of grade A O-levels and the number of A-levels attempted				
All pupils	2.08	G	2.05	
	1.82	C	1.97	
	2.04	B	2.03	Not significant
Single-sex only	2.08	G	2.07	
	2.04	B	2.05	Not significant
AT LEAST 3 GRADE B A-LEVELS				
1. Controlling for number of grade A O-levels and the number of A-levels attempted				
All pupils	3.21	G	3.21	
	3.29	C	3.29	
	3.23	B	3.22	Not significant
Single-sex only	3.21	G	3.21	
	3.23	B	3.22	Not significant

Note: G = girls-only schools
C = fully co-educational schools
B = former boys-only schools with a co-educational sixth form

former boys-only schools is no longer significant. It appears that the number of A-levels achieved by girls in fully co-educational schools is significantly lower than their counterparts in the girls-only schools, even after controlling for academic achievement at intake and the number of A-levels attempted.

A similar pattern of results is observed for the second measure of academic achievement or total A-level score.

Table 8.3 focuses on A-level achievement at grade B and above. It has already been established that girls in the co-educational sixth form of a boys-only school are entered for and obtain a greater number of A-levels than their counterparts in girls-only or fully co-educational schools (see Table 8.1). However, in terms of the higher A-level grades, there appears to be no significant advantage for those girls chosing to complete their studies in the co-educational sixth form of a boys-only school, once an allowance has been made for prior academic achievement and the numbers of A-levels attempted.

Table 8.4 is concerned exclusively with the girls' A-level achievement in the hard sciences. The raw data show that those girls who remained in the girls-only schools are more likely to attempt at least one hard science A-level and to score higher in these subjects. While

TABLE 8.4

A COMPARISON OF A-LEVEL RESULTS* IN THE HARD
SCIENCES ACHIEVED BY GIRLS IN 1983

Measure of analysis	Before		After	Significance level
Hard science A-level score				
1. Controlling for prior O-level score and the number of hard science A-levels attempted				
All pupils	28.01	G	27.44	
	23.68	C	25.69	
	26.89	B	27.50	.01 % level
Single-sex only	28.01	G	27.76	
	26.88	B	27.81	Not significant
No. of grade A/Bs				
1. Controlling for number of grade A O-levels obtained and the number of hard science A-levels attempted				
All pupils	0.90	G	0.85	
	0.69	C	0.86	
	0.74	B	0.76	Not significant
Single-sex only	0.90	G	0.88	
	0.74	B	0.79	Not significant
Physics only				
1. Controlling for O-level score in Physics				
All pupils	14.03	G	14.03	
	13.53	C	13.53	
	14.30	B	14.35	Not significant
Single-sex only	14.03	G	14.02	
	14.30	B	14.34	Not significant

Note: G = girls-only schools
C = fully co-educational schools
B = former boys-only schools with a co-educational sixth form

*Only hard science O- and A- levels were included in the analyses that form the basis of these results.

these data seem to support the view that a girls-only school is the most conducive environment for girls to succeed in the hard sciences, the remaining results do not altogether sustain this. For it appears that once an allowance has been made for prior achievement and the number of A-levels attempted, the girls in girls-only schools have little or no significant advantage over their peers in boys-only schools. The science results of girls educated in fully co-educational schools remain almost consistently lower.

DISCUSSION

Once an allowance has been made for prior academic achievement and the number of A-levels attempted, it appears that girls who are educated in the sixth form of a fully co-educational school achieve poorer academic results than their peers in single-sex schools. A similar pattern is observed for overall A-level results and achievement in the hard sciences. Those results focusing on girls' achievement in the hard sciences appear to confirm the findings of research carried out in the maintained sector, such as that of Steedman (1983), which show a small advantage in favour of girls educated in girls-only schools. However, this conclusion cannot be extended to those girls who chose to complete their secondary studies in the co-educational sixth form of a boys-only school.

Preliminary findings suggest that the boys-only schools are successful in attracting the most academically able girls, in terms of their prior O-level achievement, and that these girls are encouraged to take a higher number of A-levels than those who remain in girls-only schools. The ultimate outcome of this may not necessarily be a positive one, particularly if the number of A-levels to be entered for is set at an unrealistically high level. It is possible that the pressure to take more examinations may be at the expense of a more rounded and balanced education.

Differences between the overall achievement of girls in girls-only and girls in boys-only schools may largely be explained by the high number of A-levels taken by girls in the boys' schools. Furthermore, there is little to suggest that the type of school attended is significant in explaining girls' academic achievement, in terms of the higher A-level grades that are required to gain entry to the more prestigious universities and higher-education establishments. However, it is important to note at this point that the measure used to compare the higher A-level grades made no distinction between subjects. It is quite possible that the higher A-level grades achieved by girls in girls-only schools may relate to an entirely different group of subjects than those obtained by girls in former boys-only schools.

One of the most persuasive claims made by the boys-only schools is that they possess superior facilities, particularly with respect to the teaching of maths and science. In the absence of any hard evidence to the contrary, it is likely that this is one of the main attractions influencing girls to complete their studies in the co-educational sixth form of a boys-only school. One of the final issues that the research had hoped to explore was the extent to which girls who enter boys-only schools profit from the superior science facilities that are used to attract them at the onset.

Findings from the research suggest quite a different scenario, for it appears that it is the girls who remain in single-sex schools who are most likely to be entered for a hard science A-level and subsequently to obtain better results. It is particularly interesting to note that girls in girls-only schools are more likely to achieve the higher A/B grade A-levels in the hard sciences, than those who may have been attracted by polished marketing skills and the claims of superior science facilities to enter the co-educational sixth form of a boys-only school. Although tests carried out on these results fell short of the levels normally associated with statistical significance, the results in themselves are interesting and require further analysis.

The data that form the basis of this chapter relate to a sample of girls who took A-level examinations within the independent sector in 1983. As the study had an additional objective that has not been covered here – to obtain information on the girls' career destinations – it was decided to collect information on those who had taken examinations in the summer of 1983, rather than a more recent year. It is quite possible that a replication of this study, using more recent information, would produce quite a different pattern of results reflecting the continuing changes taking place within the independent sector.

By choosing to focus exclusively on quantitative measures of girls' achievement at A-level, it was not possible to explore the more qualitative issues (of girls' education) that may have helped to shed some light on the reasons why girls chose to move to the co-educational sixth form of a boys-only school. Similarly, qualitative work would be extremely valuable in helping to explain why girls in the girls-only schools achieved better science results. Researchers working both within the maintained and independent sectors have offered a number of possible explanations for the superior academic achievement of girls in girls-only schools. It has been suggested that the environment of a girls-only school offers girls a wide range of potential role models. Moreover, it has been shown that women teachers are more likely to occupy positions of higher status, particularly as the heads of science and mathematics departments, in single-sex rather than co-educational schools. Although recent years have seen an increase in the number of women teachers working in boys-only schools affiliated to the HMC, Walford (1986) has identified that most are concentrated in positions of low status and power.

At the same time as this research was being carried out, detailed plans were made to redress this perceived imbalance (of quantitative versus qualitative research) by following up this work with an in-depth qualitative study, to explore the attitudes and experiences of those girls educated within the independent sector. Sadly, the sudden and untimely death in autumn 1987 of Irene Fox who initiated and led the research, and whose enthusiasm for the subject influenced all of those involved, meant that these plans have yet to be realized. It is hoped that the inclusion of this chapter in this book may provoke the further research that is required to answer some of the questions that a quantitative study of girls' academic achievement is unqualified to answer.

ACKNOWLEDGEMENTS

I would like to acknowledge the help and assistance offered by the following individuals and organizations. First and foremost, the Girls' Schools Association (GSA) provided funding for a full-time researcher. I am most grateful to Dick Wiggins, formerly of the Polytechnic of Central London, for his support and expert statistical advice, and also to Peter Cuttance, formerly of the Department of Educational Sociology, Edinburgh University. I would also like to thank Maria Tuck at the Polytechnic of Central London Computing Centre, who provided the all-important computing assistance. Last, but not least, I would like to thank all of the staff in the participating schools who helped to provide us with the information; without this, the research would not have been possible.

REFERENCES

Bone, A. (1983) *Girls and Girls-only Schools: A Review of the Evidence*. Manchester: Equal Opportunities Commission.
Dale, R.R. (1969) *Mixed or Single-sex School? Volume I Pupil–Teacher Relationships*. London: Routledge & Kegan Paul.
Dale, R.R. (1974) *Mixed or Single-sex School? Volume III Attainment. Attitudes and Overview*. London: Routledge & Kegan Paul.
DES/HMI (Department of Education and Science) (1980) *Girls and Science: A Report on an Enquiry Carried out in 1978 into the Teaching of Science to Girls in Co-educational Comprehensive Schools and an Assessment of the Factors Influencing Their Choice of Science Subjects*, HMI Series, Matters for discussion, 13, 1080. London: HMSO.

Ferguson, G.A. (1966) *Statistical Analysis in Psychology and Education*. London: McGraw–Hill.

Fox, I., and Cresser, R. (1986) 'The Class of 1983: A Comparison of the A-level Results Obtained by Girls in Different Sixth Forms within the Independent Sector', unpublished research.

Goldthorpe, J. (1980) *Social Mobility and Class Structure in Modern Britain*. Oxford: Clarendon Press.

ILEA (Inner London Education Authority) (1982) *Sex Differences and Achievement*, RS 823/82. London: Inner London Education Authority Research and Statistics Branch.

Kelly, A. (1981) *The Missing Half: Girls and Science Education*. Manchester: Manchester University Press.

Steedman, J. (1983) *Examination Results in Mixed and Single Sex Schools: Findings from the National Child Development Study*. Manchester: Equal Opportunities Commission.

Walford, G. (1983) 'Girls in Boys' Public Schools: A Prelude to Further Research', *British Journal of Sociology of Education*, 4, 1: 39–54.

Walford, G. (1986) *Life in Public Schools*. London: Methuen.

9

Religion in the Girls' Independent Schools

BRENDA GAY

The majority of independent schools in England claim a religious affiliation either by foundation or tradition. In an earlier study (Gay, 1985), I examined the public statements made about themselves by 458 independent schools listed in either *The Public and Preparatory Schools Yearbook* or *The Girls' School Yearbook*, for 1983. This study yielded a considerable amount of information. The statements made by the 46 per cent of schools that described themselves as Church of England were subjected to detailed analysis. This revealed a considerable input by clerics as governors, teachers, chaplains and heads; opportunities for worship at Assembly, Sunday services and major school services; the place of religious studies and religious education in the curriculum; and the stated effect of a school's religious affiliation on its corporate life and ethos. The study concluded with a plea for further in-depth research to investigate what lay behind the public statements, as it was clear from a review of the literature on independent schools that little empirical research had been done on the independent schools in general or the religious dimension in particular since the late 1960s and early 1970s. Although there have been some research on the independent schools (for example, Rae, 1989; Walford, 1986, 1989), the religious dimension is not treated in any great depth.

To remedy this gap in our knowledge of an important aspect of the schools, a number of strategies were considered. As my own career in the independent sector as a head and a teacher has been in girls' schools, I decided to make a study of a number of girls' independent schools. Initial wide-ranging discussions were conducted with a number of girls' school heads and pupils. From the discussions with heads, a number of themes emerged: religion was perceived to be a great help in handling personal crises – particularly in helping pupils cope with grief; school worship both at Assembly and special services offered

187

opportunities for pupil involvement in a way that was not possible in the context of a parish church service, and could be oriented to the needs of pupils; major school services provided occasions for worship that reached beyond the immediate school community to the families of pupils. It was argued that the Christian school could show pupils how to use their talents and money in the service of others, and this began in the school community as pupils learnt to take responsibility for others.

Informal discussions with pupils revealed more about their attitudes to religion in general than to specific aspects of institutional practice. Like the heads, many pupils talked of the help of religion in times of difficulty or crisis. Religious education lessons were valued for the opportunity they provided for working out images of God and for examining moral, social and ethical issues. Interestingly, even at age 13 or 14, many pupils retained traces of an anthropomorphic picture of God. School was seen as supporting their home practices by those whose parents were church-goers, whereas for others their only contact with church services was through school. The greatest scepticism, and even hostility, was from pupils who resented the compulsory nature of school religion.

These discussions helped identify areas that needed more detailed examination. To gain a broad picture of current practice in schools, a questionnaire was sent to the heads of the 56 independent schools in the South East region of the Girls' Schools Association (GSA), seeking both qualitative and quantitative information. There were six groups of questions that were concerned with: the style of the school (in terms of size, age range, religious affiliation and proportion boarding); chapels and chaplaincy provision; worship; religious education; school ethos; and parental interest in the school's religious dimension. As well as giving factual information, heads were invited to comment freely on the perceived importance of school worship and religious education and the effect of the school's religious affiliation on school ethos and corporate life.

The questionnaires were sent out in September 1990 at the beginning of the school year. The high response rate, 49 out of 56 (87 per cent), suggests that heads viewed the topic as one of concern. Many commented in considerable detail on the open-ended questions, and a selection of these comments is included at appropriate points in the discussion below. Where there were significant differences between style of school in terms of either residential or religious dimension, the analysis reflects this. However, interestingly, on many issues, denominational differences were not apparent. In the numerical totals and percentages only the results of the 49 schools that responded to the questionnaire are used.

CHARACTERISTICS OF THE SURVEY SCHOOLS

The South East region of the Girls' Schools Association covers part of Hampshire and the Isle of Wight, Surrey, East and West Sussex and part of Kent. The Schools are located in urban and rural settings, outer London, and parts of the Home Counties commuter belt. The

TABLE 9.1

SCHOOL SIZE

School size	No. of schools	% of total
200 and under	4	8.2
201–300	14	28.6
301–400	5	10.2
401–500	15	32.6
501–600	4	8.2
601–700	3	6.1
over 700	4	8.2
Total	49	100.1

region includes large, medium and small schools, day schools, and schools with a boarding element. Some schools have junior departments and some carer for kindergarten pupils. Thus a variety of schools providing a fairly typical cross-section of girls' independent schools was included in the survey, although the geographical concentration on the South East means that the results may not be generalizable to the rest of Britain.

Table 9.1 shows that only a small number of schools had fewer than 200 pupils, or more than 600. The majority, 34 (71 per cent), were in the range 200 to 500.

Thirty-seven of the schools (76 per cent) had junior departments and, of these, 32 had pre-prep departments starting at age five, or in some cases age three. Only two schools did not have a sixth form.

Heads were asked to categorize their schools on a residential continuum from total day to total boarding. In day/boarding schools it is the day pupils who form the majority; and in boarding/day schools, it is the boarders. Table 9.2 shows that almost two-thirds of the

189

schools have a boarding element and only two schools are exclusively boarding.

TABLE 9.2
THE RESIDENTIAL DIMENSION

Residential style	No of schools	% of total
Total day	17	34.7
Day/boarding	13	26.5
Equal nos. day/boarders	5	10.2
Boarding/day	12	24.5
Total boarding	2	4.1
Total	49	100.0

Heads were asked to describe the religious affiliation of their school according to one of six categories – Church of England, Roman Catholic, Free Church, Inter-denominational, Non-denominational and Other (see Table 9.3). Thirty-two schools claimed specific denominational allegiance with the 24 Church of England schools forming the largest single denominational group. There were six Roman Catholic, one Free Church, and one former Quaker school. Thirteen of the schools were inter-denominational. Two of the five non-denominational schools considered themselves 'non denominational but with an Anglican ethos', and 'officially non denominational but with an Anglican tradition – school chaplain, confirmation', respectively.

TABLE 9.3
RELIGIOUS AFFILIATION

Religious affiliation	No of schools	% of total
C of E	24	49.0
R. C.	6	12.2
Free Church	1	2.0
Other	1	2.0
Inter-denom.	13	26.5
Non-denom.	5	10.2
Total	49	99.9

When the residential and religious affiliation are taken together just over half the day schools were either inter- or non-denominational (see Table 9.4). The boarding schools were more likely, however, to be affiliated to a particular denomination. Nineteen of them are Church of England, four Roman Catholic and one Free Church.

190

CHAPELS AND CHAPLAINS

My 1985 study showed that, among Church of England schools, girls' schools were less likely than boys' schools to have a chapel. It is difficult to assess whether the presence or absence of a chapel building affects the religious dimension and general ethos of a school. One head raised this point in our informal discussions, comparing her present school – which did not have a chapel – with her previous school, which did. In the latter, she had found there were certain occasions when the separateness and special identity of the chapel building had proved beneficial.

Among the survey schools, chapels appeared to be a feature more of the predominantly boarding schools and of schools with a specific denominational affiliation. Thus only three day schools (two Church of England and one Roman Catholic) and only three day/boarding schools (all Church of England) had chapels. The two totally boarding schools (both Church of England), four schools with equal numbers of day pupils and boarders (three Church of England one Roman Catholic) and nine boarding/day schools (four Church of England, three Roman Catholic, one Free Church and one inter-denominational) had chapels. When schools of all residential type are taken together, all the Roman Catholic, the one Free Church, but only half of the Church of England and one inter-denominational school, had chapels.

Independent schools offer a significant opportunity for ministry by the ordained clergy. In boys' schools, clerics feature as heads, chaplains, teachers and housemasters. Girls' schools are less likely to have full-time chaplains or ordained members of staff. Chaplains are more likely to be either jointly appointed to the school and parish, or

TABLE 9.4
RELIGIOUS AFFILIATION AND RESIDENTIAL DIMENSION
(the percentage refers to the proportion in each residential category)

	Day		Boarding		Equal Nos. day and boarding		Day/ boarding		Boarding/ day	
	No.	%	No.	%	No.	%	No.	%	No.	%
C of E	5	25	2	100	4	80	8	61.5	5	41
R. C.	2	12.5	0	0	1	20	0	0	3	25
Free Church	0	0	0	0	0	0	0	0	1	8.3
Other	1	6.2	0	0	0	0	5	38.5	0	0
Inter-denom.	6	37.5	0	0	0	0	0	0	2	16.6
Non-denom.	3	18.6	0	0	0	0	0	0	1	8.3
Total	17	99.8	2	100	5	100	13	100	12	100.0

191

to be the local parish priest who allots a certain amount of time to duties in school. Among the sample of girls' schools, only three Church of England, the one Free Church, and one Roman Catholic school had full-time chaplains. The latter was the only day school to have a full-time chaplain. Among the day schools, only two (one Roman Catholic and one Church of England) used the local parish priest. Both the totally boarding schools and 15 of all the other schools with a boarding element had part-time chaplains, some of whom were also stated to be parish priests. Therefore, although full-time chaplains are rarely found in the girls' schools, there is a considerable involvement on the part of Anglican clerics in both the Church of England and the inter- and non-denominational schools and of Roman Catholic priests in their schools.

The effectiveness of any chaplain depends partly on his or her personality. In the case of part-time chaplains and local priests who undertake chaplaincy duties, a further factor is the extent to which he becomes a familiar figure in the school and the impact he makes at Assembly, Sunday services, major school services, confirmation classes and through personal contact. His ministry extends beyond the staff and pupils to their families. Often he is the only cleric with whom parents have more than casual contact. It is therefore the school chaplain to whom parents as well as pupils turn for pastoral help. Several heads drew attention to the role of the chaplain. In describing the appointment she had just made, one head said, 'I am expecting new developments, having just made an appointment with a local parish. Our new chaplain is half time with us. We hope for strong local links.' Another head clearly valued her chaplain highly: 'My chaplain is *wonderful* – the confirmation classes are superb and the confirmation service is invariably a moving occasion.' Another head drew attention to the benefits for pupils of being able to turn to the chaplain for help in times of crisis:

> X's father died in particularly harrowing circumstances and I was asked to suggest someone to counsel her, with specialist skills in grief counselling. Instead I referred her to the school chaplain who already knew X well from his confirmation classes. The support he gave X and her close friends was tremendous.

The chaplain of one school filled in the questionnaire and he highlighted the similarity between the school community and a parish: 'As chaplain it is difficult to be objective but there is a feeling of community associated with the Church connection. It is like a small parish and there is an added dimension to pastoral care.'

SCHOOL WORSHIP

An important part of the religious dimension of a school is the opportunity provided for worship at Assembly, special services and Sunday services, some of which may be held in the parish church, others in school. School Assembly or morning chapel has been seen in both positive and negative terms. The Durham Report (1970) saw it as 'an opportunity for a variety of inspirational, reflective and other activities appropriate to the community'. In contrast, some of the studies of boys independent schools reported that Assembly or morning chapel was often used as a focus for resentment against authority – with boys perceiving, for example, a contradiction between the hierarchical seating arrangements and the Christian view of equality in the eyes of God.

To see the part played by Assembly in the life of the survey schools, heads were asked to state the frequency of Assembly/morning service, the people involved in taking it, and to comment on its importance. There was no correlation between denominational affiliation or residential dimension and the frequency of Assembly. Over half the schools held Assembly or morning service daily (51 per cent), 13 schools (26 per cent) held it four times a week, and seven schools (14.2 per cent) held it three times a week. In two schools, Assembly was held only twice a week. In one Church of England boarding school, whole school assembly was held in the school chapel once a fortnight, while the Christian girls met in the chapel three times a week. One Roman Catholic school held one whole school assembly a week, and on other days held class or year Assemblies. Several heads commented on the difficulty of physically assembling the whole school in one place, and therefore had to hold separate assemblies for juniors and senior or middle-school pupils.

In most schools, a number of different people conducted Assembly, and there were only four schools where the head assumed sole responsibility. In 32 schools, other members of staff took Assembly, and one head commented specifically on the value of this: 'Assembly is a chance for staff to expand beliefs/philosophies.' School chaplains, local parish priests and other clergy and visiting speakers were used on an occasional or regular basis by several schools.

One feature of school worship highlighted by the informal discussions was the opportunity it provided for pupil involvement in planning and preparing services. Several heads in the survey drew attention to the value of pupils' taking Assembly, both in promoting understanding of religious issues and in helping build up confidence. In 30 schools, pupils regularly conducted Assembly. One head stated: 'The pupils prepare the liturgy – a different class each week. This too helps understanding and personal involvement.' Another explained: 'It instils confidence and encourages leadership qualities' and 'enables pupils to express their views'.

The responses on the perceived importance of Assembly could be divided into a number of categories. The largest number in any single category were those that reflected Durkheim's view of religion as a cohesive force. For Durkheim, religion was primarily concerned with the key distinction between the sacred and the profane, with ritual serving to express and reinforce the sentiments necessary for integration and cohesion. Twenty-seven heads considered that one of the values of Assembly lay in binding the community together and reinforcing school values. The very act of gathering together at the beginning of the day was significant for establishing corporate identity and ethos. One head argued that, 'Assembly is important for cementing bonds in worship.' Two others stated:

> It gives the opportunity to establish and maintain the ethos of the school – a sense of community and belonging. The only time of the day when some pupils see the Head.

It is a time for the Head to encourage the whole school to work together in the direction set by the Head.

A second frequently cited value of Assembly lay in the opportunities it provided for corporate and individual worship. One head stated, 'It is a short, informal, quiet opportunity for worship as a family bearing in mind an international audience.' Another believed that assembly 'provides a gathering time for reflection in individual and common concerns – ends with prayer and is thus a time when we worship as a community'. Several heads emphasized that individuals cannot be compelled to worship: 'You cannot make people worship but you can provide stimulus, challenge, awe, beauty and other triggers.' The effect of worshipping together was seen by nearly a third of the heads as 'providing a worshipful start to the school day', which helped set the tone for the day. This time of reflection, peace and contemplation was perceived by some heads as helping prepare the staff and pupils for the demands of the day.

As part of the 'hidden curriculum', Assembly was seen to be one way of making pupils aware of the spiritual dimension to life. Part of this was the setting of personal, school, national and international events in a religious context. One head expressed this as: 'It allows for community consideration of important world events in a religious context.' Another aspect of the spiritual dimension was the communication of philosophical, spiritual, moral and ethical values. Assembly was viewed as 'an opportunity for religious and moral ideas to be shared'. Another head argued that, 'Through Assembly it is possible to keep ever present a moral and spiritual dimension to life as the students grow up and develop their own values.' By allowing pupils familiarity with the Bible, hymns and prayers, Assembly was also seen as 'Education – they should know the hymns and prayers.'

The administrative side of Assembly – which included giving notices, handing out awards, and congratulating girls on individual, team and house successes – was seen as one function of Assembly by nine heads, although they all said this was of secondary importance. In four schools, the 'worshipful', 'reflective' Assembly was kept separate from the administrative assembly with daily notices being given out on a separate daily or weekly occasion at which the school gathered together to 'congratulate those who have achieved on behalf of the school'. In schools with a chapel, this distinction was further marked by holding the former in the chapel and the latter in an Assembly Hall.

From the survey, Assembly was seen to be a highly valued aspect of life in both the denominational and non-denominational schools. It was perceived as an essential ingredient in building up corporate identity, social cohesion and in the affirmation of the school's ethos. It exposed pupils to worship and the spiritual dimension of life, and offered a time for sharing ideas, joys and sorrows; it helped give pupils a knowledge of the Bible, prayers and hymns. It set an appropriate tone for the day and provided a framework in which to reflect upon individual and community concerns. The views of the heads in this survey can be thus seen to support the sentiments of the Durham Report.

Sunday services were also seen as important where girls boarded. In all the schools with a boarding element, pupils attended services on Sundays. In six schools the service was always held in school and in five it was either held in the school or the parish church. The majority of schools (20) always took the boarders to the parish church, and one school made a conscious attempt to introduce pupils to different local churches – Anglican, Methodist and Baptist. Such links with local churches were clearly valued by a number of heads who typically stated, 'Our school is very much part of the parish of X and the girls and staff value their connection with a thriving parish.' Involvement in the parish often led to involvement in the community and to opportunities for service: 'We are building links with the parish church. This will lead to a greater involvement in the community.' Heads explained that sometimes girls help run various parish organizations or provide music for special services: 'We play our part in running parish church services – youth clubs, etc.' Additionally, 'The girls take an active part. Participating in the services, helping at the church fete, helping care for the elderly in the parish. This activity forms not so much part of the curriculum as part of life.'

It is not only the daily and Sunday services that provide opportunities for worship in the school context. Another significant aspect is the major school services which mark particular occasions in the church and school year. Such services reach beyond the immediate school community, for they are public events attended by the families of pupils, for some of whom they provide their only contact with institutional religion. Major school services included carol services, founders day or speech day, confirmation, Ash Wednesday, Easter, harvest festival, Advent Carol Service and Remembrance Day. Fewer special services were held by the non-denominational schools, but only one non-denominational school did not hold any major services.

A slightly different pattern of special services was found among the Roman Catholic Schools. In the four schools with a boarding element and one of the day schools, weekly Mass and special Masses on the Days of Obligation were seen as the major services. The other day school held special Masses on Days of Obligation.

Thirty-six heads answered a question on their perceptions of the importance of such services and their responses were in many ways similar to those given for the importance of Assembly. Again, the largest single category of response was for statements to do with the effect of such occasions in providing corporate identity and cohesion. Emphasis was given by ten heads to the public expression of the school's Christian ideals and the affirmation of shared values. For example, one head stated, 'Services are important for the affirmation of our Christian principles and ethos.' Another commented, 'They act as a focal point for communicating common values.' Over all, the vast majority of the heads regarded these major services as a significant part of corporate life, providing opportunities for worship for both pupils and their families, reinforcing a sense of community, and helping highlight the spiritual dimension to life.

The Schools Council identified two approaches to Religious Education (Schools Council, 1971), which have influenced much subsequent discussion of religious education. The first, the confessional, is a dogmatic approach that begins with the assumption that the aim is indoctrination and the purpose evangelism, although this may be carefully moderated in practice. The second, the phenomenological or undogmatic approach, seeks the promotion of understanding and aims at sensitivity to the issues involved without seeking to promote any one religious viewpoint. Over the past 20 years, the shift has been towards the latter approach with religious education syllabi including world faiths alongside Christianity and the consideration of personal, moral and social issues. At the same time, religious education, particularly in the maintained sector, has often become the 'Cinderella' subject, under-resourced, with a low timetabled allocation and taught in many cases by non-specialists. Another trend was for religious education to be the 'dustbin' subject – a repository for bits that did not fit neatly elsewhere in the curriculum, such as moral education, civics and Third World issues. To gain some information about the position of religious education in the curriculum of these private schools, heads were asked to state the number of periods allocated to it in the junior school, the lower years (11–14), the fourth fifth and sixth years of the senior school; whether it was taken as an examination subject at GCSE and A-level and the proportion of pupils taking it; and to comment on its importance.

The information relating to the timetabled provision and status of religious education was analysed by denomination. Twenty-one of the Church of England schools had junior departments. Thirteen of these schools allocated two periods each week to religious education, seven gave one period, and in one school no time was allocated. In the lower years of the senior school, three of these Church of England schools (13 per cent) allocated three, twelve (50 per cent) had two periods, and nine (37 per cent) had one period per week. In the fourth and fifth years, 14 schools allocated one period a week for general religious studies, and in 11 of these schools religious studies was an option at GCSE. In only two schools was there no provision at all for religious studies at this stage, but there were a further seven schools in which

197

only pupils who took religious studies at GCSE level received any religious education during the fourth and fifth years. In the sixth form, 12 schools provided a timetabled lesson for general religious education.

In 19 of these Church of England schools, religious education could be studied as a GCSE option, and in 13 it could be studied to A-level. In only two schools was GCSE religious studies taken by all pupils. The proportion of pupils in the other schools taking it as an option varied from five to 80 per cent. The popularity of religious studies as an examination subject declines further at A-level. In three of the schools that offered it, heads described demand as 'minimal' or 'occasional'. Even in schools with large sixth forms, the number of A-level candidates varied between six and ten. In medium and small schools, there were usually only one or two candidates, and in some years none at all.

Somewhat similar pictures were evident for the other groups of schools. For example, ten inter-denominational schools had junior departments, half of which allocated two periods of religious education per week and the other half allocated one period. In the lower years of the senior school, nine schools allocated two periods and four had one period for religious education. In the fourth and fifth years, 11 schools had a general religious education course of one period per week. Only one school made no provision for religious education at this stage, and in one school only pupils following the GCSE course received any religious education at this time. In the sixth form, five of the schools allocated one period a week for religious education, and in three more schools it was subsumed under 'general studies'. Nine of these schools offered religious education at GCSE level. In one school, only eight per cent of pupils took it, but in seven schools it was taken by between 20 and 30 per cent and in one school by 80 per cent of the pupils. Religious education was offered at A-level by nine schools, but the numbers taking it were small – usually between two and six, and in one school only 'three girls in the last three years had taken it'.

As might be expected, in the Roman Catholic schools the allocation for religious-education periods tended to be more generous, with three periods allocated in the middle years of the senior school by four, and two periods by two schools. In five of the six Roman Catholic schools, religious studies was taken at GCSE by all pupils, and in the other school there was a general period of religious education in the fourth and fifth years. In the sixth form, five schools allocated two periods for general religious education. In only two schools was it taken as an A-level subject by about 10 per cent of the pupils.

Table 9.5 shows the overall provision of religious education in the sample schools. It can be seen that the position of religious studies/ religious education in the curriculum seems to be secure. In the junior and lower years of the senior schools, the majority of schools allocate two periods a week to the subject, which compares favourably with the allocation for other humanities subjects such as history. The majority (77 per cent) of schools offered religious studies as a GCSE subject, and as a general subject in the fourth and fifth years. Slightly over half (51 per cent) of the schools included religious education as

TABLE 9.5

THE POSITION OF RELIGIOUS STUDIES/RELIGIOUS EDUCATION IN THE FOURTH, FIFTH AND SIXTH FORMS
(percentage refers to the proportion of schools in each denomination)

	RE as general subject in fourth and fifth form		RE as GCSE subject		RE as general subject in sixth form		RE at A-level	
	No. of schools	%	No. of schools	%	No. of schools	%	No. of schools	%
C of E	14	58	19	79	12	50	13	54
R.C.	1	17	5	83	5	83	2	33
Free Church	0	0	1	100	1	100	1	100
Other	1	100	1	100	1	100	1	100
Inter-denom.	11	84	9	69	5	38	7	53
Non-denom.	4	80	3	60	1	20	2	40
Total	31		38		25		26	

part of the sixth-form course, and it is offered as an A-level by 68 per cent of the schools, although numbers taking it were small. The only significant denominational differences to emerge were the more generous allocation in the Roman Catholic schools, and that schools linked to a specific denomination were more likely than inter- and non-denominational schools to offer religious studies at A-level.

Forty-three heads responded to a question on the importance of religious education. The only significant denominational difference appeared to be the more 'confessional' approach of some of the Roman Catholic heads; therefore the findings are not reported by denomination. Heads clearly had high and diverse expectations of the purposes of religious education. By far the largest single category of response (23 heads) concerned religious education as a way of communicating values, morality and the Christian way of life. For some heads, this went beyond informing to helping shape pupils' attitudes to themselves and others. For example, one stated: 'It helps instil a sense of morality, uphold values, care for others – a general Christian way of life.' Another felt, 'It gives students a different dimension and causes them to approach values and themselves from an academic stand-point, not only (or as well as) having a practising faith or being uncertain.' One head pointed out that religious education, 'must not be indoctrination but sound teaching of Christianity and wise counselling in discussion of moral issues for teenagers'.

For over half the heads, religious education was seen as important for helping pupils appreciate the spiritual dimension to life, as part of the development of the whole person. It was important for 'developing spiritual awareness' and 'catering for a child's spiritual needs is essential in providing for the development of the whole person'. Some heads were careful to maintain a distinction between religious education and nurture in the Christian faith. For example,

> The nurture of any particular faith should be performed by the officials of that particular faith or within the family. Distinct from that it is an educational *necessity* for everyone to follow an academic R.S. course where evangelism is not the aim but the promotion of tolerance and understanding is.

The academic aspect of religious education was stressed by several heads, including knowledge of Christianity and the Bible, other faiths and showing Christianity as an historic part of Western culture: 'We treat this as a totally academic subject, include knowledge of other faiths but hope it brings the realization of man's natural propensity to worship.' Its value lies in giving 'children a basic understanding of Christianity'. Another argued that, 'As a curriculum subject I feel its value is cultural rather than ethical or spiritual'.

However, giving a sound academic basis and understanding of Christianity was seen by some heads as providing pupils with a basis on which to form their own beliefs later in life as well as at present. For one head, the 'central objective has to be keeping the possibility of faith open to all'. Another head saw classroom teaching as one dimension of religious education in the broader sense:

> All religious education is beneficial in terms of the sound values and social conscience it encourages. Knowledge of the Christian religion and regular church attendance allows girls to make an informed choice in later life about religious affiliation and commitment.

Religious education, then, is visibly seen as communicating or helping shape values, as one of the principal means of making pupils aware of the spiritual dimension to life, and as an academic subject imparting knowledge of Christianity, other faiths and contemporary issues. None of the responses indicated a hard 'confessional' approach; that is, one aimed specifically at indoctrination. However, in a number of responses there were elements of a confessional approach in that some heads saw the function of religious education as being more than academic, and to do with what has been described as 'the numinate', a term that refers to the vast area of enriching human experience.

THE EFFECT OF RELIGIOUS AFFILIATION ON CURRICULUM, CORPORATE LIFE AND SCHOOL ETHOS

To assess whether a school's religious connections went beyond those areas such as worship and religious education where it might be expected to have an impact, heads were asked to identify any ways in which, if their school had a church connection, this was reflected in the curriculum, corporate life and ethos of the school.

Only a few heads saw that the curriculum was directly or indirectly affected by the school's church connection, and this was usually in relation to the place of religious education. One head emphasized that: 'Religious education is taught throughout the school with a generous allocation – all take it at GCSE.' In one school there was 'a doctrinal emphasis in the lower school curriculum'. In contrast, several effects of the church connection on corporate life were identified – including the strong links with local parishes that have been discussed earlier, the importance attached to Assembly and chapel services, provision for confirmation, and opportunities for voluntary religious activities such as Christian Union and service to the community. This included: 'Parish links, Christian Unity, Social work at X'. One head describes her school as not having 'a church connection, but historically we have always been a Christian school. This is reflected in the high profile of caring and the inclusion of Religious Education and Assemblies.'

The concept of 'school ethos' is not easy to define. Rutter et al. (1979), however, write of ethos as 'the values, attitudes and behaviours which are characteristic of the school as a whole'. Ethos exerts a powerful effect on the school and is made up of a combination of factors. One contributing factor is likely to be the religious dimension and, in turn, this may be mediated through the whole of the school. It is interesting to speculate on the extent to which a school with a Christian tradition is likely to produce a different and distinctive ethos, and how much of a school's ethos can be attributed to it.

In some of the survey schools, the religious influence on ethos was seen to be all-pervasive, even if it was difficult to pin down precisely the ways in which it operated: 'It pervades our life – it is hard to say how. The curriculum is not affected. Many do not realize its importance until after they have left.' One head stated, 'I hope the Christian atmosphere is apparent in all that we do.' Some heads tried to define more precisely what this atmosphere was: 'It creates the whole atmosphere – a caring family' or 'It permeates our whole ethos and helps build a community where Christian values and a spirit of service are presented to the pupils. Each pupil is encouraged to achieve her best in every aspect of school life'. Behaviour and attitudes to others were seen to be a product of the Christian ethos, and the influence of the Christian ethos on decision-making was highlighted by one head: 'We hope Christian values invest all our policies and attitudes.'

Several heads, however, pointed to the difficulty of separating the influence of the religious dimension or of claiming that particular aspects of school life are a product of it. Typical of remarks from these heads was: 'So much of influence is intangible – how can one tell whether a friendly and caring feel in a school has any relation to its Christian ethos? Concern for others is an express aim of non-religious foundations too and I would not wish to claim exclusivity.' Some of the fundamental teachings about consideration and love for one's fellows form 'the common teaching of most of the world's faiths and indeed of the humanists'.

The effects of school ethos described by the heads confirm some of the suggestions that I made in a previous article (Gay, 1988). Here I argued that one might expect the ethos of a Christian school to be reflected in the quality of relationships between staff and pupils and among pupils, in the concern for the individual and the emphasis on the communication of values as well as in the general atmosphere of the school.

PARENTAL INTEREST IN THE RELIGIOUS DIMENSION

Parental interest in the religious dimension of a school is shown both when parents look at the school as prospective parents and in their support and interest once their daughters are at the school. Over the past 20 or so years, different views have been put forward concerning the extent to which the religious dimension influences parental choice of school. Ollerenshaw (1967), the Public Schools Commission (1970) and the Durham Report (1970) all concluded that one of the reasons parents sent their children to independent schools was in order for them to receive a Christian education. This view was supported by Dancy (1984) and Devlin (1984), the former arguing that 'many non-religious parents are willing, even keen, for their children to have some exposure to religion' (Dancy, 1984, p.164). Rae (1989), the ex-head of Westminster School, was more specific about the number of prospective parents who asked about this aspect of the school. He stated that about 50 per cent of prospective parents asked about Westminster's religious dimension and were keen to explore issues such as the style and content of religious education and Assembly. When they did not ask, Rae referred to the school's religious foundation and current attemps to reflect it. By contrast, Fox (1984), using material gathered from interviews with 190 Headmasters' Conference school parents, found that religion was not among the reasons for their choice of school, while Barnett (1984) quoted the head of a famous public school who said that in five years he had not been asked a single question about religious education or chapel. In informal discussions, the majority of pupils in several Church of England schools showed surprise that the religious dimension might have played a part in their parents' decision to send them to that particular school, although they often stated that the general atmosphere of the school had been a decisive factor.

While it is only from questioning parents that a more valid view can be obtained of the degree to which the religious dimension influenced their choice of school, it was possible to ascertain from the heads whether prospective parents ignore or express an interest in the religious dimension. Heads were asked to state whether they were frequently, sometimes, occasionally or never asked questions to do with religion. The results were categorized according to religious affiliation. Only two Church of England schools did not answer the question, and in all the others heads were asked questions about religion in varying degrees of frequency – 14 sometimes, seven occasionally and one frequently. Only one Roman Catholic school head omitted the question and, of the rest, one head stated religion was always a matter for discussion, two others were asked frequently, one sometimes, and one occasionally. All the heads of the inter- and non-denominational schools answered the question. Two heads of inter-denominational schools stated that they were asked frequently, four sometimes, and seven occasionally. In one of the non-denominational schools, parents frequently asked, and in the other four they asked only occasionally. The Free Church head was asked frequently, and the head of 'other denomination' sometimes.

The analysis indicates some degree of interest among prospective parents in the school's religious dimension as the heads of all the schools (unlike the head quoted by Barnett, 1984) were questioned on it by some prospective parents. One head made a point of telling parents about it, even if they did not ask. Because of the difficulty in assessing the influence of the religious dimension in parental choice of a particular school, heads were not asked to make this judgement, but a few expressed the view that it was a factor: '70–80 per cent of parents give one reason for choosing the school is that it has this religious ethos'. Another head claimed that: 'parents normally choose this school because it is a Christian school'. One head attributed the wide range of religious affiliation among pupils to the fact that 'the school has a religious influence upon its standards and takes a middle ground in its practices'. However, one head wondered whether the school's Christian image 'sells or deters'.

Parental interest can also be gauged by their support of the services to which they are invited, although it is possible that parents support the major services because they are high points of the school year rather than because of their religious significance. In only three schools did heads feel that parents did not support the major services to which they were invited. Only a small minority of parents, however, attended the regular weekly services in the schools that invited them.

Another indication of parental interest in the religious dimension is the extent to which current parents commented on various aspects. In 14 of the Church of England schools, five Roman Catholic, the one Free Church, the 'Other' category, six of the inter-denominational and two of the non-denominational schools, parents were said to comment on things to do with religion, often on the particular service they had attended. Some parents appeared to make more general observations, usually appreciative. They 'are delighted we do not just pay lip service'. Parents were often supportive even if they did not have any particular religious commitment themselves, feeling it right to give their child a foundation on which to build. In one school, parents commented: 'Occasionally – mainly with reference to carol services and Confirmation rather than the day-to-day observances. I think they like the idea of a nice traditional C of E grounding without having much personal commitment'. Other parents were pleased that the school was reinforcing their own beliefs and practices: 'When they do, it is usually parents who are trying themselves to inculcate religious values at home and are keen on church attendance. They indicate their approval for what is being done at school.'

The findings from the survey tend to support the view that for some prospective parents, questions about the religious dimension of the school are important and the answers they receive may be one factor in influencing their eventual choice. Once their daughters are at a particular school, the majority seem to support major services and some take a deeper interest – commenting on the services, Assembly, religious education and school ethos.

CONCLUSIONS

The schools used in the survey cover a cross-section of girls' independent schools in terms of size, age range, residential style and religious affiliation. In all the schools, the religious dimension is taken seriously in terms of the position of religious education in the curriculum and the provision of opportunities for worship. The role of religion in helping foster corporate identity and ethos, the importance of religious education in communicating values as well as in informing, and the contribution of both religious education and worship to the spiritual development of pupils was recognized by the heads. The survey has thus helped to expand upon the public statements made about religious affiliation and practice by these 49 girls' schools. The perspectives gained from the heads were immensely valuable. However, it is recognized that the next stage in any study of religion in girls' independent schools should be to investigate the perspectives of the girls themselves.

REFERENCES

Barnett, J. (1984) 'Religious Education and Theology in the Anglican Independent Schools,' in J. Bennett (ed.), *Theology at 16+*. London: Epworth.
Dancy, J.C. (1984) 'Independent Schools,', in J. Sutcliffe (ed.), *A Dictionary of Religious Education*. London: SCM.
Devlin, T. (1984) *Choosing Your Independent School*. London: Arrow Books.
Durham Report (1970) *The Fourth R*. London: National Society and SPCK.
Fox, I. (1984) 'The Demand for a Public School Education: A Crisis of Confidence in

Comprehensive Schooling?', in G. Walford (ed.), *British Public Schools: Policy and Practice*. London: Falmer.

Gay, B.M. (1985) *The Church of England and the Independent Schools*. Abingdon: Culham College Institute.

Gay, B.M. (1988) 'The Christian Dimension of the Independent Schools: Reality or Pious Hope,', *Encyclical*, 52: 15–21.

Ollerenshaw, K. (1967) *The Girls' Schools*. London: Faber & Faber.

Public Schools Commission (1970) *Second Report of the Public Schools Commission*. London: HMSO.

Rae, J. (1989) *Too Little Too Late? The Challenges that Still Face British Education*. London: Collins.

Rutter, M., Maughan, B., Mortimore, P., and Ouston, J. (1979) *Fifteen Thousand Hours*. London: Open Books.

Schools Council (1971) *Religious Education in Secondary Schools. Schools Council Working Paper 36*. London: Schools Council.

Walford, G. (1986) *Life in Public Schools*. London: Methuen.

Walford, G. (1989) (ed.), *Private Schools in Ten Countries: Policy and Practice*. London: Routledge.

Index